THE
SEATTLE TIMES
COOKBOOK

Compiled and edited by the staff of
The Seattle Times Food section
Sharon Lane, Food Editor, Nicole Mindt,
Ruth De Rosa, Alf Collins, Tom Stockley,
Judy Borreson Groom, Dawn Clark,
Maurene Edwards, Maxine Jeffery,
CeCe Sullivan

Peanut Butter Publishing
Seattle, Washington

Dedicated to the readers of The Seattle Times weekly Food section, whose varied questions and comments have taught us to respect the basics while we explore the culinary riches of the Northwest.

Contents

Foreword

Apples and asparagus, sablefish and strawberries, walnuts and wild mushrooms. Five kinds of salmon and innumerable shellfish. How lucky you are in the Northwest! On each visit to Washington state, I discover something new. Last time, it was the mellow Johannisberg Riesling and the musty Fume Blanc wines. One spring I found fresh wild morels, available for so fleeting a season. And I've kept my eye on oysters ever since I tasted little Olympias 20 years ago. Now there are Westcotts, Shoalwater Bay oysters and delicate French "Belons." What riches!

It's a pleasure, therefore, to introduce a cookbook which celebrates Northwest cuisine. *The Seattle Times Cookbook* contains more than 400 recipes, favorites which have appeared in the food pages of the newspaper over the years. You'll find everyday dishes like Lasagne and party ideas such as Salmon Newburg with green onions, mushrooms and peas, or Mussels Marinières flavored with basil. A particular favorite of mine is Oyster Stew, but I wouldn't say no to a freshly baked fish with Pesto Butter or a fresh Strawberry Tart with cream-cheese filling.

Sharon Lane is food editor of *The Seattle Times*. She heads a team of two cooks and three writers, all of them experienced professionals. Like many of her colleagues, Sharon is a home economics graduate. She is also a Seattle native with 16 years on the newspaper behind her, combining an appreciation and understanding of local cooking with a love of good food. "Give me a fillet of salmon and plenty of local strawberries and I'm happy!" she declares.

The Seattle Times Cookbook is very much a family affair involving Food section readers. All recipes have been rigorously tested. first in the kitchens of *The Times*, then by you in your own homes.

For ease in reading and preparation, ingredients are listed in order of appearance and, when more than one preparation is involved, they are broken into segments. The method is clearly described step-by-step. Any recipe which survives the scrutiny of readers has got to be reliable. "We know the cooks behind each one," says Sharon Lane.

It is the cooks of the Northwest who have created this book, with its emphasis on the fine ingredients which so forcibly impress any visitor. One reason for this abundance is the climate, ruled by the Cascade mountains. To the east, potatoes and Walla Walla sweet onions thrive in rich volcanic soil; wheat fields, orchards and vineyards stretch for mile after mile; and fruits last all year around, from spring rhubarb to winter pears. This is the home of the rich, creamy cheddar cheese, Cougar Gold.

To the west, between the Cascades and the sea, the many rivers and high rainfall bring fine green vegetables, herbs, berries and an astonishing variety of fish and shellfish. Seattle's Pike Place Market is famous nationwide for its produce.

Northwest cuisine is unimaginable without salmon—silver salmon, poached or baked whole; deep pink king salmon; and the rare white king. Most ancient of all is the Indian barbecued salmon where the filleted fish is flattened with strips of alder and cooked in front of an alderwood fire so the smoke permeates the flesh.

Well known outside the state are Northwest apples, from the best-selling but bland red and golden Delicious to the crisper Granny Smiths and Spartans, a lively new hybrid of McIntosh. Mainly from Oregon come pears like the early Bartletts, the firm, green Anjou and Comice, queen of them all. Unfortunately, the berries of the Northwest travel less well: To enjoy the wonderful raspberries, blackberries, wild huckleberries, loganberries and boysenberries, you really need to be on the spot.

Reading *The Seattle Times Cookbook* makes me wish I were, indeed, on the spot. The late James Beard, the greatest Northwestern cook of them all, summed it up: "My own grandparents, who crossed to Oregon in a covered wagon, passed down recipes that had game, wild berries and the green plants of plain and forest as ingredients. From them I learned to love dried apples and corn, and small bits of game impaled on sticks and roasted. By them I was introduced to vinegar pie, and to cornmeal cakes and loaves cooked on a griddle . . . Northwestern cooking is simply good cooking. Nothing more, nothing less."

Anne Willan
President of La Varenne

Preface

Two things make this more than just another newspaper cookbook.

One is The Seattle Times' location in the Pacific Northwest, a region where fresh ingredients routinely enrich a cook's palette. The other is the newspaper's exceptional commitment to quality food coverage.

All of the recipes in this book have been prepared in The Seattle Times' test kitchen. The home economists on our staff test each recipe, making sure the ingredient list is complete, understandable and presented in the order in which the ingredients are used. They also make sure the steps are easy to follow and thoroughly detailed. We'd rather tell readers too much than too little, so almost all our recipes specify when to preheat the oven, what size pan to use, when to remove the food from the pan and how to serve it.

Once the home economist is done with a recipe, the result — be it seaweed soup or chocolate torte — is presented for tasting to the staff. This group of artists, writers and editors possesses a wide range of food preferences.

We ask this assortment of testers to answer a brief questionnaire rating the finished dish on its appearance, texture and taste. Later, the food staff uses the forms to help decide whether to publish the recipe or try to improve it. No recipe appears in The Seattle Times without surviving this process.

But that's only one kind of testing. The recipes which appear in this book have been through another, even more rigorous process: They've passed the test of reader reaction.

In selecting the recipes for this book, the entire food staff — two home economists, two food writers, one columnist and the section's editor — went through all of the nearly 30,000 recipes in our files. We looked for those which seemed particularly Northwestern in flavor and for those which reflect the ethnic heritage of the area. We also looked for dishes we know readers like.

The recipes in this book do have certain peculiarities. For one thing, in typical newspaper fashion, we write our recipes in a staccato prose that omits articles and conjunctions. In transposing the recipes to book form, we have tried to impose a more conversational tone; however, it won't take a grammarian to realize that much of our old style remains.

More important, readers should note that in our seafood recipes, we use the Canadian cooking method. This timing produces fish that is firm but opalescent, a just-cooked-through style many Northwesterners prefer to fish that can be flaked with a fork. If you are not used to the Canadian method, you may consider the fish underdone in our recipes; if you don't like it, by all means, use longer times.

Finally, we urge you to amend these recipes to suit yourselves. Because we have so many fresh ingredients available to us, we have avoided frozen or canned equivalents in almost all cases. In only a few instances — such as recipes calling for artichoke hearts — we've decided that starting from the basic, fresh ingredient would amount to culinary excess. Nevertheless, in most instances you can substitute the frozen version for the fresh if time or availability dictates such a compromise.

It must be obvious by now that this book is not the product of a single person. It's the collective effort of The Seattle Times food staff, including our regular employees and those who help during the holidays and vacations. Food editor Sharon Lane found a way to produce this book while putting out a weekly Food section; writer Nicole Mindt, who has worked on other cookbooks, kept the manuscript organized during the many months and phases of production. Dawn Clark, Judy Borreson Groom, Maurene Edwards, CeCe Sullivan and Maxine Jeffery are all home economists who have contributed testing and expertise to this volume. Columnist Alf Collins used his considerable knowledge of Northwest cuisine to write the book's chapter introductions and both wine columnist Tom Stockley and food writer Ruth De Rosa contributed their knowledge of the region and its tastes.

A number of recipes in this book have been contributed by area residents, or come from the personal files of our staff. In those cases, the individual cook is credited in a note following the recipe.

The design of this book is a joint effort of Peanut Butter Publishing and The Seattle Times, specifically art director Rob Covey and designer Celeste Ericsson. The illustrations are the work of free-lancer Craig K. Smith. The cover photograph was taken by Barry Wong, a Seattle Times photographer.

Peanut Butter Publishing wants to thank Judy Weisfield who was a driving force in bringing this project to fruition.

Cyndi Meagher
Assistant Managing Editor
The Seattle Times

Appetizers

Little wonder that, with the Northwest dining preferences for quick, light meals, the appetizer course sometimes becomes a light meal in itself.

For the cook with access to the best foods from around the world along with a continuous supply of fresh-from-the-garden Northwest ingredients, the appetizer is an intriguing culinary challenge. In a one-bite burst of flavor, it should excite the taste buds, express the complexity of contrasting flavors and not be too filling. Cooks can tailor a selection of high- and low- calorie appetizers, strong and mild flavors, and meats and non-meats for drop-in diners.

While most other parts of a menu usually are restricted to one cuisine, appetizers are free to roam the world. Only the unadventurous would think it exceptional to find sushi, pâté and caponata on the same table.

Northwesterners have the added advantage of diversity in seafoods, vegetables and fruits to make the appetizer course a memorable introduction to the meal to follow.

Our Skewered Oysters recipe takes on a character of its own with the Quilcenes and Willapas only minutes from the shell, firm and tasting of their native waters. The distinctive flavor and texture of the body meat of the Dungeness crab make our Crab Terrine different from what such a dish would be anywhere else in the country.

Smoked Salmon-Cheese Spread

Makes about 1 pound

12	ounces cream cheese, softened
½	pound smoked salmon, finely chopped
½	teaspoon white pepper
1½	teaspoons lemon juice
	Salt
2	tablespoons chopped chives or green onions

1. In a small bowl, cream the cheese with a wooden spoon. Add the salmon, white pepper, lemon juice and salt to taste. Continue to beat until the ingredients are well blended.

2. Line a deep, 16-ounce bowl or mold with plastic wrap. Pack the cheese mixture tightly inside. Cover with plastic wrap and refrigerate for 2 to 3 hours or longer.

3. To serve, invert the cheese mixture onto a dish; remove plastic wrap. Garnish with chopped chives or green onion.

Salmon-Stuffed Tomatoes

Makes 25 to 30 appetizers

25-30	cherry tomatoes
3	ounces thinly sliced Nova Scotia salmon
1	(3 ounce) package cream cheese at room temperature
1½	teaspoons lemon juice
1½	tablespoons sour cream
2	tablespoons unsalted butter
1	tablespoon minced watercress leaves
	Salt and pepper
	Watercress sprigs

1. Cut a thin slice from the stem end of each tomato; scoop the pulp and seeds from the center with a small, sharp-edged spoon. Turn the tomatoes, cut side down, on paper towels to drain.

2. Using a food processor or a blender, chop the salmon finely. In a medium bowl, stir the cream cheese until smooth. Stir in the chopped salmon, lemon juice, sour cream, butter and 1 tablespoon watercress. Season with salt and pepper to taste.

3. Fill each tomato with the salmon mixture, mounding it slightly. Top each tomato with a small sprig of watercress. Cover and refrigerate until serving time.

◇

Smoked Salmon Mousse

Makes 2½ cups

⅓	pound smoked salmon
2	green onions, chopped
3	(3 ounce) packages cream cheese, softened
3	tablespoons butter, softened
2	tablespoons sour cream
3	tablespoons lemon juice
	Tabasco sauce
	Lettuce leaves
	Crackers or thin-sliced French bread

1. In the bowl of a food processor, combine the salmon and green onion. Blend well.

2. With the processor running, gradually add the cream cheese, butter, sour cream, lemon juice and Tabasco to taste and blend until smooth.

3. Line a quart mold with plastic wrap, pack the mousse into the mold and chill until set.

4. To serve, unmold the mousse onto a serving platter lined with lettuce leaves and surround it with crackers or thinly sliced French bread.

Shrimp in Mustard Sauce

Serves 8

2	pounds raw shrimp, in the shell
	Salt
1	lemon slice
3-4	sprigs parsley
2	bay leaves
1	teaspoon dried thyme, crushed
2	tablespoons lemon-flavored mustard or
	1 tablespoon Dijon mustard
3	tablespoons lemon juice
¾	cup olive oil
1	teaspoon dried tarragon, crushed

1. Place the shrimp in a saucepan and cover them with boiling water. Add 1 to 2 teaspoons salt, lemon slice, parsley, bay leaves and thyme. Bring to a boil and cook 4 to 6 minutes, depending on the size of the shrimp. Drain and chill. Peel the shrimp, and devein if necessary.

2. Place the mustard in a bowl and add lemon juice. Beat with a wire whisk, adding the oil a little at a time. Add salt to taste and tarragon. Pour over the shrimp and marinate 1 to 2 hours. Stir before serving.

Crab Terrine

Makes 1 quart

1	cup whipping cream
1	tablespoon unflavored gelatin moistened in ¼ cup water
1	cup mayonnaise
1	pound fresh crab meat
1	tablespoon minced onion
1½	tablespoons Worcestershire sauce
1	tablespoon lemon juice
3	tablespoons chopped parsley
¼	teaspoon salt
	Dash pepper
	Lettuce leaves
	Assorted crackers

1. Heat the cream and moistened gelatin in a saucepan, stirring until dissolved. Add the mayonnaise, crab meat, onion, Worcestershire sauce, lemon juice, parsley, salt and pepper. Blend well. Turn into a greased 1-quart mold and chill until firm.

2. Unmold on a platter or serving tray lined with lettuce leaves. Serve with assorted crackers.

Easy Crab Sushi

Makes 3 to 4 dozen

6-8	ounces cooked crab meat, including some legs
1	cup long grain rice
2¼	cups water
¼	cup white vinegar
3	tablespoons sugar
1	teaspoon salt
3	tablespoons grated carrot
3	tablespoons finely chopped green onion

1. Finely slice the crab legs, reserving some bright pieces for garnish.

2. Bring the rice and water to a boil. Cover, reduce heat and simmer 20 to 25 minutes or until the water is completely absorbed.

3. While the rice cooks, combine the vinegar, sugar and salt; stir until sugar dissolves.

4. Remove the rice from heat and turn it into a large bowl. Gently stir in the vinegar mixture until absorbed. Let stand 30 minutes. Fold in the crab meat, carrot and onion. Shape into small balls or logs. Keep your hands moistened for easier handling. Top each sushi with a bit of red crab meat. Serve immediately.

Sushi
Serves 6

Tray:

⅓	cup rice vinegar
2	medium carrots, peeled, cut into 3-4 inch pieces, then cut lengthwise into fine julienne strips
1	pound spinach, washed, stems discarded
2	small ripe avocados
½	cup lemon juice
½	English cucumber, cut into 3-4 inch pieces, then cut lengthwise into fine julienne strips
1	(3½ ounce) bag fresh enoki mushrooms, ends trimmed
½	pound crab, cooked and shelled
½	pound medium prawns, cooked and shelled
¼	pound Nova Scotia smoked salmon, thinly sliced then halved
1	(1½ ounce) package nori (dried seaweed)
¼	cup sesame seeds
	Soy sauce

Sushi Rice:

3	cups short-grain rice
3½	cups water
⅓	cup rice vinegar

Wasabi Paste:

3	tablespoon wasabi powder (Japanese hot horseradish)
3½	teaspoons water

Sesame Sauce:

1	cup mayonnaise
4	teaspoons honey
4	teaspoons toasted sesame seeds
1½	teaspoons sesame oil

1. To prepare the tray: In a 2- to 3-quart pan, bring the rice vinegar to a boil. Add the carrots; cook and stir 1 to 2 minutes, or until carrots are tender-crisp. Drain and set aside.

2. Rinse the cooking pan. Add 1 inch of water and bring it to a boil. Gently push the spinach down into the water. Cook and stir 1 minute, just until limp. Drain and set aside.

3. Pit and peel the avocado. Slice it lengthwise into strips, about ⅛-inch thick. Place in a bowl with lemon juice; moisten each slice to prevent browning. Set aside.

4. On a large tray, separately arrange the carrots, spinach, avocado, cucumber, mushrooms, crab, prawns and salmon. If made ahead, cover and chill up to 5 hours.

5. With scissors, cut the nori into quarters. Stack on a plate or in a basket.

6. In a 10- to 12-inch frying pan, over medium-high heat, stir the sesame seeds until golden, 3 to 5 minutes. Spoon into 1 or 2 small serving bowls. Place soy sauce in a small serving bowl on the tray.

7. To prepare sushi rice: In a 3- to 4-quart saucepan, cover the rice with water and stir; drain. Rinse repeatedly until water is clear; drain. Add 3½ cups water to rice. Cover and bring to a boil over high heat. Reduce heat to low and cook without stirring until all water is absorbed, about 15 minutes. Stir in the rice vinegar. Cool to room temperature. Spoon sushi rice into a serving bowl.

8. To prepare wasabi paste: Stir the wasabi powder with water until smooth. Divide into 6 equal portions. Pinch into small cones and place 1 cone on each serving plate.

9. To prepare sesame sauce: Stir together the mayonnaise, honey, toasted sesame seeds and sesame oil. Spoon into 1 or 2 small serving bowls.

10. To assemble sushi: Lay a piece of nori in the palm of your hand. Spoon a small quantity of sushi rice into the center. Top with any of the several foods from the sushi tray and wasabi paste or sesame sauce and seeds. Overlap corners of nori to enclose the filling. Dip bite by bite into soy sauce.

Rumakis
Makes 2 dozen

12	chicken livers
½	cup soy sauce
¼	teaspoon ground ginger
1	small clove garlic, crushed
12	water chestnuts, halved
	Brown sugar
12	slices bacon

1. Cut the chicken livers in halves. Marinate in the refrigerator for 4 hours in a mixture of the soy sauce, ginger and garlic. Drain.

2. Preheat oven to 400°.

3. Make a slit in each piece of liver and insert a half water chestnut. Dip the liver in the brown sugar.

4. Cut the bacon slices in halves. Wrap each half around a piece of liver. Secure with toothpicks. Dip again in the brown sugar.

5. Arrange on a rack in a baking dish and bake for 30 minutes or until the bacon is brown and crisp, turning occasionally. Serve immediately.

Skewered Oysters
Serves 6

Maitre d'Hotel Butter:

½	cup butter
2	tablespoons chopped parsley
2	tablespoons chopped shallots, green onions or chives
1	tablespoon lemon juice
	Salt and pepper

Oysters:

24	shelled oysters (18 to 20 to the pint)
12	slices bacon, cut in half
4	slices toast
	Parsley sprigs
	Lemon wedges

1. To prepare maitre d'hotel butter: Cream the butter until light. Blend in parsley, shallots, green onions or chives, and lemon juice. Season to taste with salt and pepper. Set aside.

2. To prepare oysters: Put the oysters in a saucepan with their own juices. Bring the liquid to a boil; remove from the heat and let stand for several minutes. Drain thoroughly.

3. Pat the oysters dry. Roll each one in a half-slice of bacon. Secure with toothpicks. Broil lightly, turning often, about 3 inches from the source of the heat.

4. Serve on toast points with a spoonful of maitre d'hotel butter and garnish with a parsley sprig and lemon wedge.

Oyster-Stuffed Mushrooms

Makes 18 appetizers

18	mushrooms, 2 inches in diameter
7	tablespoons butter, melted
1	onion, minced
5	ounces oysters, drained and minced
1	teaspoon lemon juice
1	tablespoon chili sauce
2	tablespoons dry sherry
½	teaspoon salt

1. Preheat oven to 375°.

2. Wipe the mushrooms clean with a damp cloth. Remove and mince the stems. Set the caps aside.

3. Melt 3 tablespoons butter and sauté the minced onion over medium heat, stirring from time to time, for 5 minutes.

4. Add the minced mushroom stems and cook until all the moisture has been drawn out of them, about 5 minutes.

5. Scrape the onion and mushroom-stem mixture into a bowl and add the oysters, lemon juice, chili sauce, sherry and salt. Mix well.

6. Melt the remaining butter. Dip the mushroom caps in the melted butter to get them well-covered. Place them on a cookie sheet, dome side down. Stuff each mushroom with the oyster mixture. There will be some of the mixture left over, so mound it on toast rounds. Bake for 20 minutes, or until done.

Flaming Mushrooms
Serves 4

1	pound fresh mushrooms
3	tablespoons butter
2	tablespoons vegetable oil
¼	teaspoon salt
¼	teaspoon pepper
¼	teaspoon garlic powder
1½	teaspoon chopped fresh basil or ⅛ teaspoon dried basil, crushed
⅔	cup burgundy
⅔	cup sweet port
¼	cup brandy

1. Clean the mushrooms with a damp towel and cut off the stems even with the caps. In a large, heavy skillet, melt the butter and add the oil. Sauté the mushrooms until lightly brown.

2. Add the salt, pepper, garlic powder, basil, burgundy and port. Stir over high heat until the wines have been reduced completely and the mushrooms are glazed.

3. Remove from heat and stir in the brandy. Stand back and ignite with a long fireplace match; let the flames die down. Serve hot.

Fried Pepper Jack
Serves 8

8	ounces very cold pepper jack or Monterey jack cheese,
	cut in ½-inch thick slices
4	tablespoons flour
1-2	eggs, well beaten
1	cup unseasoned dry bread crumbs
4-8	tablespoons butter

1. Roll the cheese slices in flour, shaking off any excess. Dip the slices in beaten egg, then roll in bread crumbs.

2. Heat the butter in a skillet until hot, and fry the cheese. When crumbs are brown on one side, turn cheese quickly to brown on the other. Do not overcook. It is important to move quickly, or the cheese will melt and seep through the coating. Drain on paper towels. Serve at once.

Macadamia Nut-Stuffed Mushrooms

Makes 3 dozen

Béchamel Sauce:

3	tablespoons butter
3	tablespoons flour
½	teaspoon salt
1	cup milk, scalded

Stuffed Mushrooms:

36	mushrooms, at least 2 inches in diameter
¼	cup butter
¼	cup thinly sliced green onions
1	teaspoon finely chopped parsley
1	(3½ ounce) jar macadamia nuts, chopped
2	tablespoons bread crumbs
¼	cup grated Swiss cheese
1	tablespoon grated parmesan cheese

1. Preheat oven to 375°.

2. To prepare sauce: Melt the butter in a heavy saucepan. Add the flour and salt and cook until light and bubbly. Add the hot milk and cook until thickened.

3. To prepare mushrooms: Clean the mushrooms carefully with a damp cloth. Finely chop the stems plus 4 whole mushrooms. Place chopped mushrooms in a towel and squeeze out the moisture.

4. Heat a skillet and add 2 tablespoons butter. Sauté the mushroom stems and green onions. Stir in the parsley, béchamel sauce and ½ cup of the macadamia nuts. Cook for about 30 seconds. Remove from heat.

5. Combine the bread crumbs, the remaining macadamia nuts, Swiss cheese, parmesan cheese and the remaining 2 tablespoons butter; mix with fingers.

6. Place the mushroom caps in a baking dish. Fill the caps with sautéed mixture. Place a ball of cheese mixture on top of each mushroom. Bake for 15 minutes, or until done. Cooking time will vary slightly depending on size of mushrooms.

Broiled Avocado Italiano

Serves 6

2	tablespoons olive oil
3	green onions, chopped
1	(16 ounce) can whole tomatoes, well drained and chopped
¼	cup soft bread crumbs
¼	cup grated romano cheese
3	avocados, each about 4 inches long
1½	tablespoons butter, melted
½	teaspoon salt
½	teaspoon white pepper

1. In a saucepan, heat the oil. Add the green onions and cook gently until limp. Stir in the tomatoes and simmer until blended and slightly reduced, about 5 minutes.

2. Add 2 tablespoons of the bread crumbs and stir well. Keep hot over very low heat.

3. In a cup or small bowl, stir together the remaining bread crumbs and the cheese and set aside.

4. Cut the avocados in half, lengthwise. Remove the seeds and peel.

5. Brush the edges and cavities with the melted butter, then sprinkle with the salt and pepper.

6. Fill the cavities with the hot tomato mixture. Sprinkle the crumb and cheese mixture over the tomato filling.

7. Broil the avocado halves about 4 inches from the heat, just long enough to brown the topping, about 2 minutes or so. Serve at once.

Sun-Dried Tomato-Cheese Mold

Serves 12

Crumb crust:

4	tablespoons butter, melted
1	cup flavored bread crumbs
1	tablespoon dill weed
	Black pepper
2	cloves garlic
2	tablespoons chopped green onion

Filling:

1½	pounds cream cheese at room temperature
4	eggs
3	ounces tomato paste
1	(12 ounce) jar sun-dried tomatoes, drained and chopped into ¼-inch pieces
4	tablespoons finely chopped green onion
2	tablespoons dried basil, crushed
2	teaspoons coarsely ground black pepper
2	cloves garlic, minced
¼	cup white vermouth
	Juice of 1 lemon
4	tablespoons chopped parsley

1. Preheat oven to 300°.

2. To prepare crumb crust: Place all ingredients in a food processor and blend with the large blade until well mixed. Pack around the sides and bottom of an 8-inch springform pan.

3. To prepare filling: Blend the cream cheese and eggs until smooth. Fold in the tomato paste, chopped tomatoes, green onion, basil, pepper, garlic, vermouth, lemon juice and parsley, blending only until well mixed. Pour into the crumb crust; place the springform pan inside a larger pan.

4. Bake for 1½ hours. When done, cool on a wire rack, then chill. Serve cold surrounded by crackers or rye bread.

Fennel with Bagna Cauda
Makes 2 cups

Bagna Cauda:

¼	cup butter
8	anchovy fillets, chopped
3-4	cloves garlic
2	cups whipping cream
1½	tablespoons cornstarch

2-3	fennel bulbs, washed, trimmed and cut into small wedges
	French bread, thinly sliced

1. To prepare bagna cauda: Melt the butter in a saucepan; add the chopped anchovies and garlic and sauté a few minutes. Add the cream and heat to just below a boil.

2. Dissolve the cornstarch in 2 to 3 tablespoons of water and add; cook until thickened.

3. To serve, transfer the bagna cauda to a fondue pot or small chafing dish and place the fennel wedges and French bread on a serving platter. Dip the fennel into the bagna cauda and use bread as a sort of individual plate. The bagna cauda is excellent as a dip for any number of vegetables. Use whatever the season offers.

Caponata
Makes 2 quarts

2	pounds eggplant
	Salt
1	pound onions
¼	cup plus 3 tablespoons olive oil
¼	cup dry white wine
1½	pounds tomatoes, peeled, seeded and cut in chunks
2	tablespoons capers
¼	pound celery stalks, diced
1	(12 ounce) can black olives, drained
3	tablespoons vinegar
1	teaspoon sugar
¼	cup tomato sauce

1. Wash the eggplant, cut into cubes and spread on absorbent paper toweling. Sprinkle with salt and allow to sit for 1 hour to draw out the moisture.

2. Slice the onions thinly and sauté them in ¼ cup oil until tender. Add the wine and cook for a few minutes.

3. Add the tomatoes, capers, celery and olives. Cook until the tomatoes are done and well mixed throughout.

4. Dry the eggplant slightly and sauté in 3 tablespoons oil until tender. Drain, if needed, and add to the tomato mixture.

5. Add the vinegar, sugar and tomato sauce and cook for about 1 minute longer.

6. Serve cold as an antipasto or as a vegetable.

Hot Artichoke Appetizers

Makes 24

3	(14 ounce) cans artichoke hearts
1	(8 ounce) package neufchatel cheese at room temperature
¼	teaspoon dried fines herbes, crushed
¼	teaspoon dried Italian herb seasoning, crushed
4	tablespoons butter, melted
1	cup grated parmesan cheese
	Pecan bits

1. Preheat oven to 475°.

2. Drain artichoke hearts, rinse and pat dry with paper towels. Slice the bottom of each artichoke evenly so it will stand up straight. Spread the center of each artichoke apart and if necessary remove a few leaves from the center so it can be stuffed with cheese.

3. Combine cheese with fines herbes and Italian herb seasoning, mixing well. Fill each artichoke with cheese, mounding over the top.

4. Using tongs, dip each artichoke into melted butter, then roll each one in parmesan cheese. Set each one on a 10-by-15-inch jelly roll pan.

5. Press several pecan bits on top of each artichoke. Chill several hours or overnight.

6. Bake about 8 minutes or until golden brown and hot. Serve immediately. These do not stand well.

Brandied Liver Pâté
Serves 8

¾	cup butter
1	pound chicken livers
2	tablespoons brandy
1	large onion, chopped
¼	pound mushrooms, sliced
½	teaspoon salt
¼	teaspoon pepper
¼	teaspoon nutmeg
	Salad greens
	Parsley
	Mushrooms

1. Melt the butter in a skillet over medium-high heat and sauté the chicken livers for about 4 to 6 minutes. Heat the brandy slightly, stand back and set aflame and pour over the chicken livers, shaking skillet until the flame dies. Remove livers from skillet.

2. Put the onion and mushrooms in the skillet and cook over medium-high heat, stirring until onion is soft, about 5 minutes.

3. Combine the onion-mushroom mixture with the chicken livers. Add the salt, pepper and nutmeg. Blend in an electric blender or food processor until smooth.

4. Mold the pâté in a well-oiled bowl or small loaf pan. Chill several hours or overnight.

5. To unmold, run a knife around the edge of pâté. For a loaf pan, dip quickly in and out of hot water. Turn over on a plate lined with salad greens. Reshape pâté if necessary. Garnish with parsley and sliced mushrooms, if desired. Refrigerate covered until serving time.

Tomato Tarts
Makes 36

Cream Cheese Pastry:

1	cup butter, semi-softened
1	(8 ounce) package cream cheese, softened
2	cups flour

Filling:

½	pound sausage
2	tablespoons finely chopped shallots
2	eggs
½	cup whipping cream
½	cup peeled, seeded and finely chopped fresh tomato
1	tablespoon finely chopped fresh basil or 1 teaspoon dried
	Salt and pepper

1. To prepare pastry: Cream the butter and cream cheese. Mix in the flour. Form into a ball. Wrap in plastic and chill 6 hours or longer.
2. Preheat oven to 400°.
3. Let the dough soften a little before rolling. Roll on a lightly floured board to about ¼-inch thickness. Cut into 3½-inch circles and fit into 2-inch tart pans. Pierce with a fork and bake for 10 minutes.
4. To prepare filling: Sauté the sausage and shallots in a skillet until the meat is cooked. Drain the fat.
5. Beat the eggs and cream in a bowl. Add the tomatoes, basil and salt and pepper to taste.
6. Put about 1 teaspoon meat mixture in each tart shell, fill with the cream-tomato mixture. Bake for 12 minutes.

Port Wine Cheese Crock

Makes 3 cups

1	pound sharp cheddar cheese
1	(3 ounce) package cream cheese
3	tablespoons butter
1½	teaspoons dry mustard
½	teaspoon garlic powder
2	tablespoons port

1. In a food processor fitted with a grating blade, grate the cheddar cheese; empty onto wax paper. Change to the steel blade, return the cheddar cheese to the food processor. Add the cream cheese, cut in thirds, and process until smooth.
2. Add the butter, dry mustard, garlic powder and port, turning the food processor on and off until well blended. Place in a serving bowl and chill.

Pâté de Veau, Porc et Lapin

Serves 12

Rabbit:

1	pound boneless rabbit meat
3	tablespoons brandy
	Pinch salt
	Dash pepper
	Pinch dried thyme, crushed
	Pinch ground allspice
1	tablespoon finely minced shallots or green onion

Farce:

½	cup finely minced onion
2	tablespoons butter
½	cup brandy
¾	pound lean pork
¾	pound lean veal
½	pound fresh pork fat
2	eggs, slightly beaten
1½	teaspoons salt
⅛	teaspoon pepper
⅛	teaspoon ground allspice
½	teaspoon dried thyme, crushed
1	clove garlic, minced

Pâté:

½	pound thinly sliced bacon or pork fat back
1	bay leaf
	Cornichons

1. To prepare rabbit: Cut the rabbit meat into ¼-inch strips. Marinate the strips in brandy, salt, pepper, thyme, allspice and shallots or green onions in a glass dish in the refrigerator 6 hours or overnight. Turn the meat in the marinade occasionally.

2. To prepare farce: In a skillet, cook the onion slowly in the butter until tender and translucent. Place in a large mixing bowl.

3. Pour the brandy into the skillet and boil down until reduced by half. Add to the onion in the mixing bowl.

4. Grind the pork, veal and pork fat with the medium blade of a hand meat grinder or run the meat through a food processor, using the on and off pulse. The mixture should be fairly coarse. Add it to the onion-brandy mixture along with the eggs, salt, pepper, allspice, thyme and garlic. Beat vigorously with a wooden spoon until thoroughly blended and light in texture. Sauté a spoonful of farce in a small skillet. Taste and adjust seasonings if necessary. Refrigerate until ready to use.

5. To prepare pâté: Line bottom and sides of a 6-cup terrine with bacon, letting the bacon slices hang over the rim.

6. Preheat oven to 350°.

7. Drain the rabbit strips from the marinade, reserving marinade. Add the marinade to the farce, mixing well. Spread a third of the farce in the terrine and cover with half of the rabbit. Repeat. Top with remaining third of the farce. Make sure everything is tightly packed.

8. Bring the slices of bacon over the pâté, trimming them if necessary so they barely overlap. Place a bay leaf on top of bacon. Cover the terrine with lid. Seal the edges with a flour-and-water paste.

9. Place the terrine in a pan of boiling water. Water should come about halfway up the outside of the terrine. Bake about 1½ hours.

10. Remove the terrine from oven and set on a wire rack to cool. When cool enough to handle, remove the cooked flour paste and lid. With a baster, drain off excess fat. (There'll be quite a bit.)

11. Place a board or plate over the pâté and weight it down with a heavy food can until pâté is cold. Remove weight and replace lid. Chill pâté. Let the pâté age for 3 or 4 days to improve its flavor.

12. To serve, slice ¼-inch thick. Accompany with cornichons.

Note: Pâté will keep in refrigerator for about 10 days.

Terrine de Campagne
Serves 12

½	pound thinly sliced bacon
1	tablespoon butter
1	onion, finely chopped
½	pound lean pork
½	pound pork fat
½	pound veal
½	pound chicken livers
2	cloves garlic, minced
¼	teaspoon ground allspice
	Pinch ground cloves
	Pinch ground nutmeg
2	eggs, slightly beaten
2-3	tablespoons brandy
	Salt and pepper
½	cup shelled pistachio nuts, blanched, peeled and coarsely chopped
1	(8 ounce) slice cooked ham, cut into strips lengthwise
1	bay leaf
½	teaspoon dried thyme, crushed
	Water
	Flour
	Cornichons

1. Line a 6- or 8-cup terrine mold with bacon, letting the slices hang over the rim. Set aside until ready to fill.

2. Melt the butter in a small skillet. Add the onion and sauté until soft and translucent. Set aside to cool.

3. Grind the pork, pork fat and veal by using the medium blade of a hand grinder or by running the meat through a food processor, using the on and off pulse. The mixture should be fairly coarse to give texture to the pâté.

4. Snip the chicken livers into small pieces using scissors.

5. Mix the onion, ground pork, pork fat, veal and chicken livers in a large bowl. Add the garlic, allspice, cloves, nutmeg, eggs, brandy, salt and pepper. Beat with a wooden spoon until all ingredients are well blended.

6. Sauté a spoonful of the meat mixture and taste for seasonings; it should be quite spicy. Beat the chopped pistachios into the uncooked meat mixture.

7. Preheat oven to 350°.

8. Carefully spoon a third of the meat mixture into the bacon-lined terrine. Pat down gently. Place half the ham strips lengthwise over the mixture. Spoon another third of the meat mixture over the ham strips. Pat down gently. Place the remaining ham strips on top. Add remaining meat mixture and pat down. Everything should be tightly packed.

9. Bring the slices of bacon over the meat, trimming them if necessary so they just slightly overlap each other. Place the bay leaf in the center and sprinkle the thyme all over. Cover with terrine lid. In a small bowl make a paste with some water and flour and spread it around edge of the lid to seal terrine.

10. Place the terrine in a large roasting pan. Add boiling water to the pan halfway up the terrine. Bake for 1½ hours. Remove the terrine from oven and cool on a wire rack until you can handle, about 1 hour.

11. Remove the cooked flour paste and lid. Using a baster, remove extra fat. Weigh terrine down with a heavy food can resting on a board or plate until cool. Remove weight; replace lid on terrine and refrigerate it 3 to 4 days before serving. Serve cut into ¼-inch slices with cornichons.

Sesame Chicken

Makes 48 pieces

1	tablespoon vegetable oil
1	small clove garlic, minced
2	whole chicken breasts, skinned, boned and cut into 1-inch cubes
2	tablespoons soy sauce
3	tablespoons firmly packed brown sugar
½	teaspoon ground ginger
3	tablespoons toasted sesame seeds

1. Heat the oil in a heavy skillet. Add the garlic and chicken. Sauté over high heat for 3 minutes or until chicken is about half cooked.

2. Combine the soy sauce, sugar and ginger. Add to the chicken. Continue to sauté over high heat until most of the liquid is evaporated and the chicken is glazed, about 4 minutes.

3. Remove from heat. Chill. Sprinkle with the sesame seeds and toss before serving. Serve with toothpicks.

Gougère with Chicken-Almond Spread

Serves 8

Chicken-Almond Spread:

2¾	ounces chopped blanched almonds, toasted
1	pound boneless chicken breast, poached, skinned and cut in small chunks
4	tablespoons butter
5	tablespoons half-and-half
1	tablespoon tomato paste
2	tablespoons sherry
¾	teaspoon dried tarragon, crushed
	Salt and pepper

Pastry:

⅓	cup butter
1	cup milk
½	teaspoon salt
	Dash paprika
1	cup sifted flour
4	eggs
1	cup shredded Gruyère or Swiss cheese

1. Preheat oven to 300°.

2. To prepare spread: Put the almonds on a cookie sheet and toast them for 15 minutes. Shake the pan occasionally. Watch carefully so they do not burn.

3. Using a food processor or blender, mix together the chicken, butter, half-and-half, tomato paste and sherry. Season with the tarragon and salt and pepper to taste. Blend in the almonds by hand. Chill for 2 to 3 hours before serving.

4. Reset oven to 375°.

5. To prepare pastry: Heat the butter and milk in a saucepan. Add the salt and paprika. Bring to a rolling boil. Remove from heat and add the flour all at once. Beat constantly and vigorously with a wooden spoon until mixture leaves the sides of the pan and forms a ball.

6. Beat in the eggs, one at a time, until smooth. Beat in ¾ cup cheese.

7. Using a soup spoon, drop eight spoonfuls of dough on a greased baking sheet, forming a ring and leaving a 2½-inch circle in the center. Using a teaspoon and the remaining dough, make eight smaller mounds on top of the initial layer. Sprinkle with remaining cheese.

8. Bake for 45 minutes or until puffed and golden. Serve hot, accompanied by the chicken-almond spread.

South Seas Chicken

Makes 48 appetizers

1	cup sour cream
2	tablespoons finely chopped cashews
¼	cup finely chopped mango chutney
2	cups chicken stock or broth
2	whole chicken breasts, halved
4	teaspoons curry powder
48	small curly lettuce leaves
½	cup toasted coconut

1. Blend the sour cream, cashews and chutney in a small bowl. Refrigerate.

2. In a medium saucepan, combine the stock with the chicken breasts and curry powder. Bring to a boil. Lower heat and simmer 25 minutes or until the chicken is tender. Refrigerate the chicken in stock until cool.

3. Remove the chicken breasts from the stock. Skin and bone the breasts. Cut each half breast into six strips, lengthwise. Cut each strip in half crosswise.

4. Place a strip of chicken across one side of each lettuce leaf. Spoon a little of the sour cream-chutney mixture on the chicken strip. Top with a sprinkling of coconut. Roll the lettuce leaf around the chicken strip and secure with a toothpick. Refrigerate 1 hour before serving.

Spring Rolls

Makes 2 dozen egg rolls or 5 dozen appetizers

Spring Rolls:

½	pound lean pork
2½	tablespoons soy sauce
1½	teaspoons Chinese rice wine
1½	tablespoons plus 1 teaspoon tapioca flour or starch
8-10	Chinese dried mushrooms
½	pound Chinese cabbage
½	pound fresh bean sprouts
4	cups peanut or vegetable oil
½	teaspoon salt
½	cup chicken stock or broth
2	tablespoons water
24	spring-roll wrappers or 2 packages won-ton skins
4	tablespoons flour mixed with 6 tablespoons water

Dipping Sauce:

4	tablespoons soy sauce
2	tablespoons Chinese red rice vinegar

Accompaniments:

Hot Chinese mustard

Plum sauce (see index)

1. To prepare spring rolls: Slice and cut the pork into julienne strips if using egg-roll wrappers or in smaller pieces if using won-ton skins. Mix 1 tablespoon soy sauce, the rice wine and 1 teaspoon tapioca flour. Add the pork and marinate while preparing the vegetables.

2. Soak the dried mushrooms in hot water for 15 minutes. Discard the stems and shred the mushrooms. Wash and shred the cabbage. Rinse the bean sprouts with cold water and drain.

3. Heat 2 tablespoons oil in a wok; add the marinated pork and stir-fry for 30 seconds; drain and remove to a plate with a slotted spoon. Add the cabbage to the wok and stir-fry 1 minute. Add the shredded mushrooms, 1½ tablespoons soy sauce, salt and chicken stock; cover and cook about 2 minutes. Add the pork and bean sprouts to the wok and stir-fry about 30 seconds over high heat.

4. Dissolve 1½ tablespoons tapioca flour into 2 tablespoons water. Add to the wok and cook briefly to thicken liquids. Using a wire strainer, remove meat-vegetable mixture to a plate. Let cool.

5. Place 2 tablespoons filling diagonally below the center on each egg-roll wrapper and 1 teaspoon if using won-ton skins. Roll up a little, fold each side of wrapper toward center. Brush some flour paste on the outer edge of skin to seal and roll up into a tight roll.

6. Heat about 3½ cups oil in a wok over high heat; lower heat to medium and fry rolls, a few at a time until golden brown. Keep warm in a low oven until all the rolls are fried.

7. To prepare dipping sauce: Mix together the soy sauce and red rice vinegar in a metal measuring cup. Heat until warm.

8. Serve the spring rolls accompanied by the dipping sauce, mustard and plum sauce.

Note: Be sure the filling is cool before stuffing the rolls so the wrappers won't get soggy.

Chinese Roasted Pork

Serves 10

1	(3 pound) boneless pork loin
2	tablespoons rice wine
4	tablespoons sugar
1	tablespoon salt
2	tablespoons soy sauce
2	tablespoons hoisin sauce
	Chinese mustard
	Toasted sesame seeds

1. Slice meat into 2-inch wide sections and place in a bowl.

2. Blend together the rice wine, sugar, salt, soy sauce and hoisin sauce. Pour over the pork. Marinate for 2 hours at room temperature, turning several times.

3. Preheat oven to 400°.

4. Place the pork on the broiling rack. Bake for 20 minutes in middle of the oven. Turn on broiler (leave rack in middle of oven) and broil for 15 minutes on each side, basting often.

5. Serve, hot or cold, thinly sliced with Chinese mustard and toasted sesame seeds.

This recipe is from Masako Davison.

Italian Sausage in Brioche

Makes 8 brioches

1	package dry yeast
1	tablespoon sugar
¼	cup warm milk
2	cups unbleached flour
1	teaspoon salt
½	cup frozen butter, cut in 8 pieces
2	eggs, lightly beaten
8	Italian sausages (5-to-a-pound size)
	White vermouth
1	egg yolk, slightly beaten
1	tablespoon half-and-half

1. Dissolve the yeast and sugar in the warm milk (105-115° F.). Fit a food processor with the metal blade and add the flour, salt and butter to the work bowl. Process until the butter is cut into the flour mixture, about 20 seconds.

2. Add the yeast mixture and process until combined, about 5 seconds. Add the eggs and process until a ball of dough forms on the blades.

3. Turn out onto a lightly floured board and knead until smooth, about 1 to 2 minutes. Place in a greased bowl, turning to coat all sides.

4. Cover and let rise in a warm place until doubled in bulk, about 1½ to 2 hours.

5. Punch down and knead several times. Place in the bowl again. Refrigerate for a couple of hours for easier handling.

6. Meanwhile, simmer the sausages in a heavy, covered pan with the bottom just barely covered with vermouth, about 15 minutes. Liquid should be boiled away, but if any remains, pour it off. Pierce sausages to release fat and brown slowly on all sides, turning frequently. Cool.

7. Preheat oven to 375°.

8. Remove dough from the refrigerator and roll out on a lightly floured board to ⅛- to ¼-inch thickness. Cut dough in 8 equal rectangular pieces. Wrap each sausage in dough, stretching it to bring the sides up around the sausages, tucking in the ends and pinching the edges together to overlap. Any excess dough should be cut away.

9. Place seam side down on a buttered baking sheet. Cover and let rise in a warm place for 10 minutes. Brush the dough with an egg wash of egg yolk and half-and-half.

10. Bake for about 25 minutes or until brioche is lightly browned. Slice and serve with a variety of mustards.

◇

Oeufs en Gelée

Serves 4

2	cups clear chicken stock or broth
⅛	teaspoon dried tarragon, crushed
1	envelope unflavored gelatin
	Fresh tarragon leaves or black olive slices
1	(4 ounce) package thinly sliced ham
4	eggs
	Oil
	Salad greens

1. Pour the chicken stock into a small saucepan, reserving ¼ cup to soften gelatin. Add the tarragon to the stock and simmer over medium heat for 5 minutes to blend flavors.

2. Soften the gelatin in ¼ cup cold stock for 5 minutes. Add to the hot chicken stock, stirring until gelatin is dissolved. Set aside.

3. Place a fresh tarragon leaf or thin slices of black olives in the bottom of 4 individual ramekins. Carefully fit a slice of ham on top. Trim the ham even with the edges of the ramekins.

4. Break each egg into a separate dish. Add water to your poacher pan. Slightly oil the wells of the poacher. Place on top of the pan. Cover and bring water to a boil.

5. Slip each egg into one of the wells. Cover the pan and simmer the eggs 4 to 5 minutes or until white is set.

6. Remove from heat immediately and place the eggs on top of the ham. Spoon the gelatin over the eggs until it fills the ramekins. Pour the remaining gelatin into a small dish. Chill immediately until it is partly set. Cover with plastic wrap and chill for several hours or overnight.

7. To serve, run a knife around the edges of the ramekins and invert on a platter garnished with salad greens. Cut the remaining gelatin into small cubes and use to garnish platter.

Soups

In a part of the world where fogs, mists and early dark dictate the menu so much of the year, soups mean comfort and sharing of hospitality as much as nutrition. With year-round access to some vegetables fresh out of the ground, soups make winter almost as exciting for a cook as when the Pike Place Market is at its summer fullness and the only question is how to get all the harvest eaten.

Soups are a preferred method of dealing with "a bunch of" anything from the Northwest's bounty, be it watercress found in a slow-running clear-water creek bed, clams from a trip to a remote beach or zucchini that has overtaken a neighbor's yard. The fine and aromatic art of simmering to blend ingredients slowly creates its own social ambiance. Nothing will bring people into the kitchen faster than the delightful steaming of a bubbling soup pot.

The skillful Northwest cook can deal in subtleties, such as making Vichyssoise to bring out the flavors of the various varieties of potatoes available here, or in magnitudes of culinary grandeur, such as adding Northwest seafood to make something regional out of a basic Bouillabaisse or Cioppino.

The best thing about soups is that the recipes in this chapter allow a cook to sample many cuisines and the products that are abundant in the Puget Sound area.

◇

Brown Beef Stock

Makes 2 quarts

2	pounds beef shanks
3	pounds cracked beef bones
2	carrots, scrubbed and quartered
2	onions, halved
½	pound turnips, scrubbed and halved
2	celery stalks
½	pound leeks, washed
2	teaspoons salt

Bouquet garni (¼ teaspoon dried thyme, 1 bay leaf, 6 parsley sprigs, 2 whole cloves, 2 unpeeled garlic cloves, tied in cheesecloth)

1. Preheat oven to 450°.

2. Arrange the shanks, meat bones, carrots, onions and turnips in a large roasting pan and place on the middle rack of the oven. Roast until the meat and vegetables are brown, turning occasionally. This will take 40 to 45 minutes.

3. Remove from the oven and transfer the browned meat and vegetables to a 12-quart stockpot or soup kettle. Drain the fat from the roasting pan. Deglaze the drippings with 1 to 2 cups water; add to the stockpot.

4. Fold the green tops of the celery and leeks down around their stalks. Tie with string into bundles and add to the stock.

5. Cover with cold water to a depth of at least 1 inch above the ingredients. Bring to a simmer over low heat. Skim off the scum as it rises to the surface.

6. Add the salt and bouquet garni. Continue simmering slowly for at least 5 hours, leaving the cover partly ajar to allow steam to escape. Accumulated scum may be skimmed occasionally.

7. Remove the bones and vegetables from the stock. Strain the stock into a large bowl through a colander lined with cheesecloth. Cool in a sink filled with cold water. Refrigerate overnight to allow the fat to congeal on top.

8. Next day, remove the fat from the surface of the stock. Reheat the stock slowly. Pour it into a plastic container and refrigerate or freeze.

Fish Stock

Makes 1 quart

1	large onion, peeled and coarsely chopped
1	cup chopped celery
1	carrot, scraped and chopped
3-4	tablespoons butter
3	pounds white fish trimmings, such as heads and tails
1½	cups dry white wine
6-8	large peppercorns
	Bouquet garni (1 teaspoon dried thyme, 5-6 sprigs parsley, 1 bay leaf, 2 celery stalks, tied in cheesecloth)
1	cup chopped parsley
3	tablespoons lemon juice
	Salt

1. In a large, heavy enamel casserole, sauté the onion, celery and carrot in the butter over low heat until soft but not brown.

2. Add the fish trimmings, wine, peppercorns, bouquet garni, parsley, lemon juice and salt to taste. Add enough water to cover. Bring to a boil slowly.

3. Reduce heat and simmer, partly covered, for 30 to 40 minutes, skimming the stock frequently.

4. When the stock is done, strain it into a large bowl through a colander lined with cheesecloth. Cool in a sink filled with cold water. Pour the stock into plastic containers and refrigerate or freeze.

Note: Fish stock will not keep more than 1 or 2 days in the refrigerator.

Chicken Stock

Makes 1½ quarts

3-4	pounds chicken necks and wings
2-3	quarts water
	Salt
3	carrots, scrubbed and cut in chunks
1	large onion, peeled and quartered
2	stalks celery, cut in pieces
	Bouquet garni (¼ teaspoon dried thyme, 3-4 sprigs parsley, 1 bay leaf, 6 black peppercorns, tied in cheesecloth)

1. Put the chicken pieces into a stockpot. Cover with cold water to a depth of 1 inch over the chicken. Bring to a boil over low heat. Skim off the scum as it rises to the surface, occasionally adding a little cold water to bring the scum to the surface. Remove as necessary.

2. Add salt to taste, carrots, onion, celery and bouquet garni. Continue to simmer 2 to 3 hours, or until the stock has developed a good flavor. Leave the cover partly ajar to allow steam to escape.

3. Strain the stock into a large bowl through a colander lined with cheesecloth. Cool in a sink filled with cold water. Refrigerate overnight to allow the fat to congeal on top.

4. Next day, remove the fat from the surface of the stock. Reheat the stock slowly. Pack into a plastic container and refrigerate or freeze.

Oyster Stew

Serves 4 to 6

¾	cup butter
1	cup finely diced celery
2	carrots, finely shredded
6-8	green onions, white part only, finely minced
½	cup flour
2	cups half-and-half
	Salt and pepper
1	cup clam nectar or juice
1	pint extra small oysters, cut in half
½	cup white wine or dry sherry

1. Melt ¼ cup butter in a large saucepan. Add the celery, carrots and green onions and stir until coated with butter. Cover and simmer for 20 minutes over very low heat. Set aside.

2. Melt the remaining ½ cup butter in another saucepan; add the flour. Cook together until bubbly, about 1 minute. Add the half-and-half and cook over medium heat until smooth and creamy.

3. Add the flour mixture to the vegetable mixture and mix thoroughly. Season to taste with salt and pepper. Set aside.

4. Bring the clam juice to a boil. Add the oysters and wine. Simmer over low heat for about 8 to 10 minutes or until the edges begin to curl. Do not boil.

5. When very hot, pour the oyster mixture into the creamed vegetable mixture. Stir over low heat, again being careful not to boil. Serve immediately.

This is a special family recipe of Dawn Clark.

Easy Clam Chowder

Serves 4

3-4	slices bacon, diced
¼	cup finely chopped onion
3	(6½ ounce) cans chopped clams
2	large potatoes, peeled and diced
1	cup half-and-half
	Salt and pepper

1. In a large saucepan, fry the bacon slowly until done but still transparent. Remove and drain on a paper towel.

2. Add the chopped onion to the bacon drippings and cook over low heat, stirring once in a while, until it is soft and transparent.

3. Drain the clams, reserving liquor. Set aside.

4. Add the potatoes to the saucepan, along with the reserved bacon and the clam liquor plus enough water to make 2½ cups liquid.

5. Cover; bring to a boil; reduce heat and cook until the potatoes are tender, 20 to 30 minutes.

6. Add the reserved clams and half-and-half and heat thoroughly. Adjust seasonings before serving.

Cioppino

Serves 4 to 6

¼	cup salad oil
1	cup chopped onion
1	cup chopped green pepper
½	cup chopped parsley
4	cloves garlic, minced
1	(16 ounce) can tomatoes
2	cups tomato sauce (see index)
2	bay leaves
1	teaspoon salt
¼	teaspoon dried thyme, crushed
¼	teaspoon dried marjoram, crushed
½-¾	teaspoon hot pepper sauce
1½	cups dry white wine
1	pound halibut steaks, or other firm white fish, cut into 1-inch cubes
1	dozen fresh clams in the shell, scrubbed
1	pound shrimp, shelled and deveined

1. In a large saucepan, heat the oil. Add the onion, green pepper, parsley and garlic; cook until tender. Add the tomatoes, tomato sauce, bay leaves, salt, thyme, marjoram and hot pepper sauce. Simmer, covered, 2 hours, stirring occasionally.

2. Add the wine; cook uncovered for 10 minutes.

3. Add the halibut; cover and cook 3 minutes. Add the clams; cook, covered, 2 minutes. Add the shrimp and cook, covered, 3 minutes or until the fish is cooked and the clams are open. Be sure not to overcook. Serve in soup plates.

Note: Discard clams that didn't open during cooking.

Manhattan Clam Chowder

Serves 6

6½	pounds steamer clams
½	pound bacon, cut into ¼-inch pieces
3	medium onions, finely chopped

1	small green pepper, finely chopped
4	cups peeled, seeded and chopped tomatoes
3	cups tomato sauce (see index)
3	medium potatoes, diced
4	carrots, diced
2	stalks celery, diced
1½	quarts water
	Salt
	Freshly ground black pepper
1	teaspoon dried thyme, crushed
1	bay leaf

1. Shuck the clams, reserving the liquor. You should have about 1 quart of clam meat.

2. Cook the bacon in a Dutch oven until almost crisp. Remove with a slotted spoon and drain on paper towels.

3. Sauté the onions and peppers in the bacon fat until the onions are a pale gold. Add the tomatoes, tomato sauce, potatoes, carrots, celery and water. Season with salt and pepper to taste; add the thyme and bay leaf. Bring to a boil, lower heat and simmer gently, uncovered, for 15 to 20 minutes or until the potatoes are tender.

4. Add the prepared clams and their juice. Cover and heat about 3 minutes to cook the clams and blend flavors. Taste for seasonings. Add the bacon and serve immediately.

Bouillabaisse

Serves 10

Fish Stock:

	Head and tail of 1 red snapper
	Head and tail of 1 mackerel
2-2½	quarts water

Fish Soup:

3	pounds red snapper
2	pounds mackerel
2	large Dungeness crabs, cooked and cleaned
2	pounds steamer clams
25	prawns
¾	cup olive oil
2	medium onions, sliced
2	leeks, white part only, sliced
2	celery stalks, sliced
3	tomatoes, peeled, seeded and chopped
5-6	cloves garlic, minced
1	bouquet garni (1 small bay leaf, ¼ teaspoon dried thyme, 3-4 stems parsley, ½ teaspoon dried red chili pepper, tied in cheesecloth)
	Thin strip orange peel
2	sprigs fresh fennel or 1 teaspoon dried fennel
¼	teaspoon saffron
	Salt and pepper
¼	cup chopped parsley

Croûtes:

½	cup olive oil
20	slices French bread, cut on the diagonal
	Several cloves garlic, halved

1. To prepare fish stock: Place the fish heads and tails in a large saucepan and cover with water. Bring to a boil. Reduce heat and simmer 15 minutes. Strain. Set aside.
2. To prepare fish soup: Cut the fish in 2- to 3-inch chunks.

3. Using a cleaver, chop the crabs in pieces, shells included. Scrub the clams thoroughly and wash the prawns.

4. Heat the olive oil in a large pot. Stir in the onions, leeks and celery and sauté until soft but not browned. Add 2 quarts fish stock, tomatoes, garlic, bouquet garni, orange peel and fennel. Sprinkle the saffron and salt and pepper to taste over the mixture. Bring to a boil; reduce heat and simmer 30 to 45 minutes. (The dish can be prepared to this point 8 hours ahead, covered and refrigerated.)

5. Bring the soup broth to a boil, uncovered, 20 minutes before serving. Add the mackerel, clams and prawns. Boil hard 5 minutes. Do not stir, but shake the pot occasionally to prevent sticking.

6. Lay the snapper and crab on top of the mixture and boil 5 minutes longer until the fish begins to flake easily. Keep the liquid at a rolling boil during the entire cooking time so the oil emulsifies with the broth and does not float on surface. Remove from heat.

7. Transfer the fish to a warm platter, arranging each kind separately. Discard any unopened clams. Cover with foil; keep warm.

8. Taste the broth for seasoning. Pour into a tureen. Sprinkle the broth and fish pieces with parsley. Serve immediately with croûtes, letting each guest take fish and spoon broth over it.

9. To prepare croûtes: Heat the olive oil in a large skillet until very hot. Add the bread slices so they fit comfortably. Toss until the croûtes are evenly browned on both sides. Remove and drain on paper towels. Repeat with remaining bread slices. Rub each croûte with the cut side of a half clove of garlic.

Hot-and-Sour Soup
Serves 8

6½	cups chicken stock or broth
3	medium carrots, cut into julienne strips
2	cups sliced fresh mushrooms
½	pound uncooked boneless pork, cut into julienne strips
1	tablespoon soy sauce
2	cups shredded Chinese cabbage
½	pound tofu, cut into ½-inch cubes
¼	cup cider vinegar
½	teaspoon pepper
¼	cup cornstarch
¼	cup water
⅓	cup sliced green onions

1. In a large saucepan, combine the stock, carrots, mushrooms, pork and soy sauce; bring to a boil. Reduce heat to low and simmer 3 minutes. Add the cabbage and simmer 1 more minute.

2. Add the tofu, vinegar and pepper; return to boiling.

3. Combine the cornstarch and water; stir into the soup. Boil 1 minute longer or until the soup thickens slightly. Serve in heated bowls, topped with green onions.

Won Ton Soup
Serves 4 to 6

Won tons:

¼	pound fresh shrimp, shelled and deveined
¼	pound lean pork, finely ground
½	teaspoon grated fresh ginger root
½	teaspoon salt
1	tablespoon soy sauce
1	egg
1½	teaspoons sesame oil
½	teaspoon sugar
1	teaspoon dry sherry

2	tablespoons minced green onion
30	won ton wrappers
8	cups boiling water
1	cup cold water

Soup:

½	pound fresh mushrooms
4	cups chicken stock or broth
1	teaspoon sesame oil
½	teaspoon salt
½	teaspoon pepper
2	green onions, chopped

1. To prepare won tons: Rinse the shrimp and pat dry with paper towels. Chop the shrimp to a fine paste in a food processor. Combine the shrimp paste with the pork, ginger root, salt, soy sauce, egg, sesame oil, sugar, sherry and minced green onion in a large bowl; mix well.

2. Place 1 won ton wrapper on the counter with one point toward you.

3. Place 1 rounded teaspoon of filling just below the center of the wrapper. Fold the bottom point of the won ton wrapper over the filling and tuck under. Roll to cover filling, leaving 1 inch unrolled at the top of the wrapper.

4. Moisten the right corner of the wrapper with water. Grasp the corners and bring them below the filling. Place the left corner over the right and press to seal. Repeat with remaining won tons. As each won ton is finished, place it on a plate under a towel.

5. Bring 8 cups water to a boil in a large kettle. Carefully lower the won tons into the boiling water with a slotted spoon. Stir gently to prevent the won tons from sticking to the bottom of the kettle. Bring to a second boil. Add 1 cup cold water and bring to a third boil. Won tons will float when done. Remove won tons from water and set aside.

6. To prepare soup: Thinly slice the mushrooms. Pour the chicken stock into a saucepan. Bring to a boil over high heat and add the mushrooms. Reduce heat to medium and cook 5 minutes. Add the sesame oil and season with salt and pepper. Add the precooked won tons to the stock along with the chopped green onions. Heat and serve immediately.

Italian Vegetable-Meat Soup

Serves 6 to 8

1	tablespoon oil
1	pound stewing beef, cut into ½-inch cubes
1	pound Italian sausage links, sliced
1	(28 ounce) can tomatoes, broken up
3	cups water
1	cup chopped onion
½	teaspoon salt
1	tablespoon Worcestershire sauce
2	large potatoes, peeled and cut into ½-inch cubes
1	cup sliced celery

1. In a large, heavy kettle, heat the oil. Add the beef and brown on all sides. Remove the meat with a slotted spoon and set aside.

2. Add the sausage to the kettle and brown on all sides. Drain off drippings. Add the tomatoes, water, onion, salt, Worcestershire sauce and browned beef. Heat to boiling. Reduce heat to simmer; cover and cook 1½ hours or until almost tender.

3. Add the cubed potatoes and sliced celery and simmer until the vegetables and meat are tender, about 20 minutes longer.

Black Bean Soup

Serves 6 to 8

1	pound black turtle beans
	Water
2	ham hocks
2	tablespoons bacon drippings
1	cup minced onion
1	carrot, minced
1	stalk celery, minced
3	sprigs parsley
⅛	teaspoon dried thyme, crushed
	Pinch cayenne pepper flakes
1	bay leaf
2	tablespoons Worcestershire sauce

| Salt and pepper |
| ¼ cup sherry |

Garnishes:

| Minced parsley |
| Finely chopped hard-cooked egg, or sieved egg yolk |
| Sour cream or yogurt |

1. Two days before serving: Wash the beans. Cover them with cold water and soak at least 6 hours or overnight.

2. Place the ham hocks in a large kettle and cover with enough water to make 6 cups of stock. Bring to a boil and simmer for about 1 hour or until the ham is tender. Let the ham cool in the stock 1½ hours. Remove the ham and refrigerate to use in other recipes. Place the ham broth in jars and refrigerate.

3. One day before serving: Discard any floating beans; drain. Discard the congealed fat from the top of the ham broth.

4. Melt the bacon drippings in a skillet, add the onion, carrot, celery, parsley, thyme, cayenne and bay leaf. Sauté the vegetables until golden brown. Place in a soup kettle. Add the Worcestershire sauce, salt, pepper, beans and 6 cups of ham stock. Simmer slowly, covered, 5 hours. Add more stock or water if the soup becomes too thick. When done, let the soup cool and refrigerate overnight.

5. On the day of serving: Place the soup over medium heat and bring to a boil. Force the soup mixture through a sieve, a little at a time to remove skins and make it smooth. It is a thick mixture, so keep scraping the outside of the sieve to get the thicker bean mixture into the soup. Discard the excess skin and very thick mixture left in the sieve.

6. Taste and add more salt, pepper and Worcestershire sauce if needed. Add the sherry, stirring well. Heat and serve hot in soup bowls with your choice of garnishes.

Hearty Hominy Soup
Serves 8

1	large fresh pork hock, halved
1	whole stewing chicken or fryer, washed, giblets removed
2	quarts water
1	(16 ounce) can stewed or whole tomatoes
2	(16 ounce) cans yellow hominy, drained
2	yellow onions, finely chopped
1	tablespoon salt
	Freshly ground black pepper

Toppings:

Chopped red onion

Chopped fresh green chilies or green bell pepper

Chopped avocado

Shredded lettuce

Finely chopped radishes

Shredded Swiss cheese

Sliced fresh mushrooms

2 limes, cut into wedges

1. One day before serving: Add all the ingredients, except the toppings, to a large kettle. Bring to a boil, reduce heat, cover and simmer slowly about 3 hours, until the meat begins to fall away from the bones.

2. Cool the meat in the stock 1½ hours. Remove the chicken and hock, placing them in a bowl. Cover and store in refrigerator overnight. Store the soup mixture in a large covered container in refrigerator overnight.

3. On the day of serving: Remove the skin from the chicken and shred or chop the meat. Remove the rind, fat and bone from the pork hock and shred or chop the meat.

4. Remove the soup mixture from the refrigerator and skim the congealed fat from the surface. Mix the meat and soup mixture together. Store in refrigerator until ready to serve.

5. Prepare the toppings in small separate bowls.

6. Just before serving, reheat soup to simmering. Serve in large, heated soup bowls and pass the toppings so guests can help themselves. Guests should squeeze a wedge of lime over each serving.

Three Bean Soup

Serves 6

½	cup dry baby lima beans
½	cup dry pinto beans
½	cup dry green split peas
	Water
1	teaspoon salt
1	(1½ pound) ham hock
1	tablespoon vegetable oil
1	large onion, chopped
1	large clove garlic, minced
2	cups diced celery
1	cup diced carrots
4	tablespoons butter
1	teaspoon dried thyme, crushed
⅛	teaspoon dried crushed red pepper
4	cups sliced fresh mushrooms
1	tablespoon flour

1. Soak the beans and peas overnight in 1½ quarts water and salt.

2. In a Dutch oven, brown the ham hock in the oil. Stir in the onion and garlic. Sauté until the onion is soft. Add 1 quart water, cover and simmer 1 hour. Refrigerate overnight.

3. Next day, skim off the solidified fat and discard, reserving the stock. Slice the meat from the bone; add the meat to the stock in the pan.

4. Drain the beans and peas. Add them to the meat-stock mixture along with 2½ cups water.

5. Sauté the celery and carrots in 2 tablespoons butter for approximately 5 minutes. Add to the soup mixture along with the thyme and red pepper. Cover and simmer 50 minutes.

6. Sauté the mushrooms in the remaining 2 tablespoons butter until nicely browned. Stir in the flour. Add to the soup; cover and simmer 5 to 10 minutes longer.

Lentil-Beer Soup
Serves 8

2	cups dried lentils
4	cups beer
4	cups water
1	ham hock or ham bone
2	medium onions, diced
2	stalks celery, diced
3	medium carrots, sliced
½	teaspoon pepper
2	teaspoons salt

1. Stir the lentils into the beer and water in a large kettle and bring to a boil. Reduce heat, cover and simmer for 1 hour. Add the remaining ingredients and simmer for 2 hours, stirring occasionally.

2. Remove the ham hock or bone from the soup and cut off the meat, returning the meat to the soup. Serve immediately.

Fresh Mushroom Soup
Serves 6

½	pound mushrooms
½	cup finely chopped onion
2	tablespoons butter
1	tablespoon flour
2	tablespoons finely chopped parsley
3½	cups chicken stock or broth
1	egg yolk
1	cup sour cream

1. Slice the mushrooms thinly. Sauté them, along with the onion, in butter for 5 minutes or until golden brown.

2. Sprinkle the mushrooms with the flour and parsley. Gradually stir in the chicken stock and simmer slowly 30 minutes.

3. Beat the egg yolk slightly; blend with the sour cream and pour into a soup tureen. Gradually stir the hot soup into the tureen. Ladle into warmed soup bowls.

Onion Soup

Serves 6

¼	cup olive oil
2	tablespoons butter
12	medium onions, thinly sliced
½	teaspoon sugar
8	cups beef stock or broth
3	tablespoons flour
½	cup dry white wine
½	teaspoon Dijon mustard
	Salt
	Freshly ground pepper
6	(¾-inch-thick) slices French bread, toasted
1½	cups finely grated Gruyère cheese

1. Heat the oil and butter in a large saucepan over very low heat until the butter is melted. Add the onions; sprinkle with the sugar and cook until the onions are a rich golden brown, stirring about every 10 minutes. This can take 2 hours or longer.

2. Bring the beef stock to a boil in a separate saucepan.

3. Sprinkle the flour over the onions, stirring until the flour is completely dissolved. Add the boiling stock, wine and mustard; blend well. Cover partly and simmer 30 to 40 minutes. Taste and season with salt and pepper. If the soup has cooked down too much, stir in additional beef stock for a thinner consistency.

4. Preheat oven to 425°.

5. Ladle the soup into 6 deep 2-cup oven-proof soup bowls, about 4 inches in diameter, to within about 1 inch of the rims. Top with toasted French bread. Sprinkle each serving with ¼ cup grated cheese. Transfer the bowls to a baking sheet.

6. Bake for 20 minutes. Remove the bowls and reset oven to broil. Then set the bowls under the broiler to brown the tops lightly. Serve immediately.

Potage Parmentier
Serves 8

4½	cups thinly sliced leeks
¼	cup butter
6	cups diced potatoes
4	cups chicken stock or broth
⅔	cup half-and-half or milk
	Salt and pepper
	Parsley

1. Sauté the leeks in the butter in a Dutch oven until transparent.
2. Add the potatoes and chicken stock. Cover and bring to a boil. Reduce heat and simmer 45 minutes to 1 hour or until tender.
3. Purée in a blender or run through a food mill.
4. Return to the Dutch oven, add half-and-half and reheat slowly until piping hot. Adjust seasonings. Serve in soup bowls and add a garnish of parsley, if desired.

Note: You can freeze the soup, but in this case do not add the half-and-half until you reheat it.

Potage Crécy
Serves 6

8	large carrots, scraped and thinly sliced
1	medium white onion, peeled and thinly sliced
2	stalks celery, thinly sliced
3	cups chicken stock or broth
1	teaspoon salt
¼	teaspoon white pepper
2	egg yolks
1	cup whipping cream
	Chopped parsley

1. Place the carrots, onion and celery in a Dutch oven. Add the chicken stock. Season with salt and pepper. Cover. Bring to a boil over high heat. Reduce heat and simmer 40 minutes or until the vegetables are tender.

2. Using an electric blender or a food mill, purée the soup a little at a time. Return the soup to the Dutch oven and heat until piping hot.

3. Meanwhile, beat together the egg yolks and cream. Add a little of the hot soup to the egg mixture, stirring all the while. Add the egg mixture back to the soup, stirring constantly over low heat, until the soup is hot. Do not boil.

4. Adjust seasonings to taste. Garnish with parsley and serve immediately.

Cream of Broccoli Soup

Serves 4

1½	cups chicken stock or broth
½	cup chopped onion
2	cups cut broccoli
½	teaspoon dried thyme, crushed
1	small bay leaf
	Dash garlic powder
2	tablespoons butter
2	tablespoons flour
½	teaspoon salt
	Dash white pepper
1	cup milk

1. In a saucepan, combine the chicken stock, onion, broccoli, thyme, bay leaf and garlic powder. Bring to a boil.

2. Reduce heat; cover and simmer for 10 minutes, or until the broccoli is tender. Remove the bay leaf.

3. Place the vegetable mixture in a blender container or a food processor. Cover and blend 30 to 60 seconds or until smooth. In the same saucepan, melt the butter. Blend in the flour, salt and pepper.

4. Add the milk, all at once. Cook and stir until thickened and bubbly. Stir in the vegetable purée. Cook until heated through. Serve immediately or chill and serve cold.

Broccoli-Cheese-Mustard Soup

Serves 8

1	(1¼ pound) bunch broccoli, trimmed
2	medium onions, sliced
5	tablespoons butter
7	cups chicken stock or broth
1	teaspoon dried oregano, crushed
¼	cup flour
3	tablespoons Dijon mustard
⅛	teaspoon pepper
1	cup milk
2	cups shredded sharp cheddar cheese

1. Cut the flowerettes off the broccoli and divide them into small sections. Simmer in lightly salted water 2 to 3 minutes; drain and set aside.

2. Peel the stalks and cut them into small pieces; cook with the onions in 3 tablespoons butter in a large saucepan about 5 minutes.

3. Add 3 cups of the stock and the oregano; simmer 20 to 30 minutes or until the vegetables are fork-tender.

4. Process in a blender or food processor until smooth.

5. Melt the remaining 2 tablespoons butter in a saucepan. Stir in the flour and cook until bubbly. Stir in the mustard and pepper.

6. Add the processed mixture and the remaining 4 cups of stock; heat to simmering, stirring.

7. Slowly add the milk and cheese, stirring constantly until the cheese melts.

8. Add the broccoli flowerettes; heat and serve.

Cheddar Cheese Soup

Serves 4 to 6

1	small onion
2	stalks celery
1	green pepper
2	carrots

5	tablespoons butter
4	tablespoons flour
4	cups chicken stock or broth
3	cups grated sharp cheddar cheese
½	cup milk or half-and-half
2	tablespoons dry sherry
	Salt and pepper
	Chopped parsley

1. Finely chop the onion, celery, green pepper and carrots. Sauté them in the butter until tender-crisp. Stir in the flour and let cook for about 1 minute.

2. Add the chicken stock and cook until it boils and thickens slightly. Add the cheese and stir until it melts.

3. Add the milk or half-and-half and sherry. Season to taste with salt and pepper. Garnish with chopped parsley.

Scandinavian Cherry Soup

Serves 6

2	(16 ounce) cans water-pack pitted sour red cherries
1	cup strained fresh orange juice
	Grated peel of 1 medium orange
4	teaspoons cornstarch
½	teaspoon ground cinnamon
⅓	cup sugar
	Pinch salt
1	cup dry red wine
	Sour cream

1. Combine the cherries and their liquid, orange juice and peel, cornstarch, cinnamon, sugar and salt in a blender container or bowl of food processor. Whirl until the mixture is smooth. (You may need to do this in two batches.)

2. Transfer the cherry mixture to a large saucepan. Add the wine and cook the soup over medium heat, stirring constantly, until it comes to a boil and thickens. Serve garnished with sour cream.

3. If you want to serve the soup cold, refrigerate in a soup tureen until well chilled. Serve with sour cream.

Iced Honeydew-Pear Soup

Serves 4 to 6

1	large honeydew melon
2	Anjou pears
1½	tablespoons lemon juice
½	cup dry white wine
⅛	teaspoon cinnamon
	Several sprigs fresh mint

1. Cut the melon in half; discard the seeds and scoop out the flesh. Purée, in several batches, in a food processor or blender and empty into a mixing bowl.

2. Peel and core the pears and chop into small pieces. Put them in a small, heavy saucepan with the lemon juice and slowly bring to a simmer. Cook gently, stirring occasionally, 10 to 12 minutes or until soft. (This prevents the pears from darkening.)

3. Purée the pears in a food processor or blender and stir into the honeydew purée. Add the wine and cinnamon and chill. Garnish with fresh mint.

Watercress Soup

Serves 8 to 12

2-3	bunches watercress, with stems, washed and chopped
3	tablespoons butter
2	tablespoons olive oil
1	medium onion, minced
1	clove garlic, minced
4	medium potatoes, peeled and sliced
½	teaspoon salt
¼	teaspoon pepper
6	cups chicken stock or broth
2	cups milk
2	egg yolks
1	cup whipping cream

1. Set aside ½ cup of the chopped watercress. In a kettle, heat the butter and oil and sauté the onion and garlic until translucent.

2. Add the potatoes, salt and pepper. Stir in the chicken stock. Cover and cook for 10 minutes.

3. Add the milk and all but the reserved watercress. Continue cooking for another 5 minutes.

4. Purée the contents of the kettle in a blender; return to the kettle. Bring to a near boil; add the reserved watercress.

5. Beat the egg yolks and stir into the cream. Add a little of the hot soup to the egg yolk-cream mixture. Return to the hot soup. Stir together to blend. Serve immediately.

Vichyssoise

Serves 8

4	leeks, cleaned and sliced
1	medium onion, diced
1	tablespoon butter
4-5	potatoes, peeled and diced
2	cups hot water
2	cups hot chicken stock or broth
2	teaspoons salt
1	cup hot milk
1	cup hot half-and-half
1	cup whipping cream
	Finely chopped chives

1. Cook the leeks and onion slowly in the butter in a large kettle for a few minutes or until soft, stirring occasionally with a wooden spoon.

2. Add the potatoes to the kettle along with the water and chicken stock. Season with salt. Simmer, covered, for 30 to 40 minutes or until the potatoes are soft. Purée the soup in blender.

3. Return the soup to the kettle. Add the milk and half-and-half; bring the soup back to a boil, stirring occasionally to prevent scorching.

4. Strain the soup through a fine sieve. Cool, stirring occasionally, to keep it smooth; strain again. Stir in the whipping cream and chill thoroughly. To serve, sprinkle each portion with finely chopped chives.

Chilled Zucchini Soup
Serves 6

⅓	cup butter
¾	cup finely chopped onion
1	clove garlic, minced
3	cups sliced, unpeeled zucchini
1	cup chicken stock or broth
½	teaspoon salt
⅛	teaspoon pepper
4	cups milk
2	tablespoons cornstarch
¼	cup dry white wine
	Shredded zucchini

1. In a large saucepan, melt the butter over medium heat. Add the onion and garlic and cook 5 minutes or until soft and lightly browned.

2. Add the zucchini; cook, stirring frequently, 10 minutes or until the zucchini turns soft. Add the chicken stock. Season with salt and pepper. Cover and simmer 15 minutes.

3. Place in a blender container a third at a time, each time covering and blending 30 seconds or until liquefied. Return to the saucepan.

4. Stir a little milk into cornstarch, blending to a smooth paste. Add remaining milk, blending well.

5. Add the milk mixture to zucchini in the saucepan. Bring to a boil over medium heat, stirring constantly. Boil 1 minute. Stir in the white wine.

6. Cover and chill several hours or overnight. Serve in chilled glass dishes, sprinkled with shredded raw zucchini.

Northwest Gazpacho
Makes 3 quarts

¾	cup coarsely chopped celery
1½	cups coarsely chopped onion
¾	cup coarsely chopped green pepper
¾	cup coarsely chopped carrots

3	medium ripe tomatoes
2	cloves garlic, crushed
½	cup parsley sprigs
1¼	cups chicken stock or broth
½	teaspoon salt
	Pinch celery seed
2	tablespoons chopped fresh cilantro
3	bay leaves
3-4	drops Tabasco sauce
1	tablespoon tarragon wine vinegar
1	(46 ounce) can tomato juice
	Seasoned croutons

1. Place the celery, onion, green pepper and carrots in the bowl of a food processor fitted with the steel blade. Process until the vegetables are finely chopped. Place the vegetables in a gallon jar.

2. Cut the tomatoes in quarters and place in the food processor with the garlic and parsley sprigs. Chop finely and add to the jar with the other vegetables.

3. Add the chicken stock to the jar of vegetables. Stir in the salt, celery seed, cilantro, bay leaves, Tabasco, tarragon vinegar and tomato juice; mix well.

4. Cover the jar and refrigerate for 48 hours. Remove the bay leaves before serving. Serve gazpacho very cold with croutons for garnish.

This recipe is from Joanna Goodlund.

Eggs

The egg elevates spur-of-the-moment meals to culinary respectability, if not glory. The egg is the quickest of kitchen fast foods, and it provides the structure for intricate combinations of ingredients and herbs.

The techniques of egg cookery are simple and versatile and, once mastered, basic dishes such as omelets and frittatas can produce literally hundreds of variations.

The arrival of the first seafood or produce of the season, fresh from the market and too tempting to wait, can be made into simple Northwest favorites with the skillful addition of some eggs.

And, after the first rush of enthusiasm for simple, lively local produce passes, the egg is unassertive enough to accept subtle combinations of herbs and other ingredients to make even more of our seasonal bounty — when it is at its best quality and lowest cost.

Not only does Yakima asparagus make a superb side dish, but our Asparagus Frittata also can star as the main course when you are looking for an easy-to-fix dinner entrée. A broiled fillet of Chinook salmon is special, but our Salmon Quiche can make a showcase for that delicate flavor and those that complement it.

◇

Stuffed Eggs with Duxelles
Serves 10

Duxelles:

2	tablespoons butter
1	tablespoon chopped shallots
½	pound mushrooms, finely chopped
	Salt and pepper

Mornay Sauce:

3	tablespoons butter
4	tablespoons flour
2½	cups hot milk
½	teaspoon salt
⅛	teaspoon white pepper
1	cup grated Swiss cheese

Stuffed Eggs:

10	hard-cooked eggs
¼	cup minced parsley
2	teaspoons Dijon mustard
2-3	drops Tabasco

1. To prepare duxelles: Melt the butter in a skillet and sauté the shallots until soft. Add the mushrooms and cook until they look dry, about 3 to 5 minutes. Squeeze the mushrooms in a paper towel or cloth to extract as much moisture as possible. Season with salt and pepper to taste.

2. To prepare mornay sauce: Melt the butter in a saucepan, add the flour and cook for 2 minutes. Take off the heat and stir in the hot milk. Return to heat and simmer until thick, stirring constantly. Season with salt and pepper to taste. Add half the cheese, stirring until it melts. Reserve the rest of the cheese to top the dish before it goes in the oven.

3. Butter a shallow, 7¼-by-12-inch glass baking dish. Preheat oven to 375°.

4. To prepare eggs: Cut the eggs in half lengthwise and remove the yolks. Sieve or process the yolks very fine. Cut a thin slice off the bottom of the egg whites to make a flat spot so they won't slide in the baking dish.

5. Combine the yolks, duxelles, ½ cup of the mornay sauce, parsley, Dijon mustard and Tabasco in a large bowl.

6. To assemble dish: Spread the bottom of the baking dish with some of the remaining sauce. Fill the indentations in the egg whites with the yolk-mushroom mixture and arrange in the dish. Top with the remaining sauce and sprinkle with the remaining cheese. Bake 30 minutes or until bubbly and slightly brown.

Note: The dish can be prepared (but not baked) the night before and refrigerated. Be sure to use a glass dish as an aluminum pan might cause some discoloration.

Eggs in Mornay Sauce

Serves 3 to 4

6	hard-cooked eggs, halved
¼	pound mushrooms
6½	tablespoons butter
5	tablespoons flour
2½	cups milk
1	cup shredded Swiss cheese, packed
½	teaspoon salt
	Pepper

1. Place the egg halves, yolk sides up, in a baking dish.
2. Wipe the mushrooms clean with a damp cloth. Trim the stems and slice the mushrooms thinly.
3. Sauté the mushrooms in 1½ tablespoons butter until golden, stirring often. Drain on paper towels and scatter on top of the eggs in the baking dish.
4. Melt 5 tablespoons butter in a saucepan. Add the flour and blend well. Add the milk slowly, stirring constantly, until the sauce is thick. Add the cheese, a little at a time, and stir until melted and well blended into the sauce. Season with the salt and pepper to taste.
5. Pour the sauce evenly over the egg-mushroom mixture. Place under the broiler for a few minutes until bubbly and the top is tinged with brown.

Note: This recipe can be prepared ahead and refrigerated. In this case, bake in a preheated 375° oven 20 to 30 minutes.

Italian Spinach Pie

Serves 8

Sour-Cream Pastry:

3	cups flour
1	teaspoon salt
¼	teaspoon sugar
12	tablespoons butter, chilled
½	cup vegetable shortening
¼	cup sour cream
¼	cup ice water

Filling:

1	pound spinach
1	pound ricotta cheese
¾	cup grated parmesan cheese
¾	cup coarsely chopped pitted ripe olives
4	eggs
½	teaspoon salt
¼	teaspoon fennel seeds, crushed
½-¾	pound Italian sausage
1	tablespoon water

1. To prepare pastry: Combine the flour, salt and sugar. Cut in the butter and shortening until the mixture forms coarse crumbs. Beat the sour cream with the cold water; stir into the flour mixture until the dough holds together. Shape into a smooth ball.

2. Divide the pastry in half and pat into 2 small rectangles. Wrap in plastic wrap and refrigerate for 1 hour or longer before rolling.

3. To prepare filling: Wash spinach; blanch in boiling water 1½ to 2 minutes. Drain; chop and squeeze dry. Blend together the ricotta and parmesan cheeses, olives, 3 of the eggs (beaten), salt and fennel.

4. If link sausage is used, remove it from the casings. Cut the meat into small pieces. Brown the sausage; drain excess fat. Add the spinach and cook a minute longer. Remove from heat and cool slightly, then combine with the ricotta mixture.

5. On a lightly floured cookie sheet without sides, roll out half the pastry into a 10-by-14-inch rectangle. (Or roll out on a floured surface and transfer to a cookie sheet.) The dough may have to be rolled and patted into place.

6. Beat the remaining egg with the water to make an egg wash. Brush it over the pastry. Spoon the filling on the pastry, leaving a 1-inch border all around. Roll out the other half of the pastry on a lightly floured surface to the same size. Carefully roll the pastry around the rolling pin and gently lay it over the top to loosely cover filling.

7. Roll the edges of the pastry to seal. Press together with the tines of a fork. Brush the top with the egg wash. Refrigerate for 30 minutes or longer before baking.

8. Preheat oven to 375°.

9. If needed, brush the pastry with more egg wash; bake about 40 to 45 minutes until golden brown. Remove from the oven and let stand 10 minutes before cutting. To serve, cut in half lengthwise, then into crosswise sections. Serve hot or at room temperature.

Pesto-Stuffed Eggs

Makes 48 halves

1	cup packed fresh basil leaves, washed and drained
½	cup freshly grated parmesan cheese
¼	cup olive oil
2	dozen hard-cooked eggs
½	cup mayonnaise
	Salt
	Pimento or parsley

1. Put the basil, parmesan cheese and olive oil into a blender or food processor and process until a very coarse purée is obtained.

2. Cut the eggs in half lengthwise and remove the yolks. Mash the yolks; add to the pesto mixture with the mayonnaise and salt to taste.

3. Fill the egg whites with the yolk mixture. Garnish with pimento or parsley.

Eggs Germaine
Serves 4

4	tablespoons butter
¼	cup flour
2	cups milk
1	teaspoon salt
¼	teaspoon pepper
¼	teaspoon ground nutmeg
1	pound fresh spinach
8	hard-cooked eggs
2	tablespoons grated parmesan cheese
	Toast points
	Paprika
	Parsley

1. Melt 2 tablespoons butter in a skillet over low heat; blend in the flour. Add the milk all at once; cook, stirring constantly, until thickened and bubbly. Blend in ½ teaspoon salt, pepper and nutmeg; set aside.

2. Cook the spinach in boiling salted water until tender; chop and drain well; set aside.

3. Cut the hard-cooked eggs in half lengthwise; remove the yolks. Mash the yolks; combine with the spinach and ½ teaspoon salt. Refill the whites with the spinach mixture, placing the filled eggs in a 1½-quart shallow baking dish.

4. Pour the sauce over the eggs. Sprinkle with the parmesan cheese and dot with 2 tablespoons butter. Broil for 5 minutes or until lightly browned. Serve over hot toast points. Garnish with paprika and parsley.

Cheese and Bacon Pie
Serves 6

1	(9 inch) unbaked pie shell (see index)
1½	cups shredded Gruyère cheese
6	slices bacon, cooked and crumbled
¼	cup thinly sliced green onions, including tops

4	eggs, slightly beaten
1	(8 ounce) container plain yogurt
1	tablespoon cornstarch
¾	cup milk
	Dash pepper
¼	cup grated parmesan cheese

1. Prepare the pastry and line a 9-inch pie plate with it. Sprinkle the Gruyère cheese, bacon and green onions over the bottom of the pie shell.
2. Preheat oven to 375°.
3. Beat the eggs, yogurt, cornstarch, milk and pepper together. Pour the mixture into the pie shell. Sprinkle with the parmesan cheese.
4. Bake 40 minutes or until a knife inserted in the center comes out clean. Let the pie stand 10 minutes before serving.

Shrimp-Stuffed Eggs

Serves 3 to 4

6	hard-cooked eggs
3	tablespoons mayonnaise
¾	teaspoon dry mustard
	Dash salt
	Dash pepper
¼	pound tiny cooked shrimp, drained
	Paprika

1. Cut the eggs in half lengthwise. Carefully remove the yolks to a small bowl. Set the egg whites aside.
2. Mash the egg yolks until smooth. Add the mayonnaise and dry mustard, blending well. Season with salt and pepper to taste.
3. Set aside 12 of the best looking shrimp for garnish. Coarsely chop the remaining shrimp. Add them to the egg yolk-mayonnaise mixture, blending gently. Stuff the egg whites with the egg-shrimp mixture, mounding slightly. Garnish each stuffed egg with one of the reserved shrimp. Dust lightly with paprika. Cover and chill until serving time.

Piquant Poached Eggs

Serves 2

4	large eggs
1	tablespoon vegetable oil
1	small onion, chopped
4	ounces canned green chilies, diced
1	(16 ounce) can diced tomatoes in juice, drained
1/8	teaspoon garlic powder
	Pepper
1/8	teaspoon dried oregano, crushed
	Salt
3/4	cup shredded Monterey jack cheese
	Black olives
	Tortillas

1. Break the eggs in 4 individual cups. Set aside.

2. Heat a large skillet over medium heat; add the oil. Cook the onion in the oil until tender but not browned. Add the chilies, tomatoes, garlic powder, pepper, oregano and salt. Cook, uncovered, over medium-low heat until some moisture has evaporated and mixture is well blended, about 5 to 10 minutes. Stir occasionally.

3. Sprinkle 6 tablespoons cheese evenly over the tomato mixture. Cover and cook until the cheese begins to melt, 2 to 3 minutes.

4. With the back of a spoon, make 4 indentations in the tomato mixture. Place the eggs in the indentations on top of the melting cheese. Sprinkle the remaining cheese over the eggs. Cover and cook until the eggs are set and the cheese is melted, 7 to 10 minutes.

5. To serve, slip a spatula under the tomato mixture and 1 egg. Lift onto a plate. Repeat until all 4 eggs are served. Spoon the remaining tomato mixture over each serving. Garnish with black olives. Serve with warm tortillas.

Chili Omelet

Serves 6

8	eggs, beaten
1 1/4	cups milk
1	teaspoon garlic salt

7-8	ounces diced chilies
¼	cup chopped green onions
1	medium tomato, chopped
2	cups shredded sharp cheddar cheese
	Salsa
	Sour cream

1. Preheat oven to 350°.
2. Grease a shallow 1½-quart casserole dish.
3. Combine the eggs, milk and garlic salt. Mix in the chilies, green onions, tomato and cheese. Pour into the casserole and bake for 1 hour or until a knife inserted in the middle comes out clean. Serve immediately with salsa and sour cream.

Onion and Cheese Omelet

Serves 2

2	tablespoons butter
1	large onion, thinly sliced
4	eggs at room temperature
1	tablespoon water
½	cup grated Jarlsberg cheese
	Chopped parsley

1. Melt 1 tablespoon butter over medium-high heat. Add the onions and cook slowly until soft and golden, reducing heat if necessary. Keep warm while preparing the omelet.
2. In a medium bowl, whip the eggs with the water vigorously until frothy. Over medium-high heat, heat the remaining 1 tablespoon butter in a 10-inch omelet pan until sizzling. When the butter stops sizzling, pour the eggs into the pan.
3. When the eggs begin to set, carefully lift the edges with a spatula and let the uncooked portion run under the omelet. The top of the egg mixture still will be moist.
4. Pour the onions on one-half of the omelet and sprinkle with the grated cheese. Fold the omelet in half with a spatula and slide from the pan onto a warm serving platter. Garnish with the parsley and serve immediately.

Flipless Vegetable Frittata
Serves 6

2	tablespoons butter
½	pound mushrooms, sliced
½	cup chopped green pepper
1	cup diced zucchini
⅓	cup finely chopped green onions
1	medium tomato, diced
4	eggs
¼	cup water
2	tablespoons Dijon mustard
½	teaspoon salt
¼	teaspoon coarsely ground pepper
1	cup shredded Monterey jack cheese
	Paprika

1. Melt the butter in a heavy, 10-inch skillet with an oven-proof handle. Add the mushrooms and green pepper. Cook for about 2 minutes, then add the zucchini and onions. Cook and stir for 2½ minutes more. Add the tomato.

2. Lightly beat together the eggs, water, mustard, salt and pepper; pour over the vegetables in the skillet.

3. Cover and cook over low to medium heat 5 minutes or until the underside is done. The top still will be slightly runny.

4. Sprinkle with the cheese and then the paprika. Place under a heated broiler just until the cheese melts and the eggs set. Cut in wedges to serve.

Asparagus Frittata
Serves 5 to 6

12-14	asparagus spears
8	eggs, beaten
2	cups grated fontina or Monterey jack cheese
1½	tablespoons Dijon mustard
¼	teaspoon salt
¾	teaspoon freshly ground pepper

½	cup chopped parsley
4	tablespoons butter
2	cloves garlic, minced
½	pound mushrooms, sliced
½	pound ham, diced

1. Preheat oven to 350°.
2. Break the woody ends off the asparagus and discard. Wash the asparagus. Place the spears in a 10-inch oven-proof skillet with lightly salted water to just cover; bring to a boil and simmer 3 minutes. Drain thoroughly and cut into 2-inch lengths. Reserve.
3. Combine the eggs, cheese, Dijon mustard, salt, pepper and parsley in a medium mixing bowl; reserve.
4. Melt the butter in a 10-inch skillet on low heat; add the garlic and mushrooms and sauté 1 to 2 minutes. Stir in the asparagus. Cover the skillet, increase the heat slightly and cook 3 minutes, stirring occasionally. Stir in the ham and cook 2 minutes more.
5. Remove the skillet from the heat and stir in the egg mixture. Bake for 30 minutes. Let stand 5 minutes. Cut into wedges to serve.

Bacon-and-Onion-Stuffed Eggs

Makes 24 halves

6	slices bacon, diced
3	shallots, minced
12	hard-cooked eggs, cut in half lengthwise
⅓	cup mayonnaise
2	teaspoons grainy or country-style mustard
1	tablespoon lemon juice
	Freshly ground black pepper

1. Cook the bacon until crisp; pour off all but 1 tablespoon of the fat. Add the shallots and cook for 1 minute. Drain.
2. Carefully remove the yolks and put them into a food processor. Add the bacon, shallots, mayonnaise, mustard, lemon juice and pepper and blend well. Fill the egg whites with the yolk mixture and chill.

Spinach Frittata
Serves 6

½	cup sliced onions
1	clove garlic, minced
2	tablespoons vegetable oil
1	cup sliced mushrooms
2	pounds fresh spinach
⅓	cup fresh lime juice (about 3 limes)
1	teaspoon dried basil, crushed
½	teaspoon pepper
½	teaspoon nutmeg
10	eggs, beaten
4	tablespoons grated parmesan cheese

1. Preheat oven to 350°.

2. In a large skillet over medium heat, sauté the onions and garlic in vegetable oil for about 5 minutes. Add the mushrooms and cook, stirring 2 minutes.

3. Wash the spinach; blanch in boiling water 1½ to 2 minutes. Drain, chop and squeeze dry. Add to the skillet along with the lime juice, basil, pepper and nutmeg and cook, stirring, an additional 3 minutes. Remove the mixture from heat.

4. Stir the spinach mixture into the beaten eggs. Mix in the cheese. Pour into a greased 9-by-13-inch baking dish. Bake for 15 to 20 minutes until the eggs set. Check for doneness before removing from the oven. Cool slightly and cut into serving squares.

Frittata Jardinière with Ham
Serves 2

1	clove garlic, minced
3	tablespoons butter
½	medium onion, sliced
6-8	ounces fresh green beans, cut up, cooked till tender-crisp
¼	teaspoon dried oregano, crushed
⅛	teaspooon dried thyme, crushed

4	eggs
	Salt and pepper
4	cherry tomatoes, halved
½	cup shredded Swiss cheese
	Cooked ham slices or steaks, sautéed in butter till warm

1. Sauté the garlic in 2 tablespoons butter in a 7-inch oven-proof skillet until golden. Add the onion and sauté until tender. Add the green beans, oregano and thyme; cook 2 to 4 minutes.

2. Beat the eggs lightly and season to taste with salt and pepper. Pour the eggs into the vegetable mixture, spreading to cover the top. Shake the pan lightly while cooking over medium heat, lifting the bottom to allow the eggs to flow into the bottom of the pan.

3. When the bottom is just set and the top still slightly runny, garnish the top with the tomato halves and sprinkle with the cheese. Dot with the remaining butter and place under the broiler just until the eggs are golden. Serve with the ham slices.

Smoked-Trout-Stuffed Eggs

Makes 24 halves

12	hard-cooked eggs, cut in half lengthwise
6	ounces smoked trout, bones and skin removed
2	green onions, sliced
⅓	cup mayonnaise
3	tablespoons sour cream
1	tablespoon plus 2 teaspoons lemon juice
1	tablespoon horseradish
½	teaspoon dried dill weed, crushed
24	capers, drained

1. Carefully remove the yolks to a small bowl. Combine the yolks, trout and green onions in a food processor and blend well. Add the mayonnaise, sour cream, lemon juice, horseradish and dill weed and blend until smooth.

2. Fill the egg whites with the yolk mixture and garnish each one with a caper. Chill.

Salmon Quiche

Serves 6

Pastry:

1	cup flour
4	tablespoons chilled sweet butter, cut into pieces
1½	tablespoons shortening
½	teaspoon salt
⅓	cup ice water

Quiche Filling:

½	tablespoon butter
2	tablespoons chopped onions
6	ounces raw salmon, chopped
	Grated peel of 1 lemon
1	tablespoon chopped parsley
¾	cup grated Gruyère cheese
¼	cup romano or parmesan cheese
4	eggs, lightly beaten
½	teaspoon salt
	Pepper
1	cup whipping cream
½	cup milk

1. To prepare pastry: Using the metal blade of a food processor, process the flour, butter, shortening and salt for 8 to 10 seconds. While the machine is running, add the water through the feed tube. Stop the processor when the dough forms a ball. Wrap in wax paper and chill for a few hours before using.

2. Preheat oven to 425°. Roll the dough into a circle about ⅛-inch thick. Shape into a 9-inch quiche or pie pan. Pierce the sides and bottom of the pastry with a fork.

3. Partly bake the shell for 10 minutes. Remove from the oven; reset to 375°.

4. To prepare filling: Heat the butter and sauté the onions. Mix with the salmon, lemon peel and parsley and place in pastry shell. Sprinkle with the grated cheeses.

5. Combine the eggs, salt, pepper, cream and milk, mixing well. Pour into the pastry shell on top of the other ingredients. Bake the quiche for about 45 minutes or until a knife inserted near the center comes out clean.

Ratatouille Quiche

Makes two 9-inch quiches

2	9-inch pastry shells,* unbaked
1	egg white
¼	cup olive oil
2	cloves garlic, minced
½	cup sliced onion
1½	tablespoons flour
1	small eggplant, peeled and sliced
1	zucchini, scrubbed and sliced
1	green pepper, seeded and sliced
2	small tomatoes, peeled and sliced
1	tablespoon capers
3	eggs plus 1 egg yolk
1½	cups half-and-half
½	teaspoon salt
¼	teaspoon black pepper
½	cup grated parmesan cheese
¼	teaspoon nutmeg

1. Preheat oven to 450°.
2. Bake pastry shells for 10 minutes. Brush them with 1 egg white and set aside to dry. Reset oven to 350°.
3. Heat the oil in a heavy skillet. Sauté the garlic and onion for 5 to 10 minutes or until the onion is tender and golden.
4. Lightly flour the eggplant, zucchini and green pepper; add to the skillet. Cover and cook over low heat for about 30 minutes, stirring occasionally. Add the tomatoes and simmer, uncovered, until the liquid has evaporated. Add the capers and set aside to cool.
5. Beat 3 eggs and the egg yolk lightly with a wire whisk. Add the half-and-half, salt and pepper, and blend until smooth.
6. Spoon half the vegetable mixture into each pastry shell. Carefully pour half the custard mixture into each shell. Sprinkle with parmesan cheese and nutmeg.
7. Bake 30 to 35 minutes or until a knife inserted near the center comes out clean. Remove from the oven and cool on wire racks for 10 to 15 minutes before serving.

*Use pastry recipe from Asparagus and Ham Quiche.

Quiche in Zucchini-Rice Crust

Serves 6 to 8

Crust:

1¾	cups shredded zucchini
1¼	cups cooked rice
1	egg
¼	cup grated parmesan cheese

Filling:

8	slices bacon, cooked and crumbled
1	cup grated Swiss cheese
1	medium tomato, chopped and drained
½	cup chopped onion

Custard:

1⅓	cups half-and-half
4	eggs
½	teaspoon dried basil, crushed
½	teaspoon garlic salt
¼	teaspoon dried thyme, crushed
⅛	teaspoon pepper
⅛	teaspoon paprika

1. Preheat oven to 350°.

2. To prepare crust: Combine the zucchini, rice, egg and cheese and mix well. Pat the crust mixture into the bottom of a well-buttered 8-by-12-inch baking dish.

3. To prepare filling: Combine the bacon, cheese, tomato and onion; mix well and spread on top of the crust.

4. To prepare custard: Combine the half-and-half, eggs, basil, garlic salt, thyme, pepper and paprika; mix well and pour over the filling. Bake for 30 minutes or until a knife inserted near the center comes out clean. Cut in squares and serve immediately.

To prepare individual quiches:

1. Preheat oven to 350°.

2. Butter sixteen 2½-inch muffin cups. Pat 2 tablespoons of the crust mixture into each muffin cup and bake for 10 to 12 minutes or until lightly browned. Cool on a wire rack. Reset oven to 375°.

3. Spoon 2 tablespoons of the filling into each cooled crust. Pour 3 to 4 tablespoons of custard over the filling. Bake the individual quiches for 15 to 20 minutes or until the custard is set. Remove from oven and serve.

Asparagus Quiche

Serves 6

1	(10 inch) pie shell, unbaked (see index)
6	eggs, beaten
½	pound fresh asparagus, cut in 1-inch pieces
½	cup shredded Swiss cheese
1	cup milk
½	cup sour cream
¼	cup minced onion
½	teaspoon salt
¼	teaspoon white pepper

1. Preheat oven to 450°.

2. Brush the pie shell with a small amount of the beaten eggs. Pierce the bottom and sides of the pie shell with the tines of a fork.

3. Bake the pie shell until golden brown, about 5 minutes. If using a glass pie plate, bake at 425°. Cool the pie shell on a wire rack. Reduce the oven temperature to 375° for metal pan or 350° for glass.

4. In a medium saucepan over medium heat, cook the asparagus in about 1 inch of water just until tender-crisp. Drain well.

5. Arrange the asparagus and cheese in the pie shell. Beat the eggs, milk, sour cream, minced onion, salt and pepper with a wire whisk until well blended. Pour the mixture into the pie shell.

6. Bake until a knife inserted between the center and outside edge comes out clean, 35 to 40 minutes. Let stand 5 to 10 minutes before serving.

Asparagus and Ham Quiche

Makes two 9-inch quiches

Pastry Shell:

3	cups flour
½	cup butter
½	cup vegetable shortening
½	teaspoon salt
½	cup cold water

Filling:

14	whole stalks asparagus, plus 2 cups sliced, about 1½ pounds total
2	tablespoons olive oil
1	small onion, chopped
2	cups diced ham
6	eggs plus 2 egg yolks
3	cups whipping cream
1	teaspoon salt
	Pepper
	Nutmeg
⅓	cup grated Gruyère cheese
4	small plum tomatoes

1. To prepare pastry shell: With a pastry blender, cut the flour, butter, shortening and salt together until the mixture is the texture of coarse meal. Add the water and mix until the dough comes out clean from the bowl and forms a ball.

2. Divide the dough in half. Flatten it into two 8-inch rounds. Place each round between wax-paper sheets and refrigerate for 30 minutes.

3. Preheat oven to 400°.

4. Place one round of dough on a well-floured board and roll into a 12-inch circle. Gently transfer the circle of dough into a 9-inch quiche pan. Without forcing or stretching the dough, press it into the pan. Cut the dough even with the edge of the quiche pan. Repeat with the other round of dough and another quiche pan.

5. Pierce the sides and bottom of both quiches with a fork. Set a piece of wax paper on the dough and cover the bottom with rice or dry beans. Bake for 10 minutes. Discard the paper, rice or beans. Set the quiche pastries aside while preparing the filling. Reset oven to 350°.

6. To prepare filling: Bring a pot of salted water to a boil. Bend and break the whole asparagus stalks at their tender point. Wash in cold water. Drain and parboil the stalks until just tender and still bright green. Lift out the stalks to a strainer and rinse them with cold water. Set aside to drain. Add the sliced asparagus to the water and parboil until tender but still crunchy. Drain and refresh under cold water. Drain again.

7. Heat the oil in a skillet and sauté the onion for 5 minutes. Add the diced ham and sauté for another minute. Remove from heat.

8. Mix the eggs, egg yolks, cream, salt, pepper and a few gratings of nutmeg in large bowl. Stir in the cheese. Add the sliced asparagus and onion-ham mixture. Divide the mixture evenly between the pastry-lined quiche dishes. Bake 25 minutes or until the egg custard is beginning to set at the edges but is still slightly soft in the middle.

9. Cut out the stem ends of the tomatoes; peel and cut in quarters. Remove the quiches from the oven. Carefully arrange the tomatoes and asparagus spears in a pattern on top. Return the quiches to the oven and continue baking for another 20 to 25 minutes or until firm and golden and a knife inserted near the center comes out clean.

Fish

Any anthropologist who came upon us unaware probably would jot down "fish-eating people." We Pacific Northwesterners live and work just a net's throw away from some of the best fishing grounds in the country. The waters of Puget Sound and Washington's rich off-coast fishing grounds have given us one of the finest fresh-fish supplies in the world. Vastly improved flash-freezing capabilities of coastal and Alaskan fishing fleets have extended the use of our seafood beyond the fresh season.

As the traditionally large salmon runs have slacked off, the fishing industry has gone after other catches that have netted us something new to try almost every time we walk into the fish market. Our so-called "bottom fish" have given us firm-fleshed, white fish which can be baked, broiled or served in a stew, depending on the variety.

The development of the fresh albacore fishery and air shipment of fish from more remote areas such as New Zealand and Chile have shaped our cuisine into one of the most varied in the country.

Choosing a suitable cooking method, making allowances for varying fish textures and bringing out delicate flavors and balancing strong ones have kept Times cooks busy the past several years.

We have assembled a selection of fish recipes that combine ingredients in such a way that the fish, not the sauce, is the star of the table. The presentations are simple, yet elegant.

◇

Lemon-Rice Stuffed Salmon

Serves 8

1	4-pound, whole salmon
2½	tablespoons butter
½	cup finely chopped celery
¾	cup sliced fresh mushrooms
1	cup cooked rice
½	cup chopped green onions
2-3	tablespoons diced pimento
2	tablespoons lemon juice
¾	teaspoon salt
⅛	teaspoon dried thyme, crushed
	Lemon pepper to taste
	Oil
	Lemon slices
	Parsley

1. Wash the fish well and scale, if necessary. Remove the head and tail if desired. Set the fish aside while preparing the stuffing.

2. Heat the butter in a skillet. Add the celery and mushrooms and sauté about 5 minutes.

3. Combine the cooked rice, green onions, pimento, lemon juice, salt, thyme and lemon peppers in a bowl; add the celery-mushroom mixture and blend well.

4. Preheat oven to 450°.

5. Pat the fish dry and fill the cavity with stuffing. Close opening with small skewers or toothpicks. Measure fish at the thickest part, including the stuffing.

6. Brush fish with oil. Place in a greased, shallow baking pan. Bake 10 minutes per inch of thickness. Remove skewers and upper skin if desired. Garnish with lemon slices and parsley.

Orange-Rice Salmon

Serves 6 to 8

1	salmon, boned (3-4 pounds prepared weight)
	Salt
¾	cup water
¾	cup orange juice
⅔	cup uncooked long-grain rice
1	cup chopped celery with leaves
¼	cup chopped onion
¼	cup oil
2	tablespoons lemon juice
1	tablespoon grated orange peel
½	cup slivered blanched almonds, toasted
	Orange wedges
	Lemon wedges
	Parsley

1. Wash the fish and pat dry. Sprinkle it inside and out with salt.

2. Bring the water, orange juice and ½ teaspoon salt to a boil. Add the rice and cook for 20 minutes or until done.

3. Preheat oven to 450°.

4. Meanwhile, cook the celery and onion in the oil in a skillet until tender. Add the celery-onion mixture to the rice along with the lemon juice, orange peel and almonds. Mix thoroughly.

5. Stuff the fish loosely. Close the opening with small skewers or wooden food picks. Place the fish in a well-greased oven-to-table baking dish and brush with oil.

6. Bake 10 minutes per inch of thickness after stuffing. Baste occasionally with oil. Remove skewers. Garnish with orange and lemon wedges and parsley.

Northwest Salmon Pie

Serves 8

Crust:

1½ cups flour

½ cup grated parmesan cheese

¾ cup vegetable shortening

2 tablespoons cold water

Filling:

1 pound poached salmon, well drained

1 large onion, diced

1 clove garlic, minced

2 tablespoons butter

1 pint sour cream

4 eggs

1½ cups shredded Gruyère cheese

1 teaspoon dill weed, crumbled

¼ teaspoon salt

1. Preheat oven to 375°.

2. To prepare crust: Combine the flour and cheese. Cut in the shortening until the mixture resembles small peas. Sprinkle with the water. Form into a dough with your hands, adding more water as needed.

3. Press into the bottom and up the sides of an 8-inch springform pan. Bake for 10 minutes. Leave the oven on.

4. To prepare filling: Drain the salmon. Remove the dark skin and bones. Break into bite-size pieces.

5. Sauté the onion and garlic in butter until the onion is soft.

6. Beat the sour cream and eggs until blended. Stir the salmon into the sour cream mixture along with the sautéed vegetables, 1 cup Gruyère cheese, dill weed and salt.

7. Pour the mixture into the parmesan crust; top with the remaining ½ cup Gruyère cheese. Return to the oven and bake 55 to 60 minutes. Cool 15 minutes in pan. Remove the sides of pan and cut the pie into wedges.

Note: It may be necessary to cover the top loosely with foil toward the end of cooking to prevent too much browning.

◇

Salmon Steaks Provençale

Serves 6

6	salmon steaks, 1-2 inches thick
1	teaspoon celery salt
¼	teaspoon freshly ground white pepper
8	tablespoons butter
1	cup minced onion
2	garlic cloves, minced
3	fresh tomatoes, peeled, drained, seeded and minced
½	cup dry white wine
1	teaspoon minced fresh tarragon or ½ teaspoon dried tarragon, crushed
1	cup whipping cream
	Beurre manié (2 tablespoons each butter and flour, mixed well and formed into 6 marble-sized balls)
	Lemon wedges
	Parsley

1. Rub the salmon steaks with the celery salt and pepper; chill in the refrigerator.

2. Preheat oven to 450°.

3. In a saucepan, melt 6 tablespoons butter and add the onion and garlic; simmer gently until the onion becomes transparent.

4. Add the tomatoes, wine and tarragon; cook for a few minutes to blend ingredients.

5. Add the cream. When the mixture returns to a simmer, cover the pan and turn off the heat.

6. Cook the salmon steaks 10 minutes per inch of thickness, basting with 2 tablespoons melted butter during cooking.

7. While the steaks are cooking, bring the sauce back to a simmer and add the marbles of beurre manié, stirring constantly until the sauce is smooth and thickened.

8. Pour the sauce over the steaks on either a platter or individual dishes. Garnish with lemon wedges and parsley.

Salmon Newburg
Serves 8

1	pound fresh salmon
¼	cup sliced green onions
1	cup sliced fresh mushrooms
¼	cup butter
3	tablespoons flour
1	pint half-and-half
1	egg yolk, beaten
¼	teaspoon salt
	Dash pepper
2	hard-cooked eggs, sliced
1	pound fresh peas, shelled and cooked tender-crisp
3	tablespoons grated parmesan cheese
8	baked patty shells

1. Pour about 1 inch of salted water into a large shallow pan with a rack. Wrap the salmon loosely in cheesecloth and place on the rack in the pan. Cover and simmer until the salmon is done. Allow 10 minutes per inch of thickness.

2. Drain the salmon, reserving 2 tablespoons of the poaching liquid. Break the salmon into chunks with a fork, removing the bones.

3. Sauté the green onions and mushrooms in butter. Blend in the flour. Add the half-and-half. Cook, stirring constantly until thickened and smooth.

4. Combine a little of the hot sauce with the egg yolk. Return to the sauce and cook 1 minute, stirring constantly. Blend in the salmon, reserved 2 tablespoons poaching liquid, salt, pepper, hard-cooked eggs, peas and grated parmesan cheese. Heat through. Serve in patty shells.

Chilled Salmon Dijon
Serves 8

Salmon:

1	onion, cut into quarters
1	stalk celery, sliced
3	pounds fillet of salmon

Sauce:

1	cup mayonnaise
1	cup sour cream
¼	cup chopped green onions
2	tablespoons Dijon mustard
2	tablespoons lemon juice
¼	teaspoon seasoning salt
¼	teaspoon dried tarragon or herb seasoning
	Lettuce
	Lemon

1. To prepare salmon: Pour about 1 inch of salted water into a large shallow pan with a rack (such as a large roasting pan). Add the onion and celery. Wrap the salmon loosely in cheesecloth and place on the rack in the pan.

2. Cover and simmer until the salmon is done, allowing 10 minutes per inch of thickness. Lift from water, using cheesecloth. Remove and discard the skin and chill the salmon.

3. To prepare sauce: Stir together the mayonnaise, sour cream, onions, Dijon mustard, lemon juice, seasoning salt and tarragon. Serve the salmon on lettuce with the sauce. Garnish with lemon.

Albacore with Sour Cream Sauce

Serves 4 to 6

1	pint sour cream
2	tablespoons flour
5	green onions, finely chopped
	Salt and pepper
2	pounds albacore, poached or steamed

1. Mix the sour cream, flour and 4 green onions until well blended. Season with salt and pepper to taste.

2. Preheat oven to 350°.

3. Into a well-greased 2-quart casserole, place a layer of fish. Spread with one-third of the sauce. Repeat, alternating layers of fish and sauce and ending with the sauce. Bake for 25 minutes. Garnish with remaining green onion.

Halibut Oscar
Serves 6

Halibut:

2¼	pounds halibut fillets, cut into 6 equal pieces
1	tablespoon pickling spices
1	small onion, coarsely cut
1	cup dry white wine
18	asparagus spears, cooked until tender-crisp
12	Dungeness crab legs or large chunks of crab meat

Oscar Sauce:

3	egg yolks
3	tablespoons tarragon wine vinegar
1	teaspoon chopped shallots
15	whole peppercorns, crushed
1	tablespoon water
1¼	cups butter, melted and skimmed
¾	teaspoon dried tarragon, crushed
	Juice of ½ lemon
	Salt
	Cayenne pepper

1. To prepare halibut: Rinse the halibut pieces. Bring 1½ quarts salted water, pickling spices, onion and dry white wine to a boil in a large skillet. Lower heat, cover and simmer 20 minutes. Add the halibut fillets and poach just until done, allowing 10 minutes per inch of thickness.

2. Place the fish on a warm serving platter, removing any skin from the fish. Top each fish piece with 3 asparagus spears and 2 crab legs or large chunks of crab meat. Cover with foil and place in a warm oven while preparing Oscar sauce.

3. To prepare sauce: Put the egg yolks in the top part of a double boiler; add water to the bottom part and set it simmering.

4. In another saucepan, put the tarragon vinegar, shallots and crushed peppercorns. Boil until most of the vinegar is cooked away. Set aside to cool. Add 1 tablespoon water and strain into the egg yolks.

5. Beat the egg yolk mixture well and place over simmering water, beating constantly with a wire whisk, until the mixture looks foamy and just barely thick. Do not overcook the egg yolks. It is best to take the top part of the double boiler off the water toward the end of the beating to make sure the egg yolks do not overcook.

6. Pour the egg yolk mixture into a blender container. Pour the warm melted butter in a slow stream through the opening in the cover while beating at lowest speed of blender. The mixture will get thick and smooth. If too thick, add a little warm water. Add the tarragon, lemon juice, salt and cayenne to taste, while the blender is running.

7. Drain any water that formed on the halibut platter. Pour some sauce over each halibut piece and serve immediately.

Baked Salmon with Sour Cream Stuffing

Serves 6

¾	cup chopped celery
½	cup chopped onion
2	tablespoons oil
1	quart dry bread cubes
½	cup sour cream
¼	cup diced, peeled lemon
2	tablespoons grated lemon peel
1	teaspoon paprika
1	teaspoon salt
1	3-4 pound boned, ready-to-cook salmon

1. To prepare stuffing: Cook celery and onion in oil until tender. Combine with bread cubes, sour cream, diced lemon, lemon peel, paprika and salt and mix thoroughly.

2. Preheat oven to 450°.

3. Wash and dry fish. Sprinkle inside and out with salt. Stuff fish loosely. Close opening with small skewers or toothpicks. Measure fish at the thickest part, including the stuffing.

4. Place fish in a well-greased baking pan. Brush with oil. Bake 10 minutes per inch of thickness. Baste occasionally with oil. Remove skewers and serve.

Flaming Halibut

Serves 4

2 halibut steaks, about ¾-inch thick
2 tablespoons butter
2 ounces brandy
¼ cup flour
1½ cups dry white wine
1 cup water
1 (6 ounce) can tomato paste
½ cup finely chopped onion
⅓ cup finely chopped parsley
Salt and pepper
Cayenne pepper
Small boiled new potatoes

1. Cut the halibut steaks in half crosswise. In a heavy skillet or Dutch oven, melt the butter. Add the fish and cook slowly just until it turns white. This will take only a few minutes.

2. Add the brandy to the pan, stand back, and ignite. As soon as the flames die, remove the fish to a plate.

3. Add the flour to the juices in the skillet, blending well. Mix the wine with the water and add it to the skillet. Cook slowly, stirring constantly. When smooth, let simmer for 5 minutes.

4. Add the tomato paste, onion and parsley. Blend well using a whisk if necessary to obtain a smooth sauce. Let cook 5 more minutes. Season to taste with salt, pepper and cayenne.

5. Put the fish back in the sauce, including the juices that accumulated on the plate. Cook, covered, for 15 minutes. Do not stir. If the fish seems to stick, lift it gently with a spatula. Serve with small whole boiled potatoes.

Note: This dish is better prepared ahead to give its flavors a chance to blend. Keep refrigerated until serving time. Reheat over low heat for ½ hour or until piping hot.

Poached Halibut with Shrimp Sauce

Serves 6

Fish:

1	cup white wine
1	cup water
1	bay leaf
	Dash dried thyme, crushed
1	teaspoon salt
2	pounds halibut steaks

Sauce:

2	tablespoons butter
2	tablespoons flour
2	cups reserved fish stock, strained
2	egg yolks, beaten
1	tablespoon lemon juice
1	tablespoon minced parsley
5-6	ounces cooked shrimp meat

1. To prepare fish: Combine the wine, water, bay leaf, thyme and salt in a skillet or saucepan and bring to a boil; simmer a few minutes. Add the halibut steaks and simmer 10 minutes per inch of thickness. Remove the halibut from the fish stock; remove the skin and bones carefully, making sure not to break up the fish. Set the fish and fish stock aside, keeping them warm.

2. To prepare sauce: Melt the butter in a saucepan; add the flour, stirring until smooth. Slowly add the fish stock. Cook until thick and creamy. Combine the egg yolks, lemon juice and parsley. Stir some sauce into the egg yolks, stirring constantly. Then stir the egg yolk mixture slowly into the sauce. Add the shrimp and simmer 5 minutes. Spoon the sauce over the halibut. Serve additional sauce on the side.

Halibut à la Crème

Serves 2 to 4

1	(1 pound) whole halibut steak, ¾-inch thick

Court Bouillon:

1	cup dry white wine
2	cups water
1	stalk celery, cut in 3 pieces
1	carrot, peeled, cut in 4 pieces
1	large slice of onion
1	tablespoon coarse salt
10	peppercorns
1	small bay leaf
¼	teaspoon dried thyme, crushed

Mushrooms:

¼	pound fresh mushrooms, cleaned and sliced
2	teaspoons butter
1	tablespoon water

Cream Sauce:

¼	cup butter
¼	cup flour
1	cup reserved court bouillon
1	cup whipping cream
	Salt and white pepper

1. To prepare court bouillon: In a large skillet, place the wine, water, celery, carrot, onion, salt, peppercorns, bay leaf and thyme. Cover. Bring to a boil and simmer 20 minutes. Let cool. Remove the vegetables, bay leaf and peppercorns and discard them.

2. Meanwhile, wash the halibut steak and cut in half crosswise.

3. Place the halibut steak in the cooled court bouillon. Bring to a simmer and poach 10 minutes per inch of thickness or until fish is opaque. (Do not let the water boil.) Remove the bones and skin and place the fish portions in an oven-proof shallow casserole dish. Reserve the court bouillon.

4. Preheat oven to 325°.

5. To prepare mushrooms: Place the mushrooms in a small saucepan along with the butter and water. Cover and cook over medium high heat about 5 to 8 minutes, shaking the pan occasionally. Drain and reserve.

6. To prepare cream sauce: Melt the butter in a medium saucepan. Add the flour and blend well. Slowly add the court bouillon, stirring constantly, until thickened. Add the cream, stirring all the while. Season with salt and pepper to taste.

7. To serve: Add the cooked and drained mushrooms to the cream sauce. Pour over the fish. Bake 20 minutes or until bubbly. Serve immediately.

Steamed Fish with Black Beans
Serves 4 to 6

1	(1½ pound) whole trout
1	teaspoon salt

Sauce:

1	tablespoon coarsely chopped salted black beans
	(available at Oriental shops)
1	green onion, cut into 2-inch lengths
1	tablespoon shredded fresh ginger root
½	teaspoon sugar
1	tablespoon rice wine
1	tablespoon light soy sauce
1	tablespoon peanut or vegetable oil

1. Wash the fish inside and out and pat dry with paper towels. Slash crosswise on both sides at about 1½-inch intervals. Rub salt inside and outside the fish, working the salt into the slashes. Place the fish in a shallow heat-proof bowl.

2. To prepare sauce: Blend together the black beans, green onion, ginger root, sugar, rice wine, soy sauce and oil. Pour the sauce evenly over fish.

3. Place a footed rack in a large kettle. Add water to about a 1-inch depth or to the top of the rack. Cover the kettle and bring the water to a boil. Place the bowl with the fish on the rack. Cover the kettle and steam over high heat 10 minutes per inch of thickness. Remove the bowl from the kettle. Transfer the fish and sauce to a hot platter and serve immediately.

Baked Fish in Parchment

Serves 6

1½	pounds firm-fleshed fish fillets, such as sole or flounder
1½	teaspoon salt
2	slices ginger root, smashed with flat side of cleaver
3	tablespoons rice wine
8	dried Chinese black mushrooms
4	paper-thin slices prosciutto
1	tablespoon corn oil or safflower oil
1	tablespoon minced green onions
2	teaspoons minced ginger root
2	teaspoons soy sauce
1	teaspoon sugar
4	teaspoons sesame oil
1	teaspoon cornstarch
¼	cup chicken stock or broth
8	(12-inch) parchment squares

1. Cut the fish fillets into 6 to 8 pieces, about 3 to 4 ounces per piece. Place in a bowl and sprinkle with 1 teaspoon salt.

2. Place the ginger root slices in 1 tablespoon rice wine and pinch repeatedly for a few minutes to impart the flavor to the wine. Add the ginger mixture to the fish pieces, toss lightly and let marinate for 20 minutes.

3. Soften the black mushrooms in warm water to cover for 25 minutes. Remove the stems and discard; shred the caps. Cut the prosciutto slices crosswise into quarters.

4. Preheat oven to 450°.

5. Heat a wok or skillet. Add 1 tablespoon corn oil and heat until very hot. Add the minced green onions and ginger root and stir-fry until fragrant.

6. Combine the soy sauce, 2 tablespoons rice wine, sugar, remaining ½ teaspoon salt, 1 teaspoon sesame oil, cornstarch and chicken stock. Add this mixture to the wok and stir-fry until it thickens, stirring constantly. Remove from heat.

7. Lightly brush the parchment squares with the remaining sesame oil. Place a piece of fish diagonally just below the center of the parchment square. Arrange a slice of prosciutto with several mushroom shreds sprinkled on top. Spoon some of the sauce over the fish. Fold over the edges of the paper, crimping to seal completely, or fasten with

paper clips. Place finished packages on a cookie sheet and bake for 4 to 6 minutes, or until the fish is baked. Remove and serve immediately.

Sautéed Sesame Fish

Serves 4 to 6

Parsley-Onion Garnish:

¼	cup chopped parsley
¼	cup fresh squeezed lemon juice
½	cup finely chopped green onions

Sesame Fish:

2	pounds snapper, lingcod or halibut fillets
	Salt and pepper
¼	cup flour
½	cup fine dry seasoned bread crumbs
¼	cup sesame seeds
1	egg, beaten with 2 tablespoons milk
2	tablespoons salad oil
2	tablespoons butter

1. To prepare garnish: Combine the parsley, lemon juice and green onions and let stand while preparing the fish.

2. To prepare sesame fish: Cut the fish into serving-sized pieces; sprinkle each piece with salt and pepper to taste and dust lightly with flour.

3. Mix together the bread crumbs and sesame seeds. Dip the fish pieces in the egg-milk mixture, drain briefly, then turn in the crumb-seed mixture until evenly coated.

4. Heat the oil and butter in a large, heavy skillet over medium heat. Add the fish and cook, turning once, until the fish is done and golden brown. Allow 10 minutes per inch of thickness.

5. Place the cooked fish on a warm serving platter and serve with parsley-onion garnish.

Beer-Batter Fish

Serves 4

Spicy Tomato Sauce:

1	tablespoon olive oil
½	cup coarsely chopped onion
½	cup seeded, cored and coarsely chopped green pepper
1	(15 ounce) can tomato purée
¾	cup beer
⅛	teaspoon red pepper flakes
1	tablespoon Worcestershire sauce
½	teaspoon salt
1½	teaspoons sugar

Batter:

2	eggs, separated
1½	cups beer
1½	cups flour
4	tablespoons cornstarch
½	teaspoon salt
8	medium or 4 large fish fillets (haddock, cod or flounder), about 2 pounds
	Vegetable oil

1. To prepare tomato sauce: Heat the olive oil in a large skillet and sauté the onion and pepper until limp but not brown, about 3 minutes. Add the tomato purée, beer, red pepper flakes, Worcestershire sauce, salt and sugar. Bring to a boil, lower heat, cover and simmer 30 minutes. Let cool to room temperature.

2. To prepare batter: Combine the egg yolks and beer and blend well. Beat in the flour, cornstarch and salt. Let stand 1 hour. Beat the egg whites until almost firm and whisk into the batter.

3. Cut the fish into serving pieces. Dip the fish into the batter. Heat the vegetable oil in a deep frying pan until very hot. Add the coated fish pieces, a few at a time. Fry on both sides until golden brown and the fish is done. Time will vary depending on the thickness of the fish. Allow 10 minutes per inch of thickness. Serve immediately with spicy tomato sauce.

Crispy Fish in Ginger Sauce

Serves 4

Ginger Sauce:

1	cup sugar
⅔	cup vinegar
⅔	cup cold water
¼	cup soy sauce
3	tablespoons cornstarch
2	teaspoons salt
1	teaspoon ground ginger

Fish:

1	pound red snapper fillets
2	eggs
⅔	cup flour
⅓	cup cornstarch
1	teaspoon salt
	About 6 tablespoons water
	Hot oil for deep frying
	Cooked rice

1. To prepare sauce: Combine the sugar, vinegar, water, soy sauce, cornstarch, salt and ginger in a saucepan. Cook, stirring constantly until thick and clear. Set aside.

2. To prepare fish: Place the fish fillets in the freezer for about 1 hour for ease of slicing. With a large, heavy knife, slice on the diagonal into ⅛-inch thick slices, starting at the narrow end.

3. Beat the eggs; add the flour, cornstarch, salt and enough water to make a thick batter. Dip the semifrozen fish pieces into the batter.

4. Heat oil to 375°F. in a heavy skillet or deep-fat fryer. Fry a few pieces of fish at a time for 2 to 3 minutes or until golden. Drain on paper towels. Place the fish in a serving dish. Pour the ginger sauce over the fish and toss. Serve immediately to retain the crispness of the fish coating. Accompany with rice.

Puget Sound Fish Poach

Serves 4 to 6

2	pounds white fish fillets or steaks, such as cod, snapper or halibut
½	cup dry white wine
1	tablespoon lemon juice
	Salt
¼	cup butter
½	pound mushrooms, thinly sliced
1½	tablespoons flour
½	cup half-and-half
	Ground nutmeg
¾	cup shredded Swiss cheese

1. Preheat oven to 450°.

2. Wipe the fish fillets with a damp cloth. Arrange the fish in a single layer in a large shallow baking pan. Pour the white wine and lemon juice evenly over the fish. Sprinkle lightly with salt to taste. Cover and bake, allowing 10 minutes per inch of thickness or until the fish is done. Remove from oven and let cool a few minutes.

3. Holding the fish in place with a wide spatula, drain the poaching liquid from the baking pan into a measuring cup. There should be about 1 cup of poaching liquid, but this will depend on the type of fish used. If there is more than 1 cup, reduce by boiling over high heat. If less than 1 cup, add dry white wine. Reserve. Keep the fish at room temperature while preparing the sauce.

4. In a saucepan, melt 2 tablespoons butter over medium-high heat. Add the mushrooms and cook, stirring until the mushrooms are limp and the liquid has evaporated. Remove the mushrooms from the saucepan and set aside.

5. Melt the remaining butter in the saucepan and blend in the flour. Remove from heat and, using a wire whip, gradually stir in the reserved poaching liquid, half-and-half and ½ teaspoon ground nutmeg. Bring to a boil and cook, stirring, for 1 to 2 minutes, or until thickened. Remove from heat; add the mushrooms, and salt to taste.

6. Spoon the sauce evenly over the poached fish, covering completely. Sprinkle the cheese evenly over fish. Reduce oven heat to 400°. Place the pan, uncovered, in the oven and bake for 5 to 8 minutes or until the sauce is bubbling around the edges and the cheese has melted. Dust very lightly with ground nutmeg and serve.

◇

Poached Skate Wings

Serves 4

1½	quarts water
2	cups dry white wine
1½	teaspoons salt
1½	pounds skate wings
8	tablespoons butter
2	tablespoons vinegar
4-6	tablespoons capers, drained

1. Bring the water, wine and salt to a boil in a large skillet. Place the skate wings in the boiling liquid. Wait until the liquid reaches the simmering point again, then poach the fish for 10 minutes per inch of thickness.

2. Drain the fish thoroughly. Place on a serving dish.

3. Melt the butter in a small saucepan until it turns a light brown. Add the vinegar and capers. Heat until hot and pour over the fish just before serving.

Baked Grouper

Serves 2

¼	cup butter
	Juice of ½ lemon
2	(8 ounce) fillets of grouper, at least 1-inch thick
	Parsley

1. Preheat oven to 450°.

2. Melt the butter over medium heat. Add the lemon juice. Heat until butter bubbles, stir lightly and pour enough over the fish to coat the top. Reserve remainder of the lemon butter.

3. Bake the fish 10 minutes per inch of thickness. Serve with remaining lemon butter and garnish with parsley.

Shark Teriyaki

Serves 4

1½	pounds shark steaks, or other firm-fleshed fish
2½	cups fresh pineapple chunks, juice reserved
3	tablespoons soy sauce
2	tablespoons sherry
1	tablespoon grated ginger root
½	teaspoon dry mustard
2	cloves garlic, minced
1	teaspoon firmly packed brown sugar
1-2	large green peppers, cut into large pieces

1. Rinse the shark with cold water and pat dry with paper towels. Set aside.

2. Make a marinade by combining 3 tablespoons pineapple juice, soy sauce, sherry, ginger, mustard, garlic and brown sugar. Stir well and pour over the fish. Cover and marinate in the refrigerator for 1 hour, turning once.

3. Using bamboo or metal skewers, make kebabs from alternating pieces of pineapple chunks and green pepper; set aside.

4. Drain the shark, reserving marinade. Place the fish on a well-greased broiler pan and broil 5 to 6 inches from the heat for 4 to 5 minutes. Baste with marinade and turn. Broil 4 to 5 minutes more, or until the fish is done. Allow 10 minutes per inch of thickness.

5. Baste the fruit and vegetable kebabs with marinade, place on the broiler pan and broil 15 to 30 seconds on each side, or until just browned.

Stir-Fried Squid

Serves 4

1	clove garlic, minced
1	bunch green onions, cut into 1½-inch pieces
2	medium tomatoes, peeled and cut into wedges
1	green pepper, seeded and cut into julienne strips
2	tablespoons oil
1	pound squid, cleaned and cut into ½-inch strips

2	tablespoons ketchup
1	tablespoon Worcestershire sauce
½	teaspoon salt
	Dash hot-pepper sauce

1. In a large skillet, sauté the garlic, white portion of onions, tomatoes and green pepper in 1 tablespoon oil over high heat. Remove the vegetables from the skillet.

2. Sauté the squid in the remaining oil until it begins to turn white, about 1½ to 2 minutes.

3. Quickly return the vegetables and green portion of onions to the pan; add the ketchup, Worcestershire sauce, salt and hot-pepper sauce. Heat thoroughly. Serve over cooked rice.

Swordfish with Garlic

Serves 4

4	cloves garlic, minced
¼	cup plus 2 tablespoons butter
	Salt and freshly ground pepper
2	tablespoons dry vermouth
4	(½ pound) swordfish steaks
½	cup flour
2	tablespoons vegetable oil

1. Sauté the garlic on low heat in ¼ cup butter until the garlic begins to color and appears transparent. Season to taste with salt and pepper. Add the vermouth and keep warm while cooking the fish.

2. Wash the fish and pat dry with paper towels. Place the flour in a flat dish and season with salt and pepper. Dip the swordfish steaks in the seasoned flour to coat evenly.

3. Heat the oil and 2 tablespoons butter in a large, heavy skillet and fry the steaks over medium-high heat, until lightly browned and cooked through. Allow 10 minutes per inch of thickness. Transfer the fish to a heated serving platter, spoon the garlic mixture over the fish and serve hot.

Marinated Sablefish

Serves 4

1¼	pounds sablefish fillets
¼	cup orange juice
2	tablespoons ketchup
2	tablespoons soy sauce
1	tablespoon lemon juice
¼	teaspoon pepper
1	teaspoon sesame oil
1	tablespoon firmly packed brown sugar
	Vegetable oil
1	tablespoon sesame seeds, toasted

1. Rinse the fish with cold water; pat dry with paper towels. Cut the fish into 4 equal portions. Place the fish in a single layer in a glass baking dish.

2. In a small bowl, combine the orange juice, ketchup, soy sauce, lemon juice, pepper, sesame oil and brown sugar. Pour over the fish. Cover and marinate in the refrigerator for 2 hours, turning once.

3. Remove the fish, reserving the marinade. Coat the broiler pan with vegetable oil. Place the fish on the broiler pan and baste with marinade. Broil 4 to 5 inches from source of heat for 5 to 7 minutes. Turn and baste with marinade. Broil for an additional 4 to 5 minutes, or until the fish is done. Allow 10 minutes per inch of thickness.

4. Heat the remaining marinade; pour over the fish just before serving and top with the sesame seeds.

Lemon Catfish Fry

Serves 4 to 6

2	pounds catfish fillets, skinned
¼	cup lemon juice
1	teaspoon salt
1	clove garlic, minced
¼	teaspoon dried oregano, crushed
½	cup yellow cornmeal
¼	cup flour

2	tablespoons chopped parsley
2	tablespoons butter
2	tablespoons salad oil
	Parsley
	Lemon peel grated in long threads
	Lemon wedges

1. Wipe the fish with a damp cloth; cut into serving pieces, about 3 by 5 inches.

2. Combine the lemon juice, salt, garlic and oregano. Pour over the catfish and chill 30 minutes, turning the fish occasionally to marinate all sides. Remove fish from marinade and drain.

3. Combine the cornmeal, flour and parsley on wax paper in a shallow pan. Roll each fish piece in the cornmeal mixture to coat all sides evenly; shake off excess.

4. In a large skillet, heat the butter and oil until it foams but doesn't brown. Promptly add as many fish pieces as will fit without crowding. Cook, turning once, over medium-high heat if pieces are ⅝-inch thick or less; over medium heat if pieces are thicker than ⅝ inch. Cook until fish is lightly browned; measuring the thickest part of fish, allow 10 minutes total cooking time per inch. Remove each piece as it is done. Arrange on a warm serving platter and keep warm while you cook the remaining fish. Add more butter and oil to the pan if necessary. Serve immediately, garnished with parsley and lemon peel and accompanied by lemon wedges.

Sturgeon with Tarragon Sauce

Serves 6

Sauce:

6	tablespoons butter
½	teaspoon dried tarragon, crushed
3	tablespoons chopped shallots or onion
2	cups sliced fresh mushrooms
2	tablespoons dry white wine

Fish:

6	sturgeon fillets, at least 1-inch thick, skinned
	Melted butter

1. To prepare sauce: In a saucepan, melt the butter over medium-high heat; add the tarragon and stir lightly. Add the shallots or onion and the mushrooms. Sauté, stirring until the mushrooms are limp. Sprinkle with the wine and cook, stirring, 1 minute longer. Remove from heat; set aside while the fish cooks.

2. To prepare fish: Place the fillets on a greased broiler rack. Adjust the oven rack so the top surface of the fish is 2 to 4 inches from the element. Brush the fish with melted butter. Broil 10 minutes per each inch of thickness. The fish can be cooked all on one side or turned once during the cooking time. Baste with butter occasionally during cooking.

3. When the fish is done, reheat the sauce and spoon it over the fish. Serve on warm plates.

Spinach-Stuffed Sole

Serves 6

Stuffed Fish:

4	ounces fresh mushrooms, sliced
2	tablespoons butter
2	cups chopped fresh spinach
⅓	cup sliced green onions
1	cup cooked rice
½	teaspoon dried dill weed

¼	teaspoon salt
⅛	teaspoon pepper
6	fillets of sole, about 1½ pounds
	Lemon slices
	Parsley

Sauce:

2	tablespoons butter
2	tablespoons flour
1¼	cups milk
1	cup shredded Jarlsberg cheese
1	teaspoon Worcestershire sauce
½	teaspoon dry mustard
½	teaspoon salt
	Dash cayenne pepper

1. Preheat oven to 400°.

2. To prepare stuffed fish: Brown the mushrooms in the butter. Add the spinach and green onions; cook until tender. Add the rice, dill, salt and pepper. Lay out the fillets; divide the stuffing among the fillets. Roll up and fasten with toothpicks. Place in a buttered shallow baking dish. Bake 15 minutes or until done.

3. To prepare sauce: In a saucepan, melt the butter, add the flour and cook, stirring until bubbly and smooth. Remove from heat and gradually blend in the milk. Cook, stirring until thickened and smooth. Add the cheese, Worcestershire sauce, dry mustard, salt and cayenne pepper. Stir until the cheese melts. Serve over the fish. Garnish with lemon slices and parsley.

Cod with Dill Sauce
Serves 2

1	tablespoon butter
2	tablespoons finely minced shallots
1¼	cups dry white wine
2	cups whipping cream
½	teaspoon dried dill
	Salt and white pepper
1	pound cod fillets
	Small boiled potatoes

1. Melt the butter in a small, heavy saucepan over medium-high heat. Stir in the minced shallots and sauté until the shallots are tender, about 3 to 4 minutes. Add 1 cup white wine.

2. Slowly boil the wine, uncovered, approximately 15 minutes to reduce to ½ cup. Add the cream, dill, salt and white pepper. Reduce the sauce again, uncovered, for about 15 minutes, or until you have approximately 1½ cups sauce. Stir the sauce often during the reduction process to prevent scorching. The finished sauce should have a smooth, fairly thick consistency. Keep warm while baking the fish.

3. Preheat oven to 450°.

4. Lay the cod fillets in a buttered baking dish. Pour ¼ cup white wine over them and sprinkle with salt and white pepper to taste. Bake until the fish is done, allowing 10 minutes per inch of thickness. Do not overbake.

5. Remove the cod from the wine and place on two warm plates. Coat lightly with the dill sauce. Serve accompanied by small boiled potatoes.

Mediterranean Cod
Serves 6 to 8

2	pounds cod fillets
3	cloves garlic, slivered
⅓	cup plus 2 tablespoons vegetable oil
1	medium eggplant, cut into 1-inch cubes

3	medium onions, cut into wedges
2	green peppers, cut into 1-inch squares
¼	teaspoon pepper
¾	cup water
2½	teaspoons salt
1	egg
1	cup seasoned bread crumbs
1	tablespoon plus ¾ teaspoon chopped fresh dill
	or 1¼ teaspoons dried dill weed
3	tomatoes, cut in wedges

1. Rinse the fish with cold water; pat dry with paper towels. Cut the fish into the desired number of serving portions. Set aside.

2. In a large skillet, over medium heat, sauté the garlic in 2 tablespoons oil until golden. Discard the garlic, reserving the oil in the pan. Add the eggplant and onion; cook until the vegetables are browned, stirring frequently, about 5 minutes.

3. Stir in the green peppers, pepper, water and ½ teaspoon salt. Cover and cook 5 minutes, stirring occasionally. Remove the cover and continue cooking until all water has evaporated. Remove the vegetables to a bowl and keep warm.

4. Sprinkle the remaining 2 teaspoons salt over the fish. In a pie plate, beat the egg slightly. On wax paper, combine the bread crumbs and 1 tablespoon fresh dill. Dip the fish in egg; coat with bread crumb mixture.

5. In the same skillet, heat ⅓ cup vegetable oil over medium heat. Place the breaded fish portions in hot oil and cook for 6 minutes. Turn and cook for an additional 4 to 5 minutes, or until the fish is done when tested with a fork. Allow 10 minutes per inch of thickness. Transfer the fish to a warm serving platter and keep warm.

6. Return the vegetables to the skillet. Sprinkle the remaining ¾ teaspoon dill over the tomatoes. Add to the vegetable mixture in the skillet. Cook over medium heat, stirring frequently until the tomatoes are heated through. Drain the vegetables and serve in a separate bowl alongside the fish.

Glazed Poached Steelhead

Serves 4

Poached Fish:

1	(750 ml) bottle white wine or dry vermouth
6	cups water
1	small onion, quartered
1	stalk celery with leaves, chopped
¾	teaspoon salt
3	sprigs parsley
4-5	whole black peppercorns
1	teaspoon dried thyme, crushed
1	(3 pound) whole steelhead

Mayonnaise Glaze:

1	envelope unflavored gelatin
¼	cup cold water
1½	cups mayonnaise
½	teaspoon horseradish
2	tablespoons lemon juice
	Salt and pepper
	Lemon-slice halves

1. To poach the fish: Prepare a court bouillon by combining the wine, water, onion, celery, salt, parsley, peppercorns and thyme in a large kettle. Cover and simmer for about 45 minutes. Strain and refrigerate until ready to use.

2. Wrap the fish in cheesecloth. Bring the court bouillon to a simmer. Lower the fish carefully into the court bouillon. Cover and simmer gently 20 minutes or until done.

3. Lift out the fish. Drain it and discard the cheesecloth. Carefully remove and discard the skin. Cool the fish.

4. To prepare glaze: Soak the gelatin in the cold water for a few minutes; stir over hot water until dissolved. Stir in the mayonnaise, horseradish, lemon juice and salt and pepper to taste.

5. To glaze the fish: Place the fish on a serving platter. Working quickly before the mayonnaise sets, with a spatula spread the glaze over the top of the fish so that it is covered completely and smoothly. Place the glazed fish in the refrigerator until the glaze is set. Before serving, garnish with lemon slices. Pass remaining mayonnaise glaze at the table.

Snapper en Papillote

Serves 4

1½	pounds red snapper fillets
¾	teaspoon salt
¼	teaspoon pepper
⅓	cup butter, melted and cooled
2	tablespoons chopped parsley
1	tablespoon lemon juice
½	teaspoon dill weed
	Parchment or brown paper
2	tablespoons cooking oil
4	thin onion slices
1	cup thinly sliced carrots
¾	cup grated Swiss cheese

1. Preheat oven to 450°.

2. Cut the fish into 4 serving portions. Sprinkle with ¼ teaspoon salt and pepper.

3. Combine the butter, parsley, lemon juice, ½ teaspoon salt and dill weed.

4. Cut the pieces of parchment or brown paper into 4 heart shapes about 10-by-12 inches each. Brush the paper with oil. Spread 1 teaspoon parsley butter on one half of each paper heart. Place the fish portion on top of the parsley butter. Separate the onion slices into rings and place on the fish. Top each portion with ¼ cup carrots. Pour the remaining parsley butter over the carrots. Top each serving with 3 tablespoons cheese.

5. Fold the other half of each paper heart over the fillet to form an individual case. Seal, starting at the top of heart, by turning the edges up and folding, twisting the tip of the heart to hold the case closed.

6. Place the cases in a baking dish. Bake, allowing 10 minutes per inch of thickness. Serve in cases.

Bacon-Topped Snapper

Serves 6

1½	pounds snapper fillets
6	slices bacon
¾	cup thinly sliced onion rings
1	tablespoon lemon juice
	Pepper
	Garlic salt
½	cup drained, pitted and sliced black olives
½	cup soft bread crumbs
2	tablespoons chopped fresh parsley

1. Preheat oven to 350°.
2. Rinse the fish with cold water; pat dry with paper towels. Cut the fish into 6 portions.
3. In a large skillet, fry the bacon over medium heat until crisp. Remove the bacon from the skillet, reserving the bacon drippings. Blot the bacon with paper towels and crumble; set aside.
4. Sauté the onion in the bacon drippings until tender. Place the fish in a single layer in a well-greased 2-quart glass baking dish. Sprinkle with the lemon juice, pepper and garlic salt to taste. Top with the onion and olives. Combine the bacon, bread crumbs and parsley; sprinkle over the top of the olives.
5. Bake for 25 to 30 minutes, or until the fish is done when tested with a fork.

Mustard-Butter Fillets

Serves 3 to 4

½	cup butter at room temperature
1	tablespoon minced parsley
2	teaspoons lemon juice
2	tablespoons lime-flavored mustard or 1 tablespoon Dijon mustard
	Salt and pepper
1-1⅓	pounds thick white fish fillet

1. Preheat oven to 450°.

2. To prepare mustard butter: Combine the butter, parsley and lemon juice in a food processor. Whirl until well blended.

3. Add the mustard and again whirl until fluffy and well-combined. Season to taste with salt and pepper.

4. To prepare fish: Spread the fillet lightly with the mustard butter and bake 10 minutes per inch of thickness.

5. Immediately melt more mustard butter over the fish and serve. Pass any remaining butter to use with the fish or on bread.

Baked Orange Roughy

Serves 6

6	(6 ounce) orange roughy fillets
1	egg
4	tablespoons lemon juice
1¼	cups dry white wine
½	teaspoon salt
⅛	teaspoon pepper
4	tablespoons butter
2	tablespoons minced parsley

1. Arrange the fish fillets in a single layer and close together in a shallow baking pan. Beat together the egg, 3 tablespoons lemon juice, 1 cup wine, salt and pepper. Pour the mixture over the fish. Cover and chill for about 1 hour.

2. Remove the fish from the marinade and drain, reserving marinade. Heat 2 tablespoons butter in a wide heavy skillet; brown the fish fillets on both sides. Place the cooked fish on a heated platter and keep warm in a low oven while making the sauce.

3. In a saucepan, melt the remaining 2 tablespoons butter. Add ¼ cup of the marinade mixture, the remaining 1 tablespoon lemon juice and ¼ cup wine. Bring to a boil.

4. To serve, pour some of the sauce over the fish, sprinkle with the minced parsley and pass the remaining sauce at the table.

Shellfish

Puget Sound's nutrient-rich waters and gently sloping shores make it a natural shellfish hatchery.

For a long time crab and clams garnered most of the attention. Although Northwest cooks are still partial to them, they have vastly expanded their menu planning to include lots of other shellfish.

Today many of our restaurants offer a list of three or four types of local oysters, and it doesn't take much hunting to find a fish market that has that many or more available to the home cook. The comeback of the tiny Olympia oyster, almost wiped out by industrial pollution and competition with larger Pacifics, has been a national food story.

In the past 10 years, commercially raised mussels, mostly from the clear waters of Penn Cove on Whidbey Island, have made a year-round delicacy of a food that not too many years before had been ignored.

These are exciting times for innovative cooks, and the recipes in this chapter range from regional standbys to those that will stretch your imagination. It takes a real culinary effort to explore delicate flavor combinations such as Crab with Stilton Cheese or Shrimp Amaretto when just plain shrimp or crab is such good eating, but it's worth the effort.

◇

Crab with Stilton Cheese

Serves 4

Herb Butter:

4	tablespoons butter, softened
1	teaspoon chopped fresh tarragon or ½ teaspoon dried, crushed
	Pinch freshly grated nutmeg
½	teaspoon finely chopped fresh parsley
	Pinch ground fennel

Crab Ramekins:

16-20	mushrooms, thickly sliced
½	cup dry white wine
12	ounces crab meat, legs and body
4	tablespoons chopped green onions
24	seedless grapes, halved
4	ounces Stilton cheese, crumbled

1. Preheat oven to 375°.
2. To prepare herb butter: Cream the butter and blend in the tarragon, nutmeg, parsley and fennel.
3. To prepare crab ramekins: Place the mushrooms and white wine in a small saucepan. Cover; bring to a boil, then simmer for 5 minutes. Drain the mushrooms.
4. Layer equal amounts of crab, mushrooms, onions, herb butter, grapes and crumbled cheese in 4 individual ramekins. Bake 10 to 12 minutes, or until bubbly.

Spicy Shrimp Broil

Serves 4

1¼	pounds medium raw shrimp, peeled and deveined
1	large tomato, diced
4	green onions, finely chopped
½	cup butter
	Juice of 1 small lemon
4	shallots, minced

2	cloves garlic, minced
½	teaspoon Worcestershire sauce
5	drops Tabasco
2½	cups hot cooked rice, seasoned with dried dill weed to taste

1. Drop the shrimp in boiling salted water. Bring back to a boil and cook about 2 minutes or until almost done. Drain in a colander.

2. Place the shrimp in a shallow baking dish. Sprinkle the diced tomato and green onion over the shrimp.

3. Melt the butter in a saucepan. Add the lemon juice, shallots, garlic, Worcestershire sauce and Tabasco. Simmer slowly until the shallots are a little soft.

4. Spoon about half the butter sauce over the shrimp and tomatoes. Keep the remaining sauce warm.

5. Broil the shrimp and tomatoes until just tender, about 2 to 3 minutes, depending on the size of the shrimp. Serve over dill weed-seasoned rice. Pass the remaining butter sauce for those who want extra sauce for dipping shrimp.

Chili-Spiced Shrimp

Serves 4

2	tablespoons vegetable oil
1	cup chopped onion
2	cloves garlic, minced
1	slice fresh ginger root, chopped, or ½ teaspoon ground ginger
2	teaspoons chili powder
½	teaspoon salt
1	pound raw shrimp, shelled and deveined
⅓	cup amaretto
2	tablespoons lemon juice

1. In a large skillet, heat the oil and sauté the onion, garlic, ginger, chili powder and salt, stirring constantly to prevent the spices from sticking.

2. Add the shrimp and cook about 3 minutes until they are pink and tender. Stir in the amaretto and lemon juice. Serve with rice if desired.

Shrimp in Lobster Sauce

Serves 2 to 3

1	pound medium raw shrimp, shelled, deveined and blotted dry
1	egg white, lightly beaten
1	teaspoon cornstarch
1½	cups plus 2 tablespoons peanut oil
½	pound pork, coarsely ground
1½	tablespoons fermented black beans
2	tablespoons coarsely chopped garlic
1	teaspoon finely chopped ginger root
2	green onions, finely chopped
1½	tablespoons thin soy sauce
2	tablespoons dry sherry
¼	teaspoon sugar
	Pinch salt
½	cup chicken stock or broth
1	tablespoon cornstarch dissolved in 2 tablespoons chicken stock
1	egg
2	teaspoons sesame oil

1. Coat the shrimp with a mixture of the egg white and 1 teaspoon cornstarch. Let stand for 20 minutes in the refrigerator.

2. Heat 1½ cups peanut oil in a wok. Stir-fry the shrimp a few at a time until just done. Pour the oil from the wok.

3. Brown the ground pork in 2 tablespoons peanut oil. Add the fermented black beans, garlic, ginger root, green onions, soy sauce, sherry, sugar, salt and ½ cup chicken stock. Bring to a boil.

4. Add the cornstarch-stock mixture to thicken the sauce slightly.

5. Turn off the heat. Beat the egg with the sesame oil and stir into the wok, pulling the clumps of egg into thin strands with chopsticks as they cook. Stir in the cooked shrimp to coat them with the sauce. Serve immediately.

Shrimp Newburg with Avocado

Serves 4

6	tablespoons butter
4	tablespoons flour
2	cups half-and-half
12	ounces shrimp, cooked
	Salt and pepper
2-4	tablespoons pale sherry
2	cups hot cooked rice
2	soft avocados, peeled and halved
	Ground nutmeg
	Parsley

1. Preheat oven to 350°.

2. Melt 4 tablespoons butter in a saucepan. Stirring briskly with a wire whisk, add the flour gradually to form a bubbly paste. Add the half-and-half and cook over medium heat, stirring constantly, until thick and smooth. Remove from heat.

3. Melt the remaining 2 tablespoons butter in a small skillet. Reserve 8 shrimp for garnish. Sauté the remaining shrimp until warm through. Add the shrimp to the cream sauce; season to taste with salt and pepper and add the sherry.

4. Place a layer of cooked rice in each of 4 ramekins. Top the rice with an avocado half. Spoon the shrimp sauce over the avocado halves, filling the cavities. Pour in the remaining sauce to cover. Sprinkle with nutmeg.

5. Bake for 15 minutes or until hot. Garnish with the reserved shrimp and parsley. Serve at once.

Shrimp Amaretto

Serves 6 to 8

2	tablespoons peanut or corn oil
1	clove garlic, minced
1	bunch green onions, trimmed and sliced
1	green or red pepper, seeded and cut into ¼-inch strips
⅓	cup amaretto
⅓	cup soy sauce
⅓	cup red-wine vinegar
1¼	cups chicken stock or broth
2½	pounds raw shrimp, shelled and deveined
¼	pound snow peas, strings removed
½	cup toasted blanched whole almonds
2	tablespoons cornstarch
	Hot cooked rice

1. In a large wok (or skillet), heat the oil and sauté the garlic and green onions for 2 minutes over high heat. Add the green pepper. Stir-fry for 2 minutes. Add the amaretto, soy sauce and vinegar. Simmer 5 minutes.

2. Add ¾ cup chicken stock to the wok. Add the shrimp, snow peas and almonds and stir over high heat until the shrimp are cooked, 4 to 6 minutes, depending on the size of the shrimp.

3. Mix the remaining ½ cup chicken stock and cornstarch. Add to the wok and stir until thickened. Serve with hot cooked rice.

Sautéed Scampi

Serves 4 to 6

18-20	large raw shrimp, shelled and deveined
2	tablespoons olive oil
2	tablespoons butter
2	cloves garlic, minced
	Dash Italian seasonings
	Chopped parsley
	Seasoned bread crumbs
	Parmesan cheese

1. Clean the shrimp and keep in the refrigerator until ready to cook. Heat the oil in a large, heavy skillet and add the butter, garlic and Italian seasoning.

2. Sauté the shrimp in the butter-oil mixture until almost done.

3. Sprinkle with parsley, bread crumbs and parmesan cheese, mixing until the cheese is melted and the shrimp are done. Serve immediately.

Garlic-Parmesan Oysters

Serves 6

¼ cup coarsely chopped mushrooms	
3 cloves garlic	
2 whole green onions, coarsely chopped	
½ cup unsalted butter, softened	
6 tablespoons brandy	
2 tablespoons dry sherry	
24 extra small oysters, in the shell	
½ cup grated parmesan cheese	
Parsley	
Lemon wedges	

1. In a food processor using a metal blade, whirl the mushrooms, garlic, green onions and butter until the mixture is finely chopped and well combined.

2. Add 2 tablespoons brandy and the sherry, gradually, and blend well. Set aside.

3. Preheat oven to 425°.

4. Shuck the oysters, leaving them in the deeper shell. Place in a 10-by-15-inch baking pan.

5. Sprinkle the remaining brandy evenly over the oysters. Top each oyster with garlic butter. Sprinkle with parmesan cheese.

6. Bake 6 to 8 minutes. Serve immediately, garnished with parsley and lemon wedges.

Oysters Benedict

Serves 6

2	egg yolks
3	tablespoons lemon juice
¼	teaspoon salt
	Dash cayenne pepper
½	cup plus 2 tablespoons butter
3	English muffins
6	thin slices Canadian-style bacon or ham
1	pound fresh spinach
2	tablespoons chopped onion
⅛	teaspoon nutmeg
1	pint fresh oysters, cut into 1-inch pieces

1. Place the egg yolks, lemon juice, salt and cayenne pepper in a blender container. Blend for 5 seconds on low speed. Melt ½ cup butter over moderate heat and keep warm.

2. Split the muffins and toast them lightly. Reserve in a warm oven.

3. Sauté the bacon in a medium-sized skillet until lightly browned. Place the bacon on the muffins. Return to warm oven.

4. Wash the spinach. Blanch in boiling water for 1 to 2 minutes. Drain, chop and squeeze dry.

5. Add the spinach, onion and 1 tablespoon butter to the skillet and cook about 2 minutes or just until the onion is tender. Add the nutmeg. Place about ¼ cup drained spinach mixture on each slice of bacon; keep warm in the oven.

6. Melt 1 tablespoon butter in the skillet. Pour the oysters and liquid into the skillet and simmer for 2 to 3 minutes or until the oysters curl. Remove the oysters with a slotted spoon and place on the spinach, dividing evenly among servings. Keep warm.

7. Pour the ½ cup melted butter very slowly into the blender containing the egg yolk mixture, omitting the milky residue at the bottom of the pan. Continue to blend until the sauce is thick and smooth. Spoon over the oysters. Serve immediately.

Oysters Rockefeller

Serves 6

¼	cup chopped shallots
⅓	cup chopped celery
½	teaspoon dried tarragon, crushed
4	sprigs fresh parsley
1	cup washed and chopped fresh young spinach leaves
½	cup soft bread crumbs
1	cup butter, softened
1	teaspoon anchovy paste
1	tablespoon Worcestershire sauce
	Salt and freshly ground black pepper
3	dozen fresh oysters in the shell
	Rock salt
¾	cup grated Gruyère cheese

1. In the work bowl of a food processor fitted with a metal blade, whirl the shallots, celery, tarragon, parsley and spinach until chopped.

2. Add the bread crumbs, softened butter, anchovy paste, Worcestershire sauce, salt and pepper. Process with an on-and-off motion until mixed. Taste and adjust the seasonings.

3. Preheat oven to 425°.

4. Shuck the oysters, leaving them in the deeper shell. Place rock salt in the bottom of six aluminum pie plates. Set the oysters on top of the rock salt, 6 to a pie plate. Place 1 tablespoon of the spinach-bread crumb mixture to cover each oyster and sprinkle lightly with cheese.

5. Bake the oysters until the sauce bubbles (approximately 5 to 6 minutes), then place under a hot broiler for 2 more minutes to slightly brown the cheese. When serving, place each pie plate of oysters on a serving plate.

Hangtown Fry

Serves 4

8	eggs
1	pint oysters, shucked and drained
½	cup flour
1	cup soda crackers, finely crushed
½	cup butter
½	cup half-and-half
	Salt and freshly ground white pepper
4	slices bacon, broiled or fried crisp
1	cup cocktail sauce

1. Beat 2 eggs well. Roll the oysters in the flour, shaking off any excess. Dip them into the eggs and then into cracker crumbs.

2. Melt the butter in a large skillet until just sizzling but not brown. Add the oysters and brown quickly on each side, but be careful not to overcook.

3. Beat the 6 eggs in a bowl with the half-and-half. Season with salt and pepper to taste and pour over the oysters in the skillet. Reduce heat and cook until the eggs are set and the underneath begins to brown nicely.

4. With a spatula, fold the omelet over carefully into a half circle and lift onto a prewarmed platter. Top each serving with a strip of bacon. Serve cocktail sauce on the side.

Puget Sound Clambake

Serves 4

1	pound rockweed
2	whole chicken breasts, halved
4	whole medium onions, peeled
4	lobster tails (thawed, if frozen)
4	ears corn with husks on, but silk removed
4	bratwurst
2	dozen fresh clams, in the shell, scrubbed
¾	cup butter, melted

1. Put 2 cups of water in the bottom of an 8- to 10-quart kettle.
2. Place a rack in the kettle and then a layer of rockweed.
3. Proceed with layering the chicken, onions, lobster tails, corn, bratwurst and clams, in that order.
4. Top with another layer of rockweed.
5. Bring to a boil over high heat. Reduce heat to medium-high; cover and cook 25 to 30 minutes or until the chicken is fork-tender.
6. In a 1-quart saucepan over low heat, melt the butter.
7. To serve, use tongs to remove and discard the rockweed. Serve the chicken, vegetables, bratwurst, lobster tails and clams on a large heated platter. Discard unopened clams. Pass melted butter.

Steamed Mussels in Wine

Serves 3

1	small onion, chopped
2	cloves garlic, minced
2	tablespoons butter
1	cup white wine
½	cup dry vermouth
1	(16 ounce) can Italian stewed tomatoes
¼	cup fresh chopped parsley
1	tablespoon sweet dry basil
24	mussels, scrubbed and beards removed

1. Sauté the onion and garlic in butter until the onion is transparent. Add the wine, vermouth, tomatoes, parsley and basil. Bring to a boil. Add the mussels; cover and steam only until the mussels open.
2. Discard any mussels that do not open. Serve immediately with the broth.

This recipe is from Anita Van Slyck.

Mustard-Cream Scallops
Serves 6

2	tablespoons butter
2	tablespoons flour
1¼	cups milk
3	tablespoons Dijon or green pepper mustard
2	tablespoons sherry
½	teaspoon salt
1½-2	pounds scallops
	Buttered bread crumbs
	Rice, pasta or toast

1. Preheat oven to 400°.
2. Melt the butter in a small saucepan; add the flour and stir until smooth. Gradually add the milk, stirring constantly. Add the mustard, sherry and salt. Cook over medium heat, stirring occasionally, until the mixture comes to a boil. Combine with the scallops in a bowl.
3. Spoon into a shallow 2-quart casserole; sprinkle bread crumbs around the edge. Bake 15 to 20 minutes or until bubbling hot. Serve with rice, pasta or on toast.

Scallop Curry
Serves 3 to 4

1	pound scallops
2	tablespoons butter
2	tablespoons oil
1	teaspoon curry powder
¼	cup dry vermouth
1	tablespoon lemon juice
2	tablespoons finely chopped parsley
	Hot cooked rice
	Parsley
	Lemon wedges

1. Rinse the scallops in cold water and towel dry.

2. Heat the butter and oil in a medium skillet. Add the scallops and cook, stirring about 2 to 3 minutes. Sprinkle with the curry powder and mix well. Cook about 2 minutes more or until done, watching carefully so they don't toughen. Remove the scallops and keep warm.

3. To the same skillet, add the vermouth, lemon juice and parsley. Stir, scraping the bottom of the skillet to incorporate any browned bits.

4. Pour the sauce over the scallops and serve over rice in individual au gratin dishes. Garnish with more parsley and lemon wedges.

Clams Italiano

Serves 5

5	pounds clams
½	cup boiling water
1	cup marinara sauce, puréed (see index)
2	tablespoons lemon juice
2	teaspoons chopped parsley
2	tablespoons chopped chives
	Butter

1. Wash the clams thoroughly under running water using a stiff brush. Discard any that are opened.

2. Place the clams in a steamer. Add the boiling water and cover. Steam 5 to 10 minutes or until the clams open. Discard any unopened clams.

3. Remove the clams from the pan with tongs and place in a shallow pan. Twist off the top shell with hands protected by potholders.

4. While the clams are steaming, combine the marinara sauce and the lemon juice. Spoon the marinara sauce over the clams. Sprinkle with the parsley and chives and dot with the butter. Broil until bubbly hot, 5 to 10 minutes.

Mussels Marinières
Serves 4

4	dozen mussels
4	cups dry white wine
1	medium onion, finely chopped
4	cloves garlic, minced
4	whole fresh basil leaves or 2 tablespoons dried basil
3	sprigs parsley
1	tablespoon fresh lemon juice
1	teaspoon coarse salt
1	teaspoon coarse black pepper
4	tablespoons butter
4	teaspoons minced parsley
	French bread

1. Scrub the mussels thoroughly and remove the beards. Place the mussels in a large kettle with the wine, onion, garlic, basil, parsley, lemon juice, salt and pepper. Bring to a boil. Cover and cook until the mussels open, shaking the pan occasionally.

2. Remove the mussels from the kettle with a slotted spoon and divide among 4 heated soup bowls. Keep warm. Discard any mussels that did not open.

3. Add the butter to the liquid in kettle. Bring to a boil and reduce the liquid by half over high heat. Strain the liquid through a fine sieve into a small saucepan. Reheat and pour some over the mussels in each soup plate. Sprinkle 1 teaspoon parsley over each serving. Serve immediately accompanied by French bread.

Sautéed Scallops Montélimar
Serves 4

1	pound fresh small scallops
	Salt and freshly ground pepper
	Flour
4	tablespoons plus 1 teaspoon butter
1	tablespoon olive oil
2	tablespoons finely minced shallots

2	large cloves garlic, minced
2	tablespoons finely minced fresh parsley
1	cup fish stock reduced to ½ cup
1	cup whipping cream
	Chopped parsley

1. Dry the scallops thoroughly with paper towels. Season with salt and pepper to taste. Dredge lightly with flour, shaking off the excess.

2. Heat 3 tablespoons butter and the oil in a large heavy skillet. Add the scallops; do not crowd the pan. Sauté over high heat until the scallops are golden brown on all sides. Remove from heat. With a spatula, remove the scallops to a side dish and reserve.

3. Add the shallots, garlic and parsley to the pan. An additional tablespoon of butter may be needed. Return the pan to the heat and cook for 2 minutes, scraping the bottom of the pan well.

4. Add the stock, bring to a boil and reduce to 2 tablespoons. Add the cream, bring to a boil and reduce by one third.

5. Mix 1 teaspoon butter and 1 teaspoon flour. Whisk into the sauce until it coats a spoon heavily. Return the scallops to the pan and cook for 2 to 3 minutes, or until heated through. Taste and correct seasonings.

6. Transfer the scallops to a serving dish. Sprinkle with parsley and serve hot, accompanied by crusty French bread.

Beef & Veal

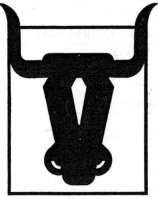

The rolling grassy hills of central Washington provide excellent grazing for cattle that have given "Ellensburg beef" a national reputation for flavor from visitors who have eaten it here.

The rich flavor and satisfying texture of beef gives us a versatile ingredient, and we take full advantage of it. The Times Food section has been able to find beef recipes among the many ethnic groups that have settled in this area. The vivid memories of many good cooks who brought their native cooking with them are represented in this international selection.

Most cuisines don't use as much beef per serving as we Americans, so many of these recipes are a plus for those watching their intake of red meats and, if done skillfully, not much of a minus for those who like their beef in large slabs.

While beef eaters have a fairly easy time at the meat market, veal fanciers who want specially grown veal may have to search a little more to find it. Supermarket veal here tends to be of good quality, but getting custom-raised veal has become somewhat of a gourmet game. The hunt is challenging, but not as much as it once was, thanks to the number of restaurants in this area that have found farmers to raise calves for them. The secret is to ask about sources whenever you find good veal on your plate.

◇

Beef Bourguignon
Serves 8

5	slices bacon
2	pounds stewing beef, well trimmed
2-2½	cups burgundy wine
2	cups beef stock or broth
1	tablespoon tomato paste
1	large clove garlic, minced
1	bay leaf
½	teaspoon dried thyme, crushed
	Salt and pepper
12-15	boiling onions
1	tablespoon oil
5-6	tablespoons butter
24	whole mushrooms, cleaned
2-3	tablespoons flour

1. Preheat oven to 350°.

2. Cut up the bacon and blanch. Drain. Sauté in a large skillet until crisp. Remove from the skillet and set aside.

3. Brown the meat in the same skillet in the remaining bacon drippings, a few pieces at a time, until nicely colored on all sides. Remove from the skillet and transfer to an oven-proof casserole. Deglaze the skillet with a little of the wine and add to the casserole.

4. To the casserole, add the remaining wine, 1½ cups beef stock, tomato paste, garlic, bay leaf, thyme and salt and pepper to taste. Cover the casserole and bake 2 to 3 hours or until the meat is tender.

5. About 1 hour before serving, brown the onions in 1 tablespoon each oil and butter in a small skillet until even in color. Add ½ cup stock; cover and braise over low heat 30 to 40 minutes or until tender.

6. Sauté the mushrooms in 2 tablespoons butter in a small skillet until brown and tender-crisp.

7. Add the braised onions and sautéed mushrooms to the casserole; cover and heat through.

8. Prepare a beurre manié by blending together 2 to 3 tablespoons each of butter and flour. Add it, a little at a time, to the gravy, stirring until the desired thickness is achieved. Serve over hot noodles or rice.

◇

Steak Rolls

Serves 6

2	pounds boneless sirloin
½	pound pork sausage
¼	pound mushrooms, chopped and sautéed lightly in butter
½	cup dry bread crumbs
1	egg, lightly beaten
1	tablespoon chopped capers
2	cloves garlic, minced
¼	cup finely chopped parsley
	Salt and freshly ground pepper
3	tablespoons vegetable oil
¼	cup beef stock or broth
¼	cup water
2	tablespoons white wine
1	tablespoon dried marjoram, crushed
1	onion, sliced
	Parsley

1. Have the butcher cut the steak into very thin slices, almost paper thin. (There should be about 12 or 13 slices.) Flatten the steak slices on wax paper.

2. Cook the sausage, breaking it into small pieces. Drain. Combine with the mushrooms, bread crumbs, egg, capers, garlic, parsley and salt and pepper.

3. Divide this mixture among the steak slices, spreading it around evenly. Roll up the steaks and fasten with toothpicks or tie with twine.

4. Heat the oil in a heavy skillet and sauté the steak rolls until brown on all sides, about 3 to 5 minutes. Drain off excess oil.

5. Add the stock, water, wine, marjoram and onion slices. Cover and simmer about 15 to 20 minutes. Remove toothpicks or twine before serving. Serve with a little of the sauce and onion on each roll. Garnish with parsley, if desired.

Beef Steak Parmesan
Serves 4

1-1¼	pounds boneless beef top sirloin, cut ¾- to 1-inch thick
3	tablespoons olive oil
⅓	cup dry red wine
2	tablespoons chili sauce
¼	teaspoon minced garlic
¼	teaspoon salt
¼	teaspoon pepper
½	cup grated parmesan cheese

1. Cut the beef into 4 equal serving pieces.
2. Combine the oil, wine, chili sauce, garlic, salt and pepper. Pour over the beef in a glass dish and marinate 4 hours or overnight.
3. Remove the beef from marinade and drain. Coat with half of the cheese. Place the steak on the broiler pan. Broil 3 inches from the top element 5 to 6 minutes on one side; turn the steaks and sprinkle generously with more cheese. Broil 5 minutes on the other side for rare.

Viennese Beef Goulash
Serves 6

¼	cup butter
2	medium onions, chopped
1½	pounds beef chuck, cut into cubes
¾	teaspoon dried marjoram, crushed
2	cloves garlic, minced
3	tablespoons paprika
¼	cup ketchup
1½	teaspoons salt
½	teaspoon caraway seeds
1½	cups water
6	medium potatoes, peeled and halved

1. Preheat oven to 350°.
2. Melt the butter in a large Dutch oven. Add the onions and brown

lightly. Add the beef cubes, marjoram, garlic, paprika, ketchup, salt, caraway seeds, water and potatoes.

3. Cover and bake for 1 hour and 45 minutes.

Stuffed Flank Steak Creole
Serves 4

1	(1½ pound) flank steak
1	(16 ounce) loaf bread, cubed
½	cup chopped mushrooms
½	cup butter
½	cup chopped onions
1	cup water
¾	teaspoon poultry seasoning
¼	teaspoon dried thyme, crushed
1	tablespoon oil
1	(16 ounce) can tomatoes, chopped
2	tablespoons tomato paste
1	clove garlic, minced
½	teaspoon dried basil, crushed
2	medium zucchini, sliced
1	cup sliced green pepper

1. Have the butcher cut a pocket in the side of the flank steak.

2. Preheat oven to 250°.

3. Spread the bread cubes on a cookie sheet; place in the oven to dry for 2 to 3 hours.

4. Brown the mushrooms in the butter in a Dutch oven; add the onions and cook until tender. Add the water and bring to a boil. Add the bread cubes, poultry seasoning and thyme. Blend well. Stuff into the flank steak and secure with toothpicks.

5. Brown the steak in the oil in a large skillet. Add the tomatoes, tomato paste, garlic and basil. Cover and simmer 45 minutes. Add a little water during cooking, if necessary. Add the zucchini and green pepper. Cover and cook 15 minutes longer or until the meat and vegetables are tender.

Beef Ragout
Serves 6 to 8

4	tablespoons butter
2	tablespoons bacon drippings
3	pounds lean round steak, cut into 2-inch chunks
3	tablespoons flour
1	teaspoon salt
½	teaspoon freshly ground pepper
1	bay leaf
1½	teaspoons chopped fresh basil or ½ teaspoon dried basil, crushed
2	cloves garlic, minced
½	teaspoon dried oregano, crushed
1	pound tiny white onions, peeled
1	pound French carrots
¾	cup burgundy
1	tablespoon sugar
¾	cup madeira
¼	cup brandy
	Chopped parsley

1. Preheat oven to 300°.

2. Heat 2 tablespoons butter and the bacon drippings in a large, heavy skillet, and brown the beef well on all sides. Arrange the browned beef in a large casserole with a lid or a Dutch oven.

3. Add the flour, salt, pepper, bay leaf, basil, garlic and oregano to the drippings in the skillet, and stir until the flour begins to brown.

4. Parboil the onions and carrots in water separately. Drain the liquid from the parboiled onions and carrots into a 2-cup measure. Add water to make 2 cups. Stir the juices into the skillet and continue cooking, stirring until the sauce is smooth and thickened. Add the burgundy, stirring until blended.

5. Pour the sauce over the meat in the casserole; cover and bake for 3 hours, or until the meat is fork-tender.

6. Melt the remaining butter in the same skillet and stir in the sugar. When the butter has melted and the sugar dissolved, add the drained carrots and onions, stirring frequently until coated with butter and sugar and slightly brown.

7. Add the vegetables and madeira to the casserole and continue baking, covered, for 30 minutes more. When done, stir in the brandy and heat thoroughly. To serve, arrange the meat, vegetables and sauce on a warm serving platter and garnish with chopped parsley.

Flaming Beef Ragout

Serves 6

2	pounds round steak or sirloin tip
4	slices bacon
1	bay leaf
1	teaspoon salt
1	teaspoon dried oregano, crushed
½	teaspoon freshly ground pepper
¼	cup red-wine vinegar
2	cloves garlic, minced
½	cup burgundy
½	cup beef stock or broth
2	tablespoons flour
12	tiny white onions, peeled
1	large green pepper, coarsely chopped
½	pound fresh mushrooms, sliced
1	cup cherry tomatoes, halved
¼	cup brandy
	Hot cooked rice or noodles

1. Preheat oven to 300°.

2. Cut the beef into 1- to 1½-inch cubes. Fry the bacon in a large Dutch oven until crisp. Remove from the Dutch oven, drain on paper towels; when cool, crumble.

3. Remove all but 1 tablespoon fat from the Dutch oven. Add the beef and brown slowly on all sides. Combine the bay leaf, salt, oregano, pepper, wine vinegar, garlic, wine and stock, and pour over the beef. Cover and bake 2 hours or until almost tender.

4. Remove from the oven and place on a surface element on low. Add some water if the liquid seems to have cooked down. Thicken the gravy with the flour mixed with a little water.

5. Add the crumbled bacon and onions, cover and simmer for about 10 minutes, until the onions begin to be tender. Add the green pepper and mushrooms and simmer about 5 more minutes. Add the tomatoes and cook about 4 minutes; do not overcook.

6. Transfer the ragout to a warm chafing dish and bring to the table. Warm the brandy, pour over the meat and set aflame. Stir gently to mix the brandy into the sauce. Serve with rice or noodles.

Sauerbraten Stew

Serves 4

Marinade:

1½	cups water
½	cup red-wine vinegar
½	cup finely chopped onion
2	bay leaves
1	teaspoon salt
¾	teaspoon ground ginger
⅛	teaspoon ground black pepper

Stew:

2½	pounds stewing beef, cut into 1½-inch pieces
2	tablespoons vegetable oil
1¼	cups beef stock or broth
1½	cups sliced celery
1½	cups sliced carrots
2	teaspoons sugar
5	tablespoons flour

1. One day before serving: Combine the water, vinegar, onion, bay leaves, salt, ginger and black pepper in a saucepan. Bring to a boil. Reduce heat and simmer, covered, for 5 minutes. Remove from heat; let cool to room temperature.

2. Place the beef in a snug-fitting bowl; pour the cooled marinade over the beef; mix well. Cover and refrigerate overnight.

3. Day of serving: Drain the beef and reserve the marinade. Pat the beef dry with paper towels. In a large Dutch oven, heat the oil until hot. Brown half of the beef at one time; return all beef to the Dutch oven. Add the beef stock and reserved marinade. Bring to a boil. Reduce heat and simmer, covered, until the beef is tender, about 40 minutes.

4. Add the celery, carrots and sugar; simmer, covered, until the vegetables are tender, about 15 minutes. Combine the flour with ½ cup water. Stir into the sauce. Cook and stir until thickened, about 2 minutes. Remove the bay leaves before serving.

Burgundy Beef with Peppercorns

Serves 6 to 8

1	(3½ pound) boneless chuck roast
1	teaspoon salt
	Pepper
2	tablespoons vegetable oil
1⅔	cups burgundy
¾	cup beef stock or broth
2	teaspoons brown sugar
1	onion, chopped
2	cloves garlic, minced
⅛	teaspoon nutmeg
¼	teaspoon dried thyme leaves, crushed
1½	tablespoons green peppercorns
3	tablespoons chopped parsley

1. Rub the meat all over with salt and pepper. Heat the oil in a heavy Dutch oven and brown the meat on all sides. Remove any fat remaining from the browning. Add the wine, stock, brown sugar, onion and garlic to the pan and sprinkle the meat with the nutmeg and thyme.

2. Preheat the oven to 350°.

3. Bake the meat for about 45 minutes in the uncovered Dutch oven, basting often with the pan liquid. Turn the meat over, cover the pan and bake for about 1½ hours or until the meat is tender.

4. Remove the meat to a plate and keep warm. Place the pan over high heat and reduce the liquid until it thickens slightly. Add the green peppercorns.

5. Slice the meat thinly across the grain and arrange the slices on a serving platter. Pour the sauce over the meat and sprinkle with parsley.

Marinated Flank Steak

Serves 4 to 6

1	(1½-2 pound) flank steak

Marinade:

1	cup light red wine
½	cup chopped onion
⅓	cup soy sauce
¼	cup oil
¼	teaspoon salt
¼	teaspoon pepper

Stuffing:

3	cups enriched white-bread cubes
½	cup chopped onion
¼	pound mushrooms, sliced
¼	cup chopped celery
1½-2	tablespoons butter
½	cup beef stock or broth
1	teaspoon dried thyme, crushed
¼	teaspoon pepper
¼	teaspoon salt

1. Cut a pocket in the flank steak, lengthwise, or ask your butcher to do it for you.

2. To prepare marinade: Combine the wine, onion, soy sauce, oil, salt and pepper in a shallow glass or enamel pan; mix well. Marinate the steak in this mixture in the refrigerator at least 3 hours, preferably overnight, turning at least once.

3. Preheat oven to 200°.

4. To prepare stuffing: Place the bread cubes on a cookie sheet and place in oven for 15 to 20 minutes.

5. Sauté the onion, mushrooms and celery in butter until tender. Stir in the stock, thyme, pepper and salt; bring the mixture to a boil. Stir in the bread cubes.

6. Remove the steak from the marinade. Place the stuffing in the pocket. Pin the sides together with metal skewers.

7. Broil the steak 2 inches from the heat for 4 to 5 minutes on each side for medium rare and 5 to 7 minutes for medium. Slice diagonally and serve immediately.

Steak Mixed Grill

Serves 6

6	sausages
6	lamb kidneys, split and cores removed
½	cup melted butter
	Salt and pepper
6	slices bacon
6	small steaks, about 1-inch thick
12	mushroom caps
6	tomatoes, halved
1	bunch watercress, washed

1. Line a broiler pan with foil. Brush the rack lightly with oil.

2. Arrange the sausages on the broiler rack. Broil 3 inches from the heat for 2 minutes. Make sure the kidneys are secured open, using wooden skewers. Brush the kidneys with melted butter and arrange on the broiler pan with the sausages. Broil for 4 minutes more. Season the kidneys with salt and pepper to taste. Turn the sausages and kidneys over and broil for 5 minutes more. Remove to an oven-proof platter and keep warm.

3. Broil the bacon for 2 to 3 minutes on each side. Remove to the platter to keep warm.

4. Brush the steaks with melted butter and broil for 5 minutes on each side. Season with salt and pepper to taste. Remove to platter to keep warm.

5. Dip the mushroom caps in melted butter; brush the tomato halves with melted butter. Season both with salt and pepper to taste. Broil about 5 minutes, turning the mushrooms once.

6. To serve, arrange one each of the sausages, kidneys, steaks and bacon slices on heated individual serving plates. Add 2 tomato halves and 2 mushrooms to each plate. Garnish with watercress and serve immediately.

Note: Because of the large amount of food to be broiled, it is better to grill the ingredients in four separate steps, keeping the food warm at the bottom of the oven.

Danish Cabbage Rolls

Serves 6 to 8

1	(2 pound) green cabbage
½	teaspoon salt
2	cups boiling water
2	tablespoons butter
½	cup finely chopped onion
¾	cup finely diced celery
1	carrot, coarsely shredded
¾-1	pound lean ground beef
	Salt and pepper
14	ounces natural Danish havarti cheese
¾	cup beer
½	cup chili sauce
3	tablespoons flour dissolved in 3 tablespoons water

1. Rinse the cabbage in cold water and remove any outer marred leaves. Cut ½- to ¾-inch slice off the bottom to make separating the leaves easy.

2. Place the cabbage in a large saucepan or kettle, add ½ teaspoon salt and boiling water. Cover tightly. Bring to a boil and reduce heat; cook approximately 3 minutes.

3. Lift the cabbage out of the water and place on a cutting board. Start peeling off the leaves and place on aluminum foil. When the leaves become hard to remove, return cabbage to the pan of boiling water for a few minutes, continuing until all the leaves are separated.

4. With a sharp knife, cut off the heavy ribs to make the filled cabbage leaves easy to roll.

5. Preheat oven to 350°.

6. For stuffing, melt the butter in a skillet; add onion, celery and carrot. Sauté until the onion is golden. Push to one side of the pan and add the lean ground beef. Cook, uncovered, stirring occasionally until the meat is no longer red, about 5 minutes. Mix in the sautéed vegetables. Season with salt and pepper to taste.

7. Take ½ pound of havarti cheese and slice it into eighths. Shred the remainder and reserve.

8. Start with 8 large cabbage leaves, placing some smaller leaves on top of each. Place a slice of cheese on each group of leaves. Fill the center of each cabbage serving with ½ cup or a little more of the meat mixture. Fold two sides over the stuffing and, starting at stem end, roll up.

9. Arrange the cabbage rolls in an 8½-by-12-inch baking dish, seam side down. Pour in the beer. Cover the dish tightly with aluminum foil. Bake for 30 minutes.

10. Remove the foil and spoon the beer over the cabbage rolls. Spoon the chili sauce blended with shredded havarti cheese on top. Return to the oven and continue baking, uncovered, about 10 minutes. Remove the cabbage rolls to a serving dish. Thicken the sauce to desired consistency with the mixture of flour and water. Pour over the cabbage rolls and serve.

Brandied Steak

Serves 4

1½	pounds boneless beef sirloin steak, cut ½-inch thick
2	tablespoons flour
3	tablespoons butter
2	teaspoons Dijon mustard
1	teaspoon Worcestershire sauce
3	tablespoons chopped chives
2	tablespoons brandy
½	cup beef stock or broth

1. Cut steak into 4 serving-size pieces. Pound the steaks to about ¼-inch thickness. Dredge the steaks in the flour. Brown the steaks in 2 tablespoons butter in a large skillet for 2 minutes on each side. Remove the steaks to a platter. Spread both sides of the steaks with mustard and sprinkle with the Worcestershire sauce; keep warm.

2. Cook the chives in the remaining 1 tablespoon butter in the same skillet for 1 minute, stirring constantly. Add the brandy and stock and cook, stirring, over high heat until reduced by half. Return the steaks to the skillet and heat through, about 1 to 2 minutes.

Pastitsio

Serves 12

Sauce:

6	tablespoons butter
6	tablespoons flour
2	cups chicken stock or broth
2¼	cups milk, warmed
4	egg yolks, beaten lightly
	Salt and pepper

Casserole:

2	pounds lean ground beef
¼	cup plus 3 tablespoons butter
2	medium onions, chopped
1	cup dry white wine
2	large tomatoes, peeled and thinly sliced
½	cup lightly packed chopped parsley
1½	teaspoons salt
1¼	teaspoons cinnamon
½	teaspoon pepper
1½	cups grated parmesan cheese
3	tablespoons dry bread crumbs
¾	pound salad macaroni or 1 pound ziti
4	egg whites
	Parsley

1. **To prepare sauce:** Melt the butter over low heat in a heavy sauce-pan. Using a wire whisk, stir in the flour and blend well. Remove from heat.

2. Bring the chicken stock to a boil and add to the flour-butter mixture along with the milk and stir vigorously.

3. Return to heat and cook, stirring constantly, until the sauce is thick and smooth.

4. Stir a little of the hot sauce into the egg yolks. Stir the yolk mixture into the sauce and cook over low heat for 2 minutes, stirring constantly. Season to taste. Set aside.

5. **To prepare casserole:** In large, heavy skillet, brown the ground beef. Drain off most of the liquid and push the meat to one side of the pan.

6. Melt ¼ cup butter in the empty side of pan and add the onions, sautéeing until soft. Stir the onions and meat together. When the meat begins to sizzle, stir in the wine. Add the tomatoes, parsley, salt, cinnamon and pepper. Simmer, covered, 30 minutes.

7. Add 2 tablespoons of the cheese and bread crumbs. Stir and set aside.

8. Cook the macaroni in a large amount of boiling, salted water for about 7 minutes or until al dente. Drain well. Return the macaroni to the cooking pan. Beat the egg whites until slightly frothy and stir into the macaroni. Add 3 tablespoons butter and all but 3 tablespoons of the remaining cheese. Toss well to combine.

9. Preheat oven to 350°.

10. Place half the macaroni in a deep, well-buttered 9-by-13-inch baking pan. (It should be at least 2 inches deep.) Cover with the meat mixture. Layer the remaining macaroni mixture on top of the meat mixture.

11. Cover with sauce. Run a spatula around the edge of the pan, working some of the sauce down the sides. Using the spatula, make several cuts lengthwise down the pan to work the sauce through the layers. Try not to disturb the layers too much. Smooth the sauce across the top with a spatula and sprinkle the reserved 3 tablespoons cheese over the top.

12. Bake about 45 minutes or until the top is golden brown. Remove from oven and let stand 15 to 20 minutes before serving. Garnish with parsley if desired.

Florentine Beef
Serves 10

Meat Shell:

2	pounds ground beef
¾	cup quick or old-fashioned oats, uncooked
½	cup tomato juice
1	egg, beaten
2	teaspoons salt
¼	teaspoon pepper
1	teaspoon dried oregano, crushed
½	teaspoon dried basil, crushed

Topping:

2	pounds fresh spinach
2½	cups chopped fresh tomatoes, drained
2	tablespoons butter
1½	cups chopped onion
¾	cup ricotta cheese
½	cup chopped parsley
	Salt and pepper
	Dried oregano
1	cup shredded mozzarella cheese
¼	cup grated parmesan cheese

1. Preheat oven to 350°.
2. To prepare meat: Combine the ground beef, oats, tomato juice, egg, salt, pepper, oregano and basil until well mixed. Pack the meat mixture evenly into the bottom and halfway up the sides of an ungreased 9-by-13-inch baking pan. Bake 10 minutes. Drain off excess juices. Leave oven on.
3. To prepare topping: Wash the spinach; blanch in boiling water 1½ to 2 minutes. Drain, chop and squeeze dry.
4. Combine the spinach and tomatoes. Melt the butter in a skillet and sauté the onion until soft, but not brown.
5. Mix the onion into the spinach mixture. Add the ricotta in small spoonfuls to the spinach mixture; then add the parsley and season to taste with salt, pepper and oregano.
6. Spread the mixture into the partly cooked meat shell. Bake for 20 minutes.

7. Remove from oven and sprinkle mozzarella, then parmesan cheese over the top; continue baking for about 15 minutes more. Cut into squares to serve.

Sukiyaki

Serves 4

6	ounces udon noodles (Japanese flat noodles)
5	large dried shiitake mushrooms
¼	head cauliflower
¼	bunch broccoli
1	onion
¼	pound green beans
2	carrots
¼	cup soy sauce
2	tablespoons sugar
2	tablespoons sake (Japanese rice wine)
2	teaspoons sesame oil
5	slices fresh ginger, ¼-inch thick
½	pound flank steak, cut into ¼-by-2-inch strips across the grain

1. Cook the noodles in boiling salted water about 8 minutes or until done. Drain and set aside.
2. Soak the mushrooms in hot water until soft. Drain. Cut out the hard stems and slice the remainder into strips. Break the cauliflower and broccoli into flowerettes. Cut the onion in half lengthwise, then slice each half lengthwise into ¼-inch slices. Slice the beans French-style and slice the carrots into 1- to 2-inch shoestring pieces.
3. Mix the soy sauce, sugar and sake in a small bowl.
4. Heat a skillet or wok. Add the sesame oil. Brown steak lightly; add the vegetables and ginger. Stir-fry over medium-high heat until the meat is tender and vegetables tender-crisp.
5. Add the soy sauce mixture and noodles and heat through. Remove the ginger slices before serving.

Moussaka Romano

Serves 8 to 10

2	pounds lean ground beef
½	large onion, chopped
2	cloves garlic, minced
2	(12 ounce) cans tomato paste
1	teaspoon sugar
2¼	teaspoons salt
1	teaspoon dried basil, crushed
1	teaspoon dried oregano, crushed
½	teaspoon pepper
4	cups water
1	medium eggplant, peeled and sliced ⅜-inch thick
	Oil
¼	cup butter
¼	cup flour
2	cups milk
1	(16 ounce) carton ricotta cheese
3	eggs
½	teaspoon ground cinnamon
1	(12 ounce) package lasagne
½	cup grated parmesan cheese

1. Brown the ground beef; add the onion and garlic and cook 5 minutes. Stir in the tomato paste, sugar, 1¾ teaspoons salt, basil, oregano and pepper. Add water and simmer, uncovered, 1 hour.

2. Preheat oven to 350°.

3. Brush the eggplant slices with oil; arrange on baking sheets and bake about 8 minutes or until partly done. Remove, but leave oven on.

4. In a medium saucepan, melt the butter and blend in the flour. Gradually add the milk. Cook and stir until smooth and thick. In a bowl, beat the ricotta, eggs, ½ teaspoon salt and cinnamon; gradually mix in the white sauce.

5. Cook the lasagne in boiling, salted water until almost tender, about 15 minutes. Drain well. Rinse in cold water.

6. Grease a 13½-by-9½-by-2½-inch pan and layer ingredients as follows:

> One-fourth of the meat sauce
> One-half of the eggplant slices
> One-third of the ricotta mixture
> One-half of the lasagne
> One-fourth of the meat sauce
> One-half of the eggplant slices
> One-third of the ricotta mixture
> One-half of the lasagne
> One-third of the ricotta mixture
> One-fourth of the meat sauce

7. Sprinkle the parmesan cheese on top. Bake 45 minutes. Let stand 10 minutes before cutting. Serve with the remaining meat sauce.

Frikadeller (Danish Meatballs)

Serves 6

1	pound ground pork
1½	pounds lean ground beef
1	onion, finely chopped
¼	cup flour
2	eggs
1	teaspoon salt
	Pepper
¼	cup milk or club soda
	Butter

1. Mix the pork, beef and onion, beating with an electric mixer until it becomes fluffy.

2. Beat the flour into the meat; add the eggs, salt and pepper, mixing well. Add the milk or club soda and mix well again.

3. The mixture is quite sticky, so it is better to scoop out the amount for each meatball with a serving tablespoon. Fry in a large frying pan in a small amount of melted butter, about 10 minutes or until it is no longer pink in the center and the meatballs are firm and brown.

This recipe is from Marianne Forssblad.

Pacific Stir-Fry

Serves 4

2	tablespoons plus 1 teaspoon soy sauce
2	tablespoons dry sherry
1	clove garlic, minced
1	teaspoon sugar
½	teaspoon ground ginger
1	pound round steak, thinly sliced on the diagonal
1	(15¼ ounce) can pineapple chunks, in their own juice
½	cup vegetable oil
2	tablespoons firmly packed brown sugar
¼	cup mild vinegar
	Pepper
2	tablespoons cornstarch
1	soft avocado, peeled and sliced
1	small papaya, peeled, halved, seeded and sliced
1	cup Chinese snow peas
	Hot cooked rice

1. In a large shallow bowl, stir together 2 tablespoons soy sauce, dry sherry, garlic, sugar and ginger. Add the beef to the marinade; let stand for 1 hour.

2. Combine the juice from the pineapple chunks, 3 tablespoons oil, brown sugar, remaining soy sauce, vinegar, pepper to taste and cornstarch. Cook over medium heat, stirring until the sauce thickens.

3. Add the remaining oil to a large skillet. Remove the beef from the marinade and stir-fry over medium heat. Stir in the thickened pineapple juice sauce. Mix so the beef is coated.

4. Add the pineapple chunks, avocado, papaya and snow peas. Mix carefully and cook over medium heat until heated through. Serve over hot cooked rice.

Chinese Orange Beef

Serves 4 to 6

1½	pounds lean beef
3	tablespoons dry sherry

1	egg white
3	tablespoons cornstarch
4-5	tablespoons cooking oil
1	(8 ounce) can bamboo shoots, rinsed and drained
2	green onions, cut into ½-inch lengths
3	tablespoons grated fresh orange peel
1	tablespoon minced ginger root
3	tablespoons water
¼	cup chicken stock or broth
3	tablespoons soy sauce
2	tablespoons sugar
1	teaspoon sesame oil
	Chow mein noodles
	Orange slices

1. Slice the beef into thin strips. This can be done more easily if the beef is sliced while partly frozen. Place the sliced meat in a bowl.

2. In another bowl, combine 1 tablespoon sherry and the egg white and whip until foamy. Add 1½ tablespoons cornstarch and 2 tablespoons cooking oil and mix well. Pour over the meat and stir thoroughly.

3. Combine the bamboo shoots, green onions, orange peel and ginger in a small bowl; set aside.

4. In another small bowl, combine 1½ tablespoons cornstarch, water, 2 tablespoons sherry, chicken stock, soy sauce, sugar and sesame oil. Set aside.

5. Heat the remaining oil in a wok or large skillet over medium-high heat. Add the meat and cook for 3 minutes or until it is lightly browned. Remove from the pan with a slotted spoon; drain on paper towels.

6. Pour off all but 2 tablespoons oil from the pan. When the pan is hot again, add the vegetable mixture. Cook, stirring constantly, about 30 seconds. Return the meat to the pan and cook, stirring, about 1 minute more. Add the chicken stock mixture, cook and stir until thickened and the meat is coated with sauce, about 15 seconds. Place the meat and vegetables on a serving platter; serve immediately, garnished with chow mein noodles and orange slices.

Note: Pork may be substituted for beef.

Veal with Brown Madeira Sauce

Serves 6

Sauce:

½	cup butter
1	small onion, chopped
¼	cup diced celery
1	large carrot, chopped
1	clove garlic, minced
3	tablespoons cornstarch
3	cups beef stock or broth
3	tablespoons madeira
½	teaspoon dried thyme, crushed
2	bay leaves
¼	teaspoon freshly ground black pepper

Veal:

2	pounds veal cutlets, thinly sliced
¼	cup butter
¾	pound fresh mushrooms, sliced
2	green onions, minced
½	cup dry white wine
3	tablespoons chopped parsley
1	teaspoon salt
	Pepper

1. To prepare sauce: Melt the butter in a heavy saucepan and sauté the onion, celery, carrot and garlic until limp.

2. Stir the cornstarch into the cold beef stock and stir into the vegetable mixture. Add the madeira, thyme, bay leaves and pepper; cook and stir until the mixture comes to a boil. Cover and simmer about 30 minutes. Strain.

3. To prepare veal: If not thinly sliced, place between 2 pieces of wax paper and pound with the flat side of a meat mallet to flatten. Melt the butter in a large, heavy skillet and brown veal on both sides. When browned, remove from the pan and set aside.

4. Add the mushrooms to the butter remaining in the skillet and cook a few minutes. Add the green onions and cook together for about 3 minutes on low heat, stirring often. Add the wine and continue cooking on low for about 10 minutes, until the liquid is reduced to about half. Remove from heat and set aside.

5. When ready to serve, add the sauce to the wine-vegetable mixture. Add the parsley, salt and pepper to taste and veal and heat through, about 5 minutes. Serve immediately.

Wiener Schnitzel
Serves 4 to 6

12	(2 ounce) veal scallops
¼	loaf fresh white bread
1	cup flour
	Salt and pepper
	Paprika
4	eggs
2	tablespoons water
½	cup clarified butter
2	tablespoons lemon juice
12	lemon slices

1. Preheat oven to 350°.

2. Place the veal between sheets of wax paper and pound until very thin.

3. Cut the crusts off the bread. Place the trimmed bread in a food processor with 1 tablespoon flour and make crumbs; set aside in a bowl. Season remaining flour with salt, pepper and paprika; set aside in another bowl. Beat eggs and water together in a third bowl.

4. Dip the veal in the seasoned flour, then in the egg mixture, then in the bread crumbs. Heat the clarified butter in a large heavy skillet. When the butter starts to bubble, add enough veal slices so they lie flat in the skillet, not overlapping, and sauté until browned. Turn over and brown the other side. Remove from the skillet and keep warm in a large baking dish. Repeat with the remaining veal. Pour the lemon juice evenly over the veal in the baking dish. Cover with foil and bake 15 to 20 minutes.

5. To serve, place 2 or 3 slices of veal on each warmed dinner plate and garnish each with a lemon slice.

Veal Véronique
Serves 4

8	(3 ounce) veal scallops
3	tablespoons flour
1	teaspoon salt
¼	teaspoon white pepper
2-4	tablespoons vegetable oil
½	cup white wine
¼	cup finely chopped shallots
2	cloves garlic, minced
1	teaspoon dried basil, crushed
1	tablespoon butter
1½	cups green seedless grapes

1. Pound the veal scallops between 2 pieces of wax paper with the smooth flat side of a meat mallet until ¼-inch thick. Mix the flour, salt and pepper. Coat the veal with the flour mixture. Shake to remove excess.

2. Heat 2 tablespoons oil in a skillet until hot. Add the veal a few pieces at a time. Cook until lightly browned on both sides (about 2 minutes on each side). Add more oil as needed. Arrange the veal in a serving dish; keep warm.

3. Add the wine, shallots, garlic and basil to the skillet, stirring to deglaze drippings. Heat the wine mixture to boiling. Boil 1 to 2 minutes. Stir in the butter and add the grapes. Spoon the sauce and grapes over the veal.

Blanquette de Veau
Serves 4 to 6

1½-2	pounds veal, cubed
1	quart cold water
3	carrots
2	leeks
2	onions
1	clove garlic
1⅓	cups water

1⅓	cups white wine
2½	cups chicken stock
6	whole peppercorns
1	teaspoon sugar
1	teaspoon salt
	Bouquet garni (1 bay leaf, 3 sprigs parsley tied in cheesecloth)
¼	teaspoon dried thyme, crushed
1	pound fresh mushrooms, sliced
1	tablespoon lemon juice
4	tablespoons butter
4	tablespoons flour
2	tablespoons madeira
2	egg yolks
½	cup crème fraîche (see index)
	Cooked rice or noodles

1. Put the veal into cold water and bring to a boil. Cook 3 minutes. Discard the water and rinse the meat in cold water to stop the cooking and to wash off the scum.

2. Cut the carrots lengthwise into quarters. Clean the leeks, then split them lengthwise. Fold over and tie in a bundle. Quarter the onions and cut the garlic in half.

3. Put the vegetables, water, white wine, chicken stock, peppercorns, sugar, salt, bouquet garni and thyme into a large saucepan or Dutch oven. Add the blanched veal. Bring to a boil; cover and simmer about 1½ hours. Skim and discard scum as it collects on the surface. (Veal, being immature meat, releases more impurities than any other meat as it cooks.)

4. When the meat is done, remove from the liquid. Discard the vegetables and bouquet garni. There should be no more than 2½ cups liquid. If more, reduce by boiling.

5. Add the sliced mushrooms and lemon juice to the liquid. Boil 3 minutes.

6. Prepare a beurre manié by blending 4 tablespoons softened butter with 4 tablespoons flour. Stir half into the liquid, then add more to thicken sauce to desired consistency. Add the cooked veal and madeira.

7. Mix together the egg yolks and crème fraîche. Add some hot liquid to them, then stir back into the veal. Heat to thicken, but do not boil. Taste and adjust the seasonings. Serve with rice or noodles.

Veal Piccata
Serves 4

1	pound veal steak, cut into small pieces
	Flour
2	tablespoons vegetable oil
2	tablespoons unsalted butter
3	tablespoons lemon juice
¼	cup dry white wine
2	tablespoons capers
	Salt and pepper
1	lemon

1. Pound the veal between 2 pieces of wax paper with the smooth, flat side of a mallet until about ¼-inch thick. Dip the veal pieces in flour on both sides, shaking off excess.

2. In a large, heavy skillet, heat the oil and butter. When bubbling, add the veal and sauté about 1 minute on each side. When the veal is nearly cooked, sprinkle with the lemon juice. Remove the veal from the pan, and keep warm.

3. Add the wine to the pan and deglaze over high heat, stirring constantly. Reduce the liquid to about half. Add the capers and pour over the veal. Sprinkle with salt and pepper.

4. Thinly slice the lemon and use as a garnish. Serve at once.

Veal Birds with Ham
Serves 6

1	cup ground ham
¼	cup chopped parsley
1	teaspoon dried rosemary, crushed
	Grating of nutmeg
	Salt and pepper
6	(4-by-6 inch) veal slices, cut from the leg and pounded ⅜-inch thick
5	tablespoons olive oil
1	bay leaf
⅔	cup white wine
	Chopped parsley

1. Combine the ham, ¼ cup parsley, rosemary, nutmeg and salt and pepper to taste. Place a small amount of the filling on each piece of veal. Roll and tie with string about ½ inch from each end.

2. Heat the olive oil in a large skillet and brown the birds, turning often to give an even color. Drain the oil from the skillet. Add the bay leaf and white wine; cover and simmer 30 to 35 minutes or until tender.

3. Remove the veal birds to a warm platter and keep warm in the oven. Reduce the sauce over high heat until it forms a glaze. Pour over the veal birds, garnish with chopped parsley and serve immediately.

Brandied Veal

Serves 4

Brandy Butter:

¾	cup unsalted butter, softened
1	tablespoon dried thyme, crushed
½	teaspoon salt
3	tablespoons brandy

Veal:

1¼	pounds veal scallops
	Flour
½	pound fresh button mushrooms
3-4	tablespoons brandy

1. To prepare brandy butter: Mix together the butter, thyme and salt. Add the brandy, and refrigerate for 1 hour.

2. To prepare veal: Lightly dust the veal with flour, shaking to remove excess.

3. Sauté the veal over medium to high heat in the brandy butter about 1 minute on each side. Remove from the pan and keep warm in low oven.

4. In the same pan, sauté the mushrooms until nicely browned. Remove from the pan, and keep warm with the veal.

5. Add the brandy to the pan, stirring to deglaze drippings, and pour over the veal. Serve immediately.

Lamb

In just a few months, a lamb has turned its mother's milk and sweet grass into firm, light-colored meat that is sought by many a gourmet diner.

In most cases, lamb sold here comes from the grasslands of eastern Washington, but a few northwestern Washington farms are making specialty lamb available to buyers willing to seek them out. Several growers, particularly in the San Juan Islands, are raising a saltmarsh lamb, which, like its famous French and Irish counterparts, is said to taste subtly different for having grazed on the salt-kissed grass next to the sea.

Lamb roasted simply with perhaps a hint of garlic or rosemary or a crown roast ringing a mint stuffing is a dinner feat in itself.

Recipes in this chapter bring sauces, condiments and stuffings into play to achieve this augmentation of one of the most distinctive of meat flavors.

Experts consider lamb to be at the height of its flavor and tenderness when cooked to a point where the meat is still pink. Hence, the cooking times and internal temperatures given for roasts and legs of lamb in this chapter reflect the trend for eating less-well-done lamb, which is tender and moist.

Stuffed Leg of Lamb

Serves 8

2	tablespoons butter
½	cup diced onion
1	clove garlic, minced
12	slices raisin bread, crumbled
¼	cup coarsely chopped walnuts
1	egg, slightly beaten
½	teaspoon salt
¼	teaspoon dried rosemary, crushed
2	dashes Tabasco
1	(6-8 pound) leg of lamb, boned and flattened
1	clove garlic, slivered
	Salt and pepper

1. Preheat oven to 325°.

2. In a medium skillet, melt the butter and sauté the onion and minced garlic until soft. Add the raisin bread, nuts, egg, salt, rosemary and Tabasco.

3. Spread the lean side of the meat with the stuffing and roll up. Tie the meat securely with a clean, white string. Make slits in the meat in several places with the point of a knife and insert a sliver of garlic in each slit. Season with salt and pepper to taste.

4. Place the meat on a rack in a shallow roasting pan. Roast about 20 minutes per pound, or until meat thermometer registers 150° to 155°F., depending on doneness desired. Let stand 10 minutes before carving.

Breast of Lamb with Curry Mustard Glaze

Serves 6

1	(3 pound) breast of lamb, cut into riblets
⅓	cup honey
½	cup Dijon mustard
2	tablespoons curry powder
1	tablespoon soy sauce
1	large clove garlic, minced

½ teaspoon salt

Parsley

1. Put the riblets in a large saucepan and add water to cover. Bring to a boil, reduce heat and let simmer for 30 minutes. Drain and place in a single layer in a 9-by-13-inch baking pan.
2. Preheat oven to 325°.
3. Mix the honey, mustard, curry powder, soy sauce, garlic and salt in a small bowl. Spoon half the sauce over the meat and bake for 30 minutes. Turn the meat over and spoon on the remaining sauce. Bake 20 to 30 minutes longer. Remove to a serving platter and garnish with parsley sprigs.

Chutney Lamb Steaks

Serves 4

1	cup chopped chutney
2	tablespoons lemon juice
2	teaspoons curry powder
1	teaspoon ginger
½	cup butter
4	lamb leg steaks, 1-inch thick

1. In a saucepan, combine the chutney, lemon juice, curry powder, ginger and butter. Cook 15 minutes over low heat, stirring occasionally. Brush the lamb steaks with the chutney mixture.
2. Broil the steaks 3 to 4 inches from the source of heat, or cook on an outdoor grill 7 to 10 minutes on each side or until lamb reaches desired degree of doneness. Brush the lamb frequently with the chutney mixture during cooking period. Serve the lamb with the reserved sauce.

Crown Roast of Lamb with Mint Stuffing

Serves 8

1 (5-6 pound) crown roast of lamb at room temperature

Stuffing:

⅓ cup sliced celery

2 tablespoons finely chopped onion

6 tablespoons butter

3 cups soft bread crumbs

1 egg

2 tablespoons water

½ cup finely chopped fresh mint

½ teaspoon finely chopped fresh sage, or ¼ teaspoon dry

½ teaspoon finely chopped fresh marjoram, or ¼ teaspoon dry

½ teaspoon finely chopped fresh thyme, or ¼ teaspoon dry

Salt and pepper

Garnish:

Paper frills

Spiced whole red crab apples

1. Have the butcher prepare a crown roast with 2 lamb-rib French racks.

2. Cover the tips of the roast bones with aluminum foil to prevent them from charring as the roast cooks. Place the meat on a rack in an open roasting pan or use the chine bones, if you wish, to rest the crown on.

3. Preheat oven to 325°.

4. To prepare stuffing: Sauté the celery and onion in the butter until soft. Add the crumbs, the egg beaten with the water, the mint, sage, marjoram, thyme, salt and pepper; mix with a fork. Put some foil over the bottom center of the roast to hold the stuffing in place. Lightly pack the stuffing into the foil-lined cavity. Insert a meat thermometer into roast.

5. Roast the meat for about 20 minutes a pound or until the internal temperature reads 150° to 155°F. on the meat thermometer. The meat will be pink. Adjust time to obtain the desired degree of doneness.

6. Remove the aluminum foil from the bones and replace with paper frills. Garnish with spiced whole red crab apples and serve immediately. Cut 2 ribs per serving.

Leg of Lamb with Garlic Sauce

Serves 8

1	(5-6 pound) leg of lamb
5	cloves garlic, slivered
1	(2 ounce) can anchovy fillets, cut up
2	tablespoons olive oil
1	teaspoon dried rosemary, crushed
1	teaspoon dried thyme, crushed
	Salt and freshly ground black pepper
12	cloves garlic, peeled and cut in halves
½	cup dry white wine
2	tablespoons chopped parsley or mint

1. Make slits in the leg of lamb and insert a sliver of garlic and a piece of anchovy in each incision. Rub the lamb with 1 tablespoon olive oil and the rosemary, thyme, salt and pepper. Let stand for 1 to 2 hours in refrigerator.

2. Preheat oven to 425°.

3. Place the meat on a rack in a roasting pan. Insert a meat thermometer, making sure it doesn't rest on the bone. Roast, uncovered, for 20 minutes. Reduce heat to 350° and roast 40 to 45 minutes longer or until meat thermometer registers 150° to 155°F. The lamb will be pink.

4. Meanwhile, heat the remaining 1 tablespoon oil in a small iron skillet and cook the 12 garlic cloves slowly for 10 minutes or until they are soft. Do not let the edges become crisp. Set aside in a small bowl.

5. Remove the lamb from the pan and keep warm. Degrease pan juices. Pour the wine into the pan; scrape brown particles and cook down the wine over a high heat to reduce it a little.

6. Add the reduced liquid to the garlic cloves. Mash well with a fork or spoon. Salt and pepper to taste.

7. To serve, slice the lamb and sprinkle with pepper. Spoon the sauce over it and sprinkle with parsley or mint.

Lamb Spanakopita
Serves 8

2	pounds fresh spinach
¼	cup chopped shallots
2	tablespoons butter
2	tablespoons minced parsley
1½	teaspoons fennel
¼	teaspoon ground nutmeg
1	teaspoon salt
¼	teaspoon black pepper
¼	cup whipping cream
¼	pound feta cheese, coarsely crumbled
3	eggs, lightly beaten
1	cup melted butter
½	pound phyllo pastry (16 sheets)
½	pound ground lamb, cooked and drained

1. Wash the spinach and blanch in boiling water 1½ to 2 minutes. Drain, chop and squeeze dry.

2. Sauté the shallots in 2 tablespoons butter until golden. Add to the spinach along with the parsley, fennel, nutmeg, salt and pepper; toss lightly. Remove from heat; add cream.

3. Combine the feta cheese with the eggs. Add to the spinach mixture and mix well.

4. Preheat oven to 350°.

5. Using a pastry brush, coat the bottom and the sides of a 9-by-13-inch baking dish with melted butter. Line with 8 sheets of phyllo, brushing each sheet with melted butter. Do not trim overhanging sections. Pour in the spinach mixture. Crumble the cooked lamb over the top of the spinach. Top with 8 sheets of phyllo, brushing each with butter.

6. The pastry may by trimmed slightly at the corners. Roll back the overhang as neatly as possible. Brush the top with butter. Score into squares or diamonds. Bake for 45 minutes. Let stand 10 minutes before serving.

Roast Leg of Lamb
Serves 6

1	(6-7 pound) leg of lamb
3-4	cloves garlic, peeled and slivered
½	teaspoon dried thyme, crushed
½	teaspoon dried oregano, crushed
¼	teaspoon paprika
	Salt and pepper
1	carrot, coarsely chopped
1	onion, thinly sliced
1	stalk celery, chopped
½	cup dry white wine
1	cup chicken stock or broth

1. Preheat oven to 325°.

2. Insert the point of a sharp paring knife ¾ inch into the meat's surface, repeating to make 15 to 20 small pockets. Press a garlic sliver in each pocket.

3. Combine the thyme, oregano, paprika and salt and pepper to taste. Rub well into the outside surface of the lamb leg.

4. Spread the carrots, onions and celery over the bottom of a large roasting pan and set the leg of lamb on top. Roast for 20 minutes per pound, or until 145°F. on a meat thermometer for rare, 170°F. for well done. Combine the wine and chicken stock and baste often during roasting.

5. Remove the roast to a warm serving platter and let rest 10 minutes while finishing the sauce. Spoon off as much excess fat as possible from the pan juices. Cook the remaining juices and the vegetables over high heat until reduced by half. Adjust seasonings and strain into a warm sauce dish.

6. Slice the roast and serve immediately with sauce.

Lamb Paprika in Sour Cream Sauce

Serves 6

1½	pounds boneless lamb stew meat, cubed
¼	cup flour
1	teaspoon salt
1	teaspoon paprika
¼	teaspoon pepper
3	tablespoons cooking oil
1	cup chopped onion
1	cup sliced celery
1	clove garlic, minced
1½	cups water
2	tablespoons prepared horseradish
1	teaspoon caraway seeds
¼	pound fresh mushrooms, sliced
⅔	cup sour cream
	Hot cooked noodles or rice

1. Toss the lamb cubes in a mixture of the flour, salt, paprika and pepper. Heat the oil in a large skillet or Dutch oven; add the lamb and brown well.

2. Remove the lamb from the skillet and add the onions, celery and garlic. Sauté, stirring occasionally, until the vegetables are soft but not browned.

3. Return the lamb to the skillet and add the water, horseradish and caraway seeds; stir gently to combine. Simmer for 40 minutes or until the lamb is tender, adding more water if necessary.

4. Add the mushrooms and simmer for another 5 minutes. Stir in the sour cream and heat thoroughly without simmering. Correct seasoning if necessary and serve over noodles or rice.

Festive Rolled Leg of Lamb

Serves 6 to 8

1	(4½ pound) boned leg of lamb, trimmed, rolled and tied
1	teaspoon salt
½	clove garlic, minced
¼	teaspoon pepper
½	small bay leaf, crushed
¼	teaspoon ground ginger
¼	teaspoon dried thyme, crushed
¼	teaspoon dried sage, crushed
¼	teaspoon dried marjoram, crushed
1	teaspoon lemon juice
1	tablespoon olive oil

1. Preheat oven to 325°.

2. With a small, sharp knife, cut small but deep slashes in the lamb, distributing them evenly.

3. In a small bowl, mix together the salt, garlic, pepper, bay leaf, ginger, thyme, sage and marjoram. Fill the slashes with the herb mixture; rub the surface of the lamb with lemon juice and olive oil.

4. Place the lamb on a rack in a roasting pan. Roast 20 minutes per pound or until a meat thermometer reaches 150° to 155°F. for rare. Make gravy from pan drippings, if desired.

Lamb Mixed Grill

Serves 4

	Oil
	Dried rosemary
4	loin lamb chops, 1-inch thick
4	lamb kidneys, split, cores removed and secured open with wooden picks
2	tomatoes, halved
8	large mushrooms, stems removed
5	tablespoons melted butter
8	sausages
	Salt and pepper
4	slices bacon
1	bunch watercress, washed
	Chopped parsley

1. Line a broiler pan with foil. Brush the rack lightly with oil.

2. Rub rosemary on both sides of lamb chops. Brush the chops, kidneys, tomato halves and mushrooms with melted butter.

3. Place the chops and sausages on broiler rack and broil 3 inches from heat for 2 minutes. Add the kidneys and continue to cook 3 to 4 minutes more. Season the lamb chops and kidneys with salt and pepper to taste.

4. Turn all the meat over and add the bacon, tomato halves and mushrooms. Season with salt and pepper to taste. Broil for 3 minutes, then turn the bacon and mushrooms over and broil 2 minutes longer or until the bacon is crisp and the meat is done.

5. To serve, place 1 lamb chop, 1 kidney, 1 tomato half, 2 mushroom caps, 2 sausages and 1 bacon slice on each of 4 heated serving plates. Garnish with watercress and sprinkle the tomato halves with parsley. Serve immediately.

Lamb Tetrazzini

Serves 8 to 10

1	pound spaghetti
7	tablespoons butter
4	tablespoons flour
2	cups milk
1	teaspoon salt
½	pound mushrooms, thinly sliced
1	cup whipping cream
3	tablespoons sherry
¼	teaspoon pepper
⅛	teaspoon nutmeg
2	pounds cooked lamb, cut into 2-inch strips, ½-inch thick (4 cups)
½	cup grated parmesan cheese

1. Preheat oven to 350°.

2. Cook the spaghetti according to package directions and drain.

3. Melt 4 tablespoons butter in a saucepan; add the flour and blend well. Add the milk and cook, stirring constantly, until the sauce is thick and smooth. Season with ½ teaspoon salt. Set aside.

4. Cook the mushrooms in 3 tablespoons butter over low heat until lightly browned; stir occasionally. Mix in the cream sauce, whipping cream, sherry, remaining ½ teaspoon salt, pepper and nutmeg. Cook over low heat 10 minutes, stirring occasionally.

5. Toss the sauce with the spaghetti and lamb. Turn into a greased 3-quart baking dish. Sprinkle with the parmesan cheese. Bake for 25 minutes or until lightly browned.

Pork & Ham

Part of the casual approach to Northwest entertaining is cooking and eating outside. Alfresco dining is handled by the enthusiastic cook with as much aplomb as a festive, formal meal inside.

Pork is as much at home in the outdoors — barbecued spareribs provide the highlight for many a patio meal — as it is indoors at a large-scale elegant party where a garnished roast leg can become the star attraction, or a loin roast provide a satisfying family meal.

Because of its mild flavor and fine texture, pork seems destined to be glorified with spices and herbs, yet can hold its own with sharp flavors such as mustard sauce or an acidic fruit glaze.

And when it comes to versatility, pork can't be beat. Deep-smoking and salt-curing turns legs of pork into hams with a different flavor, texture and use from their fresh counterpart.

As an international favorite, pork provides substance for stews and ground-meat dishes such as Italian Pork Pinwheel. It is equally at home with sweet marinades such as the Gingered Spareribs and tart accompaniments such as sauerkraut in the traditional Choucroute Garnie.

Pork also has a special affinity for one of our finest Northwest products — the apple. Be it a side dish of stewed apples or the Apple-Horseradish Sauce or Apple-Lemon Glaze in this chapter, the pig prospers with this touch of the Northwest.

Since the late 1970s, Northwest shoppers have been finding leaner cuts of pork at their meat counters. The recipes in this chapter have been geared to keeping pork, which could become dry with improper cooking, as moist as possible.

◇

Loin of Pork with Apple-Horseradish Sauce

Serves 6 to 8

1   (5-6 pound) pork loin

Marinade:

¼   cup soy sauce

2   tablespoons Dijon mustard

½   cup sherry

3   large cloves garlic, minced

2   tablespoons ground ginger

½   teaspoon white pepper

½   teaspoon dried thyme, crushed

Glaze:

1   (10 ounce) jar apple jelly

2   tablespoons sherry

3   tablespoons lemon juice

2   tablespoons soy sauce

Apple-Horseradish Sauce:

2   cups chunky applesauce

2   tablespoons lemon juice

3   tablespoons prepared horseradish

1. Place the pork loin in a large baking dish.

2. To prepare marinade: Measure the soy sauce, mustard, sherry, garlic, ginger, pepper and thyme into a small bowl and mix well. Spoon over the meat and marinate at least 2 hours in the refrigerator, turning occasionally to ensure flavor penetration.

3. Preheat oven to 325°.

4. Drain off the marinade, reserving it for the glaze. Insert a meat thermometer into the roast. Cover the roast with a loose tent of aluminum foil. Roast for 3 hours. Remove the foil tent and score the top of the roast. Return to oven and roast 30 minutes longer.

5. To prepare glaze: Bring the apple jelly, sherry, lemon juice and soy sauce to a boil in a small saucepan. Reduce heat and cook 5 minutes or until jelly is melted. Add reserved marinade. Baste the roast every 10 minutes during the final 30 minutes of baking. When the meat thermometer registers 170°F. the roast is done.

6. To prepare apple-horseradish sauce: Mix the applesauce with the lemon juice and horseradish. Serve with the pork loin roast.

Florentine Pork Chop Bake

Serves 6

2	pounds fresh spinach
1½	cups sliced carrots
⅓	cup flour
2	teaspoons salt
⅛	teaspoon pepper
6	pork chops, ½-inch thick
3	tablespoons bacon drippings
1½	cups milk
¼	cup parmesan cheese
½	teaspoon dried tarragon, crushed

1. Preheat oven to 350°.

2. Wash the spinach; blanch in boiling water 1½ to 2 minutes. Drain, chop and squeeze dry.

3. Blanch the carrots for 3 minutes in a small amount of boiling water. Drain and reserve.

4. Combine the flour with 1 teaspoon salt and the pepper; dredge the chops in the flour mixture, reserving leftover flour.

5. Lightly brown the chops in the bacon drippings and remove from pan. Pour off all but 2 tablespoons drippings and stir in the remaining flour, blending well.

6. Gradually add the milk and cook, stirring constantly until thickened. Stir in the parmesan cheese.

7. Add 1 teaspoon salt and tarragon. Fold in the spinach and carrots and place in a 7-by-11-inch baking dish.

8. Place the pork chops on top of the spinach mixture. Cover securely with foil and bake 45 minutes. Uncover and bake 10 to 15 minutes longer or until the chops are done.

Lemon Sesame Pork

Serves 4 to 6

Lemon Marmalade Sauce:

- ½ cup lemon juice
- 6 tablespoons orange marmalade
- 4 small cloves garlic, minced
- 2 teaspoons grated lemon peel
- 2 teaspoons cornstarch, dissolved in 2 tablespoons water
- 1 teaspoon sesame oil
- ½ teaspoon salt

Sesame Pork:

- 1½ pounds pork tenderloin
- 1 large egg white
- 1 tablespoon cornstarch
- 1 tablespoon lemon juice
- 1 tablespoon dry sherry
- 1 tablespoon minced fresh ginger root
- 1 teaspoon dark soy sauce
- ½ teaspoon salt
- Dash pepper
- ½ cup sesame seeds
- Peanut or vegetable oil
- ½ small head lettuce, shredded
- Lemon wedges
- Tomato slices

1. **To prepare sauce:** In a medium saucepan, stir together the lemon juice, marmalade, garlic, lemon peel and cornstarch mixture. Bring to a boil over moderate heat, stirring constantly. Stir in the sesame oil and salt. Keep warm.

2. **To prepare pork:** Slice the pork into ½-inch slices. Cut each slice into strips 1-inch long and ¼-inch wide. Set aside.

3. In a small bowl, beat the egg white until foamy; set aside. In a large mixing bowl, combine the cornstarch, lemon juice, sherry, ginger, soy sauce, salt and pepper; mix until smooth. Add the egg white and stir until blended.

4. Add the pork and toss lightly with your hands until all the pieces are coated. Set aside to marinate at room temperature about 30 to 40 minutes.

5. Put ¼ cup of sesame seeds into a 1-quart bowl. Add half the pork pieces and toss with 2 forks to partly coat each piece of meat. Transfer the meat to another dish and repeat the process with the remaining half of the sesame seeds and pork.

6. Heat about 2 inches of peanut oil in a wok. When the oil is very hot, add the pork, a few pieces at a time, and deep-fry about 3 to 4 minutes or until golden brown.

7. Remove with a slotted spoon and drain on paper towels. Keep warm in the oven while frying the remaining pork. (Some sesame seed comes off in frying.)

8. Cover a serving platter, or individual salad plates, with shredded lettuce. Arrange the pork strips on the lettuce and drizzle lemon marmalade sauce over them. Garnish with lemon and tomato wedges.

Cuban-Style Roast Leg of Pork

Serves 12

3	cloves garlic
1	(6 pound) leg of pork or loin roast
½	cup freshly squeezed lemon juice
½	cup freshly squeezed orange juice
1	tablespoon dried oregano, crushed
1	teaspoon ground cumin
	Salt and pepper

1. Cut 1 clove of garlic in slivers. Make slits in the roast with a sharp knife and insert the slivers of garlic into the slits.

2. Mash the remaining 2 cloves of garlic. Add the lemon juice, orange juice, oregano, cumin and salt and pepper to taste.

3. Puncture the meat a few more times with a sharp knife, so the flavor will penetrate. Place in an oven-proof glass dish and pour the lemon-juice mixture over the pork. Marinate at least 6 hours or overnight in the refrigerator, turning the meat often.

4. Preheat oven to 325°.

5. Roast the pork in the marinade for 3 to 3½ hours or until a meat thermometer registers 170°F. Baste with marinade, if desired. The marinade tends to burn a little, so the drippings will be too brown for gravy. When done, let set for 10 minutes, then serve.

Pork Tenderloin with Bearnaise Sauce

Serves 4

1	tablespoon cooking oil
1	tablespoon butter
1	pound whole pork tenderloin
	Freshly ground pepper
¼	cup water
¼	cup red wine

Bearnaise Sauce:

¼	cup white-wine vinegar with tarragon
2	tablespoons white wine
1	green onion, with top, sliced
¼	teaspoon dried tarragon, crushed
¼	teaspoon dried parsley flakes, crushed
3	egg yolks
½	teaspoon dry mustard
½	cup butter, melted
2	tablespoons capers
	Fresh basil

1. Combine the oil and 1 tablespoon butter in a heavy skillet over medium heat, stirring to mix as the butter melts. Add the tenderloin and cook until brown on all sides, turning occasionally. Sprinkle with pepper to taste.

2. Add the water and red wine to the skillet. Cover tightly and cook over low heat for 45 to 60 minutes, or until done.

3. When the tenderloin is done, remove to a warm oven-proof platter and keep warm in the oven.

4. To prepare bearnaise sauce: Combine the vinegar, white wine, green onion, dried tarragon and parsley flakes in a small saucepan. Cook over medium-high heat for 10 to 15 minutes or until reduced by half. Set aside.

5. Beat the egg yolks with a wire whisk for about 1 minute in the top of a double boiler. Add the dry mustard and vinegar mixture, beating well. Place the yolk mixture over simmering water. Gradually add the melted butter in a slow, steady stream, beating constantly with a wire whisk. Continue beating gently until thickened. Stir in the capers.

6. Immediately pour the sauce onto a heated serving platter. Place the whole tenderloin on top. Garnish with fresh basil, if desired.

Note: Do not allow bearnaise sauce to sit in the pan or be stirred again because it will curdle.

Pork Chops with Mustard Sauce

Serves 4

4	loin pork chops, 1-inch thick
1	tablespoon bacon drippings or lard
	Salt and pepper

Sauce:

1	tablespoon butter
1	small onion, finely chopped
1	tablespoon flour
1	cup beef stock or broth
1	tablespoon tomato paste or 2 tablespoons tomato purée
1	small clove garlic, minced
2	teaspoons prepared mustard
2	dill pickles, sliced
	Chopped parsley

1. To prepare chops: Brown the chops on both sides in drippings. Salt and pepper lightly. Cover, reduce heat and cook until tender, 30 to 40 minutes, or until thoroughly done. Place the chops on a warm platter and keep hot in a low oven. Drain the fat from the skillet.

2. To prepare sauce: Heat the butter in a small saucepan. Add the onion and sauté until golden. Stir in the flour. Add the stock, stirring constantly, until slightly thickened. Add the tomato paste, garlic, mustard and dill pickles, cooking over low heat 10 to 15 minutes.

3. Add the sauce to the skillet used for browning the chops and heat, scraping the brown particles. Adjust seasonings. Pour over the chops and top with chopped parsley.

Cassoulet
Serves 8

1	pound navy beans (small white beans)
2½	quarts water
¼	pound bacon, diced
2	whole medium onions
1	clove garlic (skewer with a toothpick for easier removal later)
2	tablespoons chopped parsley
	Pinch dried thyme, crushed
1	small bay leaf
1	pound mild Italian sausage, cut in 8 pieces, or 1 Polish ring, cut in 1½- to 2-inch pieces
1½	pounds shoulder of lamb, cut in pieces (leave bone in), or use arm or blade cut shoulder steaks
1	pound shoulder of pork, cut in pieces (leave bone in), or use arm or blade cut shoulder shanks
2	tablespoons shortening
¾	teaspoon salt
½	teaspoon pepper
1	clove garlic, minced
2	cups tomato sauce

1. Soak the beans overnight in 1 quart water. Put the beans and water in a large heavy kettle.

2. Add the remaining 1½ quarts water, bacon, onions, garlic, parsley, thyme and bay leaf. Bring to a boil and simmer for about 30 minutes.

3. Add the Italian sausage or Polish ring and simmer another 30 minutes or until the beans are tender.

4. Trim the fat from the lamb and pork. Brown the lamb and pork in the shortening. Drain any excess fat.

5. Season with the salt and pepper. Add the minced garlic and tomato sauce. Cover and cook over low heat for 1 hour or until tender.

6. Bone the lamb and pork and remove any fat from the sauce. Return the boned meat to sauce.

7. Drain the liquid from the beans and reserve. Discard the bay leaf, onions and garlic.

8. Preheat oven to 350°.

9. Layer the beans, sausage, lamb, pork and sauce into an oven-proof

casserole. Add some of the reserved bean liquid to just barely cover the beans.

10. Bake uncovered for 1 hour, basting occasionally. Add more bean liquid during baking if the casserole seems too dry. Taste for seasonings. Serve in the casserole.

Note: Use the extra bean broth as base for making a flavorful onion soup.

Pork-Stuffed Radicchio

Serves 6

¼	pound pork sausage
½	cup sliced celery
¼	cup chopped green pepper
2	tablespoons chopped green onion
1	(8 ounce) can crushed pineapple, drained
12	radicchio lettuce leaves, with bitter white rib removed
1¾	cups chicken stock or broth
1	tablespoon soy sauce
3	tablespoons cornstarch
	Hot cooked rice

1. In a 10-inch skillet over medium heat, brown the sausage, stirring to separate the meat; spoon off fat. Stir in the celery, green pepper and green onion; cook until vegetables are tender-crisp.

2. Spoon the sausage and vegetables into a bowl and add the pineapple.

3. Spoon about 1 tablespoon of the pork mixture into the center of each radicchio leaf. Roll up, folding in the edges and secure with toothpicks.

4. Meanwhile, stir the stock, soy sauce and cornstarch into the skillet. Cook, stirring constantly until thickened and smooth. Reduce heat to low.

5. Place the rolls, seam side down, in the stock mixture. Cover and cook 15 minutes. Stir occasionally, spooning sauce over the rolls. Serve with hot cooked rice.

Italian Pork Pinwheel
Serves 8

1½	pounds lean ground pork
¾	cup soft bread crumbs
1	egg
1¼	teaspoons salt
⅛	teaspoon pepper
¼	teaspoon garlic powder
1	teaspoon dried oregano, crushed
1	cup small-curd cottage cheese
⅓	cup shredded mozzarella cheese
3	tablespoons grated parmesan cheese
1	pound fresh spinach
3	tablespoons ketchup

1. Preheat oven to 350°.
2. Combine the ground pork, bread crumbs, egg, 1 teaspoon salt, pepper, ⅛ teaspoon garlic powder and ½ teaspoon oregano and mix until thoroughly combined.
3. Combine the cottage cheese, half the mozzarella, 2 tablespoons parmesan cheese and the remaining salt, garlic powder and oregano.
4. Place the pork mixture on wax paper and pat into a 10-by-14-inch rectangle, then spread the cheese mixture over the pork to within ¾ inch of the edge on all sides.
5. Wash the spinach; blanch in boiling water 1½ to 2 minutes; drain, chop and squeeze dry. Combine the spinach and remaining parmesan cheese and spread evenly over the cheese layer.
6. Beginning at the short end of the rectangle, carefully roll up, jelly roll fashion, to enclose the cheese and spinach layers, using the wax paper to help lift and roll the meat. Press the pork mixture at both ends to enclose the filling.
7. If any filling shows through, make repairs with extra meat from the ends.
8. Place the loaf, seam side down, on a rack in a roasting pan. Bake 1 hour.
9. Spread the ketchup over the loaf and continue baking 15 minutes more. Sprinkle the remaining mozzarella over the loaf. Cool slightly before cutting.

Garden Medley Pork Roast

Serves 8 to 12

1	(3-5 pound) double boneless pork loin roast (2 half-loins tied together)
1	cup thinly sliced carrots
½	cup chopped onion
1	cup thinly sliced fresh mushrooms
½	teaspoon salt
⅛	teaspoon pepper
⅛	teaspoon rubbed sage
1½	cups water
2	tablespoons flour

1. Preheat oven to 325°.

2. Place the roast on a rack in an open roasting pan. Insert a meat thermometer in the thickest part of the roast, not touching fat. Roast, uncovered, until the meat thermometer registers 165°F. Let the roast stand at room temperature 15 to 20 minutes after removal from the oven. (Temperature will rise approximately 5 degrees to reach the recommended internal temperature of 170°F., and the juices will set.)

3. Pour off ¼ cup pan drippings into a large skillet. Add the carrots and onion, cover tightly and cook 3 to 4 minutes. Stir in the mushrooms and continue cooking, covered, 3 minutes. Sprinkle the vegetables with salt, pepper and sage.

4. Combine the water and flour; mix well and stir into the vegetables. Bring to a boil; reduce heat and simmer, uncovered, 15 minutes, stirring occasionally. Serve the vegetable mixture with the carved roast.

Pork Chops à l'Orange

Serves 4 to 6

4-6	rib or loin pork chops, 1-inch thick
	Salt and pepper
¼	cup flour
	Salad oil
2	navel oranges, peeled and sliced
3½	tablespoons firmly packed brown sugar
2	teaspoons cornstarch
¾	cup chicken stock or broth
¾	cup orange juice
½	teaspoon dried marjoram, crushed
2	medium onions, sliced
¼	cup finely chopped parsley

1. Preheat oven to 350°.

2. Trim fat from the chops, removing as much as possible, and render out the pieces of fat in a large skillet until brown. Remove and discard the scraps of fat when they are browned.

3. Season the chops to taste with salt and pepper. Coat lightly with flour. Brown well in the hot fat, adding a little salad oil if necessary for browning.

4. Arrange the chops in a large oven-proof dish in one layer. Sprinkle the orange slices with 2 tablespoons brown sugar and let stand.

5. Combine the cornstarch, chicken stock, orange juice, marjoram and the remaining brown sugar.

6. Pour the sauce over the chops and arrange the sliced onions on top. Sprinkle the onions with parsley.

7. Cover and bake for about 1 hour. Remove from the oven and place the orange slices evenly over the top.

8. Return to the oven, uncovered, and bake 15 minutes longer. Serve each chop with onion and orange slices on top and drizzle sauce over each serving.

Note: If the sauce seems to have too much fat, skim the excess from the surface with a large spoon.

Choucroute Garnie

Serves 4

5	slices bacon, diced
1	small onion, chopped
1	(2 pound) jar sauerkraut, drained
1	cup dry white wine
¼	teaspoon ground ginger
10-12	peppercorns
1½	pounds boneless country-style spareribs, cut in half crosswise
1	tablespoon salad oil
	Salt
1	smoked Polish sausage ring, cut in pieces
4	Kielbasa sausages
1	pound whole new potatoes, cooked and drained
	Dijon mustard

1. Preheat oven to 325°.

2. In a Dutch oven, sauté the bacon over low heat to obtain some drippings. Add the onion and sauté until translucent, stirring often. Add the drained sauerkraut, wine, ginger and peppercorns. Mix well. Cover and bake while browning spareribs.

3. Brown the spareribs on all sides in oil. Salt lightly to taste. Add the browned ribs to the sauerkraut and continue baking for 1 hour.

4. Remove the Dutch oven from oven. Arrange the Polish sausages and Kielbasa over the sauerkraut, pushing them slightly into the sauerkraut. Cover and return to oven for 20 minutes.

5. Uncover and add the drained potatoes; cover and return to oven for 15 minutes or until the potatoes are heated through.

6. Arrange the sauerkraut on a large platter surrounded by the ribs, sausages and potatoes. Serve with Dijon mustard.

Apple-Lemon-Glazed Pork Chops

Serves 6

Apple-Lemon Glaze:

- 1 tablespoon cornstarch
- 1 tablespoon sugar
- ¼ teaspoon ground nutmeg
- 1 cup apple juice
- 1 teaspoon lemon juice

Pork Chops:

- 2 tablespoons butter
- 6 pork chops with pockets, 1-inch thick

Stuffing:

- ½ cup chopped dried apples
- 2 tablespoons raisins
- ¾ cup apple juice
- 1½ teaspoons lemon juice
- 2 tablespoons onion flakes
- ¼ cup chopped celery
- 1 clove garlic, minced
- ¼ teaspoon salt
- ¼ teaspoon ground nutmeg
- ½ teaspoon ground cinnamon
- ¼ teaspoon paprika
- ½ teaspoon poultry seasoning
- 1 tablespoon dried parsley flakes, crushed
- 2 cups ½-inch bread cubes, from day-old bread
- 1 egg, beaten

1. To prepare glaze: In a small saucepan, combine the cornstarch, sugar and nutmeg. Stir in the apple and lemon juices. Stir over medium heat until the glaze thickens and boils. Set aside.

2. To prepare chops: In a large skillet, melt the butter. Add the pork chops and brown on both sides. Remove from the skillet.

3. To prepare stuffing: In a small bowl, combine the dried apples, raisins, apple juice and lemon juice. Let stand to soften.

4. Lightly brown the onion flakes, celery and garlic in remaining butter in skillet. Stir in the apple-raisin mixture. Add the salt, nutmeg, cinnamon, paprika, poultry seasoning, parsley flakes, bread and egg. Toss lightly.

5. Preheat oven to 350°.

6. Stuff the pork chop pockets with the stuffing. Place the stuffed pork chops in a 9-by-13-inch baking pan. Pour apple-lemon glaze over the chops. Cover and bake for 40 minutes. Uncover and baste with the glaze. Bake, uncovered, 25 to 30 minutes longer.

Ginger Pork Chops Dijon

Serves 6

1	cup dry white wine
1	cup water
2	tablespoons grated fresh ginger
2	teaspoons Dijon mustard
	Dash salt
6	pork chops, ¾-inch thick
1	tablespoon vegetable oil
3	tablespoons sour cream
1	large tomato, cut in thin wedges
2	green onions, sliced

1. In a large bowl, whisk together the wine, water, ginger, mustard and salt. Add the pork chops and toss. Cover and refrigerate at least 4 hours or overnight, turning occasionally.

2. Drain the chops thoroughly, reserving the liquid.

3. Heat the oil in a large skillet over medium-high heat. Add the chops and cook until lightly browned, about 5 minutes on each side. Drain off fat. Add the reserved liquid, cover, reduce heat and simmer until the chops are tender, turning once or twice, about 30 minutes.

4. Transfer the chops to a serving platter and keep warm.

5. Gradually whisk the sour cream into the ginger mixture. Cook and stir over low heat to just below boiling. Stir in the tomato and onions and heat through. To serve, spoon some of the hot sauce over the chops. Put the remainder in a gravy boat.

Pork Steaks in Barbecue Sauce

Serves 4

⅓	cup chopped onion
3	tablespoons butter
⅓	cup honey
3	tablespoons fresh lemon juice
3	tablespoons soy sauce
1	tablespoon freshly grated orange peel
1	teaspoon salt
¾	cup fresh orange juice
1½	tablespoons cornstarch
4	blade pork steaks

1. Preheat oven to 350°.
2. In a small saucepan, sauté the onion in the butter until tender. Add the honey, lemon juice, soy sauce, orange peel and salt.
3. Gradually blend the orange juice into the cornstarch and add to onion mixture. Cook, stirring constantly, until thickened.
4. Arrange the pork steaks side-by-side in a baking dish. Pour the barbecue sauce over the steaks and cover the dish with foil. Bake for 1 hour or until tender. Remove the foil and broil until the steaks are browned.

Stuffed Barbecued Spareribs

Serves 4 to 6

2	racks spareribs (4½-5 pounds total)

Stuffing:

¼	pound Italian sausage
2	tablespoons olive oil
1	cup coarsely chopped zucchini
½	cup sliced celery
⅓	cup finely chopped onion
1	clove garlic, minced
½	cup water

1	cup chopped tomato
1¼	cups herb-seasoned stuffing mix

Barbecue Sauce:

1	cup ketchup
4	tablespoons firmly packed brown sugar
4	tablespoons cider vinegar
2	cloves garlic, minced
1	teaspoon dried basil leaves, crushed
1	teaspoon dry mustard

1. Cook the spareribs in simmering salted water for 1 hour. Drain.
2. To prepare stuffing: In a skillet, brown the sausage in the oil, using a fork to break it into bits. Add the zucchini, celery, onion and garlic. Cook until the zucchini is tender.
3. Remove from heat. Add the water, tomato and stuffing mixture and toss to blend. Lay out one rack of spareribs; top it with the stuffing mixture, spreading to cover the meat. Top the stuffing with the remaining rack of spareribs. Tie together.
4. To prepare barbecue sauce: Combine the ketchup, brown sugar, vinegar, garlic, basil and dry mustard in a small bowl.
5. Cook the spareribs 6 inches from broiler unit for 30 minutes. Brush frequently with barbecue sauce.

Gingered Spareribs
Serves 4

⅓	cup flour
1	cup ketchup
⅓	cup soy sauce
¼	cup sherry
¼	cup sugar
¾	teaspoon salt
1½	tablespoons hoisin sauce
4	cloves garlic, minced
4	slices fresh ginger, shredded
3	pounds pork spareribs (breast bone removed)
¼	cup light corn syrup

1. Preheat oven to 325°.
2. Shake the flour into a 14-by-20-inch oven cooking bag and place in a 13-by-9-by-2-inch baking dish.
3. In a glass measuring cup, combine the ketchup, soy sauce, sherry, sugar, salt, hoisin sauce, garlic and ginger. Pour into the bag. Mix the ingredients in the bag to dissolve the flour. Place the spareribs in the bag. Turn the bag gently several times to coat the ribs. Close the bag with a nylon tie and make six ½-inch slits in the top.
4. Bake 1½ hours or until tender. Remove from the bag onto a serving dish. Glaze the ribs by brushing with corn syrup while hot. Spoon the sauce over the ribs.

Hickory Country-Style Ribs
Serves 4 to 6

1½	cups cooking oil
¾	cup soy sauce
½	cup vinegar
¼	cup Worcestershire sauce
⅓	cup orange juice
2	tablespoons dry mustard
1	tablespoon coarsely ground black pepper
2	teaspoons salt

2	tablespoons chopped fresh parsley
2	cloves garlic, minced
4	pounds country-style pork spareribs

1. Combine the oil, soy sauce, vinegar, Worcestershire sauce, orange juice, mustard, black pepper, salt, parsley and garlic in a bowl; mix well.

2. Place the ribs in a shallow dish, cover with marinade and refrigerate for 24 hours, turning the meat occasionally.

3. Preheat oven to 350°.

4. Remove the ribs from marinade, reserving it and placing the ribs, meat side up, on a rack in a shallow baking pan. Spread some marinade over the ribs. Refrigerate the remaining marinade. Cover ribs with foil and bake for 1 hour.

5. Remove the baking dish from the oven and drain off drippings. Brush the ribs with more marinade and return to the oven. Bake, uncovered, for 45 minutes to 1 hour longer, or until tender. During the last 20 minutes of baking, baste frequently with marinade. Heat the remaining marinade to boiling and serve with the ribs.

Ham with Apricot Glaze

Serves 24

1	(8-9 pound) fully cooked bone-in ham
2	cups apricot preserves
2	tablespoons light rum
2	teaspoons prepared mustard
¼	teaspoon ground ginger

1. Preheat oven to 325°.

2. Place the ham on a rack in an open roasting pan and bake for 3 hours or until a meat thermometer reaches 140°F.

3. While the ham is cooking, prepare the glaze. Heat the apricot preserves until bubbling. Remove from heat and strain. Discard solids. Add the rum, mustard and ground ginger to the thickened syrup and stir to mix well. Pour the glaze over the ham 30 minutes before it is through cooking.

Maple Bourbon-Glazed Ham

Serves 12

½	cup bourbon
2	tablespoons butter
½	cup maple syrup
½	teaspoon ground cinnamon
¼	teaspoon salt
1	tablespoon cornstarch
2	tablespoons water
1	(3 pound) fully cooked ham

1. Preheat oven to 325°.
2. Combine the bourbon, butter, maple syrup, cinnamon and salt in a small saucepan. Mix the cornstarch and water until smooth and stir it into the bourbon mixture. Heat and stir until it boils.
3. Place the ham in a shallow baking pan. Make diagonal slashes, crisscrossing on the fat side of the ham. Pour the glaze over the top of the ham. Insert a meat thermometer in the thickest part of the ham.
4. Bake 20 to 25 minutes per pound, or until a thermometer reads 140°F., spooning glaze on occasionally.

Note: If you have the butcher preslice the ham and tie it back together, the glaze will penetrate through each slice. Untie before serving.

Orange-Glazed Ham

Serves 12 to 16

1	(4 pound) boneless fully cooked ham
⅓	cup honey
⅔	cup firmly packed brown sugar
⅓	cup fresh orange juice
¼	teaspoon dry mustard
1	tablespoon freshly grated orange peel
½	teaspoon ground ginger
	Peel from 2 to 3 oranges
	Peel from 2 to 3 limes
	Whole cloves

1. Preheat oven to 325°.

2. Bake ham for 15 to 20 minutes per pound.

3. Meanwhile, combine the honey, brown sugar, orange juice, mustard, grated orange peel and ginger to make a glaze. Mix well.

4. At 30 minutes, brush the ham liberally with the honey mixture. Return to the oven to glaze, brushing 2 more times with additional glaze during remaining baking time, about 30 minutes, or until a meat thermometer registers 140°F.

5. Meanwhile, prepare the peels and cloves. With an orange zipper (a little plastic device also known as a snacker and twist maker), remove the peel from oranges and limes in ¼-inch strips, as long as possible. Do this by going around the fruit.

6. Remove the ham from the oven when done and fashion strips of peel into a lattice design, securing the peels where they cross with a whole clove. It may be necessary to poke holes through the peels and into the ham with a skewer before inserting the cloves.

7. The ham may be returned to the oven to reheat or be served immediately.

Poultry

Chicken is the health-consciousness food of the '80s, from the new medical credentials of chicken noodle soup to the skinned, poached chicken breast popular with dieters and athletes.

It is a popular entrée for cooks on the go because young, fresh fryers cook quickly and are adaptable to almost any type of meal.

Thanks to the flourishing Washington chicken industry, chicken grown and processed within 100 miles is readily available and several Seattle-area farms are growing free-range chickens for local markets.

Turkey also is low-calorie and low-cholesterol. Both turkey and chicken intrigue the inventive chef because their close-grained meat has a mild flavor that can be accented by a delicate sauce or flavorful stuffing.

If health consciousness is the culinary star of this decade, then back-to-the-basic cooking has second billing. Some of the most enthusiastic response we get from readers is when we publish recipes for poultry dressings, particularly for holiday turkeys. The selection of stuffing recipes here is meant to encourage cooks to serve a "new-to-them" stuffing the next time turkey is on the menu.

The secret to good poultry cookery is to make the meat interesting. The adventurous cook can bring plenty of variety to family menus by preparing American regional specialties as well as ethnic recipes.

Rum-Basted Chicken
Serves 4

1	(2½ pound) frying chicken, cut up
½	orange
½	lemon
¼	cup butter
¼	cup dark rum
2	tablespoons Worcestershire sauce
	Salt and pepper
	Ground ginger
	Parsley sprigs
	Long strips orange peel

1. Preheat oven to 350°.

2. Wash and dry the chicken and place in a 9-by-13-inch baking pan. Squeeze the juice of the orange and lemon over the chicken pieces.

3. Melt the butter and add the rum and Worcestershire sauce. Spoon over the chicken.

4. Season with salt, pepper and ginger to taste. Bake about 50 minutes, until the chicken is tender and golden brown, basting occasionally with pan drippings.

5. Serve hot on a warm platter, garnished with parsley sprigs and long strips of orange peel.

Poulet Basque
Serves 4

1	(3 pound) chicken, cut up
1	teaspoon salt
⅛	teaspoon pepper
2	tablespoons butter
2	tablespoons oil
4	tomatoes, peeled and chopped
1	cup chopped green pepper
½	pound mushrooms, sliced
¼	pound baked ham, diced

| ½ cup dry white wine |
| 2 tablespoons chopped parsley |

1. Wash and pat dry the chicken pieces. Season with salt and pepper.
2. Brown the chicken on all sides in a mixture of the butter and oil in a Dutch oven.
3. When browned, add the tomatoes, green pepper, mushrooms and ham. Pour the wine over all.
4. Cover and cook gently for 30 to 40 minutes or until tender. Remove the chicken to a warm platter. Turn heat to high and reduce the sauce a little by letting it boil for a few minutes. Taste and adjust seasonings. Pour over the chicken. Sprinkle with chopped parsley.

Chicken Breasts with Leeks

Serves 4 to 6

| 5 tablespoons butter |
| 3 cups chopped leeks |
| 2 stalks celery, chopped |
| 4 whole chicken breasts, boned, skinned, and halved |
| 2 tablespoons dry sherry |
| Salt and white pepper |

1. Melt 4 tablespoons butter in a skillet. Add the leeks and celery. Stir to coat vegetables with butter. Cover the skillet and cook over low heat about 5 minutes.
2. Lay the chicken breasts on top of leeks. Cover and cook over medium heat for 5 minutes.
3. Remove cover. Add remaining 1 tablespoon butter, sherry and salt and white pepper to taste. Cover and cook 5 minutes longer or until chicken is tender and no longer pink. To serve, transfer the leeks to a serving platter. Arrange the chicken on top.

Chicken with Mushrooms
Serves 6

1	large chicken breast, boned and skinned
4-5	large fresh shiitake mushrooms
1	cup sliced green onions
½	rounded teaspoon instant dashi (Japanese cooking stock)
½	cup water
¼	cup shoyu (Japanese soy sauce)
¼	cup sake
6	eggs, slightly beaten
3-4	cups hot cooked rice

1. Cut the chicken into thin strips. Also slice the mushrooms thinly. Cut the green onions on the diagonal.

2. Dissolve the instant dashi in the water and combine with the shoyu and sake in a wok. Bring to a boil and add the chicken, mushrooms and green onions. Lower heat and cook 6 to 8 minutes or until the chicken and vegetables are tender. Be sure not to overcook.

3. Stir in the eggs, and cook until eggs are set, stirring gently a few times.

4. To serve, divide the rice between 6 individual serving bowls. Spoon the chicken-egg mixture over rice. Serve immediately.

Mustard-Glazed Chicken
Serves 4

1	(2½-3 pound) broiling chicken, quartered
	Onion powder
	Garlic salt
	Pepper
2	tablespoons butter, melted
¼	cup black or red currant jelly
1	tablespoon lemon juice
1	tablespoon Dijon mustard
2	teaspoons Worcestershire sauce

1. Preheat oven to 350°.

2. Sprinkle the chicken quarters on both sides with onion powder, garlic

salt and pepper. Brush with the butter.

3. Place on a rack in a shallow roasting pan. Roast for 20 minutes.

4. Melt the jelly in a small saucepan over low heat. Stir in the lemon juice, mustard and Worcestershire sauce. Brush the chicken frequently with the glaze and continue roasting 30 minutes longer, or until tender.

Chicken with White Port Wine

Serves 6 to 8

½	pound fresh mushrooms
½	cup butter
¼	cup flour
¼	teaspoon salt
¼	teaspoon pepper
¼	teaspoon plus 1 pinch ground nutmeg
3-4	whole chicken breasts, boned, skinned and halved
⅓	cup white port wine
1½	cups whipping cream
	Chopped parsley
	Parsley sprigs

1. Brush the mushrooms with a mushroom brush to clean, but do not get them wet. Slice thinly.

2. In a heavy skillet, melt the butter. Add the mushrooms and sauté until just limp. Remove mushrooms with a slotted spoon to a dish, and keep in a warm oven.

3. Combine the flour, salt, pepper and the ¼ teaspoon nutmeg in a flat dish. Dip the chicken breasts in the flour mixture and sauté each one in butter in the skillet, until golden brown and cooked through, about 3 to 5 minutes on each side, depending on the thickness.

4. Remove the chicken breasts to a warm serving platter. Cover with foil and keep in a warm oven while preparing sauce.

5. Add the port to drippings in skillet, then add the whipping cream and mushrooms. Bring to a boil. Cover, lower heat and let simmer for 20 minutes.

6. To serve, pour the sauce over the warm chicken breasts. Sprinkle lightly with the pinch of nutmeg, garnish with chopped parsley on top and a few parsley sprigs along the edge.

Golden Parmesan Chicken
Serves 8

1	small loaf day-old bread
5-6	pounds chicken parts (breasts, thighs and drumsticks)
¾	cup grated parmesan cheese
¼	cup chopped fresh parsley
1½	teaspoons salt
	Pepper
1	small clove garlic, minced
1	cup melted butter

1. Remove crusts from the bread and process in a blender or food processor to make about 3 to 3½ cups of coarse crumbs. Spread the crumbs in a flat pan and let dry a few hours.

2. Wash and pat dry the chicken pieces.

3. Mix the bread crumbs with the cheese, parsley, salt and pepper.

4. Add the garlic to the melted butter. Dip each piece of chicken in the butter then roll into crumb mixture, making sure that each piece is well coated. Place in a shallow, foil-lined roasting pan. Refrigerate for 30 minutes.

5. Preheat oven to 350°.

6. Pour remaining butter over chicken and bake for about 1 hour or until done.

7. Do not turn chicken, but baste frequently with pan drippings. Remove to platter and serve immediately.

Dungeness Chicken Rolls
Serves 8 to 10

Sauce:

3	tablespoons butter
¼	cup flour
⅔	cup milk
1	cup hot chicken stock or broth
⅓	cup dry white wine
	Salt

Filling:

2	tablespoons butter
⅓	cup finely chopped onion
7-8	large fresh mushrooms, cleaned and chopped
¾	pound fresh Dungeness crab meat.
½	cup crushed soda crackers
¼	cup snipped parsley
½	teaspoon salt
	Pepper

Chicken Rolls:

5	medium or 4 large whole chicken breasts, boned, skinned and halved
1½	cups shredded Swiss cheese
	Paprika

1. To prepare sauce: Melt the butter in a saucepan, stir in the flour and cook over low heat about 3 minutes, stirring constantly.

2. Add the milk, chicken stock and wine and stir to blend well. Bring to a boil, turn heat to low and simmer about 3 minutes longer, stirring until thick. Season to taste with salt.

3. To prepare filling: Melt the butter in a skillet and sauté the onion and mushrooms until the onion is soft. Stir in ½ pound crab meat, cracker crumbs, parsley, salt and pepper. Stir in 3 tablespoons of the sauce.

4. Preheat oven to 350°.

5. To prepare rolls: Using the side of a meat mallet, flatten chicken breasts between two sheets of wax paper until as thin as possible.

6. Place ¼ cup filling mixture on each breast. Bring sides up over the filling and then roll up so chicken is covering all filling. Place chicken rolls seam side down in a 7-by-11-inch baking dish.

7. Stir remaining ¼ pound crab meat into the remaining sauce. Pour sauce over chicken. Bake, covered, 1 hour. Remove from oven, uncover and sprinkle the cheese and paprika over the top. Bake 5 minutes longer.

This recipe is one of Ruth De Rosa's favorites for entertaining.

Chicken Nice-Style

Serves 6

4	pounds chicken parts (preferably breasts and thighs)
	Juice of 1 lemon
2	teaspoons thyme
	Salt and freshly ground black pepper
½	cup diced lean salt pork
1	tablespoon olive oil
2	cups minced onion
2	cloves garlic, minced
2	cups skinned, seeded and chopped tomatoes
2	bay leaves
½	cup dry white wine
½	cup Nice black unpitted olives
½	cup chopped parsley or basil

1. Wash and dry the chicken pieces thoroughly and sprinkle on both sides with lemon juice, thyme, salt and pepper. Set aside.

2. In a large skillet, sauté the salt pork over medium heat until golden brown. Remove to a Dutch oven.

3. Add olive oil to the skillet and sauté chicken until brown on all sides, about 15 minutes. Transfer to the Dutch oven. (You'll need to do this in 3 batches.)

4. Add onion and garlic to the skillet and sauté until onion is transparent, but not brown, about 10 minutes.

5. Add the tomatoes, bay leaves and wine and cook for 10 minutes or until a sauce starts to form. Add to Dutch oven.

6. Cover and simmer 30 to 35 minutes or until chicken is tender.

7. Uncover and reduce the sauce over high heat for about 5 minutes. Remove the bay leaves. Add the olives. Simmer 5 more minutes to heat the olives through.

8. To serve, transfer the chicken to a serving dish. Pour some sauce over it and sprinkle with parsley. Serve the remaining sauce on the side.

Chicken Breasts with Mushroom Sauce

Serves 6

½-⅔	cup uncooked white rice
⅔	cup uncooked wild rice
3	whole chicken breasts, boned, skinned and halved
¼	teaspoon salt
	Freshly ground black pepper
½	cup butter
1	pound fresh mushrooms, sliced
1	tablespoon grated onion
1	pint whipping cream
¼	cup brandy
¼	cup dry sherry
⅓	cup chopped parsley

1. Cook the white rice and wild rice, in separate pans, according to directions on packages. When the rices are done, combine and mix well. Keep warm in the top of a double boiler.

2. Meanwhile, season the chicken breasts with salt and pepper. In a heavy skillet, melt the butter. Sauté breasts over medium heat until done and a rich brown. Remove chicken breasts to a warm, oven-proof plate and keep hot in a warm oven.

3. Add the mushrooms and onion to the butter remaining in the skillet and sauté for 5 minutes, stirring constantly. Reduce heat and add the whipping cream slowly, stirring constantly. Simmer for 5 minutes. Add the brandy and sherry and simmer 5 minutes longer.

4. Place a bed of the rice combination on each of 6 warm plates. Arrange a chicken-breast half on each bed of rice. Pour equal amounts of the mushroom sauce over each serving. Sprinkle each with parsley.

Italian Chicken Rolls

Serves 6

3	whole chicken breasts, boned, skinned and halved
	Salt and pepper
3	tablespoons Dijon mustard
1½	teaspoons Italian seasoning
4-5	ounces mozzarella cheese (6 slices and remainder shredded)
½	cup flour
2-3	tablespoons olive oil
2	large green onions, minced
2	cloves garlic, minced
2	cups sliced fresh mushrooms
2	very large fresh ripe tomatoes, peeled, seeded and finely chopped
¼	cup finely chopped parsley

1. With a meat mallet, pound the membrane side of each breast until meat begins to flatten. Turn over and lightly pound the exposed-meat side with the side of the mallet, being careful not to destroy the delicate flesh. Flatten each chicken breast to an equal thickness. (Large breast halves may be cut in half so all are of equal size.)

2. Sprinkle the surface of each piece with salt and pepper. Spread about ½ tablespoon Dijon mustard over the top of each piece of meat with a spatula. Then sprinkle each piece with Italian seasoning.

3. Arrange a slice of mozzarella cheese on each piece and roll up, making a tight, neat package. Tie with a string.

4. Sprinkle the chicken rolls lightly with salt and pepper. Place the flour in a wide bowl and coat each roll in flour, shaking off excess.

5. Heat the oil in a large, heavy skillet until hot, but not smoking. Add the chicken breasts and sauté until nicely browned. This will take about 6 to 8 minutes, turning often with tongs so they brown evenly all over. Chicken is done when the meat feels springy, rather than very soft, to the touch.

6. Remove the chicken to a warm dish, cut off strings and keep in a warm oven while the sauce is prepared. To the oil remaining in the skillet, add the green onions and garlic and cook a few seconds. Add the mushrooms and sauté for about 1½ to 2 minutes.

7. Add the chopped tomatoes and sauté again for about 2 to 3 minutes, or until tomato pieces begin to soften and liquefy. Season to taste with salt and pepper and a generous sprinkling of Italian seasoning.

8. Return the chicken rolls to the sauce and simmer until sauce thickens a little, basting the chicken rolls with the sauce several times. This will take about 2 to 3 minutes. Taste and add more seasoning, if needed.

9. Place the chicken rolls on an oven-proof platter, cover with the sauce. Sprinkle with the shredded mozzarella cheese and place under the broiler a few minutes until the cheese melts. Remove from oven, sprinkle with chopped parsley and serve immediately.

Chicken Piccate

Serves 4

2	whole chicken breasts, boned and halved
½	cup flour
3	tablespoons butter
1	tablespoon olive oil
2	cups sliced fresh mushrooms
⅓	cup chopped green onions
½	cup madeira
½	cup water
3	tablespoons capers
½	teaspoon salt
½	teaspoon dried sweet basil, crushed
	Hot fluffy rice

1. Pound the chicken breasts to ¼ inch thick. Cut each in half. Dredge chicken in flour.

2. Sauté the chicken in hot butter and oil in a heavy skillet over medium-high heat until brown on both sides. Remove to a serving platter. Keep warm.

3. Sauté the mushrooms and half the onions in the same skillet. Stir in the madeira, water, capers, salt and sweet basil. Simmer 5 minutes, until sauce thickens. Pour over the chicken. Serve with hot fluffy rice. Garnish with the reserved chopped green onions.

Chawan Mushi

Serves 5

Custard:

4	eggs
2	cups chicken stock or broth
2	tablespoons sake
½	teaspoon salt
½	teaspoon shoyu (Japanese soy sauce)

Chicken:

1	whole chicken breast, boned and skinned
1	tablespoon sake
1	tablespoon shoyu

Vegetables:

1	(2-inch long) piece carrot, from wide end
8	fresh mushrooms (shiitake, matsutake or button), cleaned and sliced
5	tablespoons chicken stock or broth
1	tablespoon sake
2	teaspoons shoyu

1. To prepare custard: Beat the eggs; add the chicken stock, sake, salt and shoyu.

2. To prepare chicken: Remove any fat remaining on the chicken. Then cut into ½-inch cubes or into thin strips.

3. Combine the sake and shoyu. Add the chicken strips and marinate for 5 minutes.

4. To prepare vegetables: Peel the carrot piece and cut in half. Then cut in julienne strips lengthwise. In a small saucepan, simmer the mushrooms and carrots in the chicken stock, sake and shoyu until just barely limp. Drain.

5. To assemble and steam: Drain the carrots and mushrooms and place equal amounts of vegetables in each of five 8-ounce steamer bowls. Put equal amounts of chicken in each bowl, draining as much of the marinade as possible. Divide the custard mixture equally among bowls, pouring it over the meat and vegetables.

6. Cover bowls tightly with foil. Place in a heated steamer. Cover and steam slowly for 30 minutes or until custard is set. Serve warm.

Note: Chawan Mushi is a Japanese steamed egg dish of custard-like consistency. It is served as one of the main courses of a Japanese dinner.

Mock Abalone

Serves 4

2	whole chicken breasts, boned, skinned and halved
1	(8 ounce) bottle clam juice
1	egg
1½	tablespoons water
¾	cup seasoned dry bread crumbs
⅓	cup thinly sliced almonds
	Butter
	Lemon wedges
	Parsley
	Tartar sauce

1. Place the chicken breasts on a cutting board, membrane side up, and pound with a meat mallet until as thin as possible, without mashing the meat. Do not pound on the other side, where the flesh has been cut, or it will cut the meat up too much.

2. Either may have to be cut in half, if it pounds out too large. Place the breast pieces in a flat dish and pour clam juice over to cover. Cover the dish and refrigerate for 24 to 30 hours, turning meat over several times if necessary.

3. Combine the egg and water in a dish, beating well. Mix the bread crumbs and almonds in a second dish. Dip the pieces of chicken breast first in egg mixture, then crumb mixture.

4. Melt the butter in a heavy skillet. Brown the chicken slowly, until golden on both sides. Sprinkle a bit of lemon juice over each piece.

5. Serve with lemon wedges, parsley and tartar sauce, if desired.

Chicken Breasts in Phyllo Pastry

Serves 4

6	tablespoons butter
1	onion, minced
½	pound mushrooms, minced
2	tablespoons minced parsley
1	clove garlic, minced
1	tablespoon flour
¼	cup dry vermouth
	Salt and pepper
1-2	tablespoons vegetable oil
2	whole chicken breasts, boned, skinned and halved
8	sheets phyllo
¾-1	cup melted butter
2	cups bread crumbs
½	pound feta cheese
	Parsley

1. Melt 2 tablespoons butter in a large skillet; add the onion and sauté until golden. Remove the onion from skillet and set aside. Add 2 more tablespoons butter to the skillet and sauté the mushrooms over medium-high heat until they have rendered all their juices and the skillet is dry.

2. Add the sautéed onion, parsley and garlic to mushrooms and sauté for 1 minute. Blend in the flour. Add the vermouth and cook over moderate heat, stirring constantly until thickened. Season to taste with salt and pepper. Remove skillet from heat and set aside.

3. In another skillet, heat remaining 2 tablespoons butter with the oil. Sauté the chicken breasts until lightly browned on both sides, about 2 minutes altogether. Remove skillet from heat and set aside.

4. Preheat oven to 350°.

5. Place 1 sheet of phyllo on pastry board. Brush with melted butter and sprinkle with ¼ cup bread crumbs. Place another sheet of phyllo on top of the first; brush with melted butter and sprinkle with ¼ cup bread crumbs.

6. Place 1 chicken breast just below center of phyllo; top chicken with one-fourth of the mushroom mixture and one-fourth of the feta cheese. Fold sides of phyllo over the chicken. Repeat with the remaining phyllo dough, chicken breasts, mushroom mixture and feta cheese.

7. Brush the chicken bundles generously with melted butter. Place, seam side down, on a baking sheet. Bake 35 minutes or until golden brown. Place on a serving platter and garnish with parsley.

Champagne Capon

Serves 6 to 8

1	(6-8 pound) capon
	Salt and pepper
1	large onion, minced
1	carrot, diced
2	tablespoons butter, melted
4	fresh mushrooms, diced
2-2½	cups champagne
½	cup whipping cream

1. Preheat oven to 325°.

2. Clean the capon and season inside and out with salt and pepper. Tie wings close to the body and tie the legs together.

3. In a pan large enough to hold the capon, place the onion, carrot, butter and mushrooms. Stir to mix.

4. Pour in 1½ cups champagne and place the prepared capon in the pan. Roast until golden brown, 3 to 3½ hours depending on the size of the bird, or until a meat thermometer inserted in thickest part of the thigh registers 185° F. If it gets too brown, place a tent of foil loosely over the top.

5. Baste every 20 minutes with the champagne liquid in the bottom of the pan. Add more champagne if needed.

6. When the capon is done, remove it to a serving platter and keep it warm. Skim excess fat from liquid and vegetables in bottom of the pan. Reduce sauce over high heat to about 1 cup.

7. Add the whipping cream and ½ cup more champagne. Stir and cook until well blended. Put the sauce through a coarse sieve and season with salt and pepper to taste.

8. Slice the capon in serving pieces and serve on warmed plates with the champagne sauce over each serving.

Chicken-Sausage Gumbo
Serves 8 to 10

1½	pounds smoked, fully cooked sausage, coarsely chopped
⅓	plus ¼ cup flour
1	teaspoon salt
½	teaspoon pepper
½	teaspoon paprika
3	pounds chicken parts (breasts and thighs), skinned
⅓	cup shortening
1	cup chopped celery
1	cup chopped onion
4	cups chicken stock or broth
2	cups water
¼	teaspoon allspice
¼	teaspoon cloves
¼	teaspoon celery salt
¼-½	teaspoon cayenne pepper
½	teaspoon dried thyme, crushed
3	cups uncooked rice
¾	pound young okra
2	fresh tomatoes, chopped
½	cup chopped parsley
	Juice of ½ lemon

1. In a skillet, brown the sausage. Drain well and set aside. Discard any fat.

2. Combine ⅓ cup flour, salt, pepper and paprika and mix to combine in a flat shallow dish. Dredge the chicken parts in seasoned flour. In another large, heavy skillet, melt the shortening. Slowly cook the chicken parts in hot fat until nicely browned.

3. Remove the chicken pieces and place in a Dutch oven. Pour the fat from browning the chicken into a measuring cup and measure ¼ cup of those drippings back into the same skillet. Add ¼ cup flour and make a roux by cooking on medium heat, stirring constantly until a dark tan color. Reduce heat and add the celery and onion and cook until the onion is soft.

4. Add the roux mixture to the chicken in the Dutch oven. Add 2 cups chicken stock, water, allspice, cloves, celery salt, cayenne pepper and thyme. Simmer covered, until the chicken is tender, about 45 minutes.

5. Place the chicken on a large dish, cool slightly and remove meat from bones. Return the meat to Dutch oven. Add the browned sausage and the remaining chicken stock. Simmer 30 minutes more.

6. Cook the rice, according to package directions, while the gumbo is simmering. Steam the okra until just barely tender, about 8 minutes. Set aside.

7. When the gumbo is done, adjust seasonings, adding more cayenne if desired. Add the fresh tomatoes, parsley, steamed okra and lemon juice. Combine well and heat through. Serve hot in large soup bowls over beds of hot, cooked rice.

Honey-Rice-Stuffed Game Hens

Serves 2 to 4

¼	cup chopped onion
¼	cup chopped celery
¼	cup butter
1	cup cooked rice, cooked in chicken stock or broth
¼	cup raisins
2	tablespoons chopped walnuts
1½	tablespoons honey
2	teaspoons lemon juice
¼	teaspoon ground cinnamon
	Salt and freshly ground pepper
2	(1½ pound) Cornish game hens

1. Preheat oven to 375°.

2. Cook the onion and celery in 1 tablespoon butter over medium heat until tender. Stir in the rice, raisins, walnuts, honey, lemon juice, cinnamon and salt and pepper to taste.

3. Sprinkle the body cavities of hens with salt. Stuff lightly with the rice mixture. Twist the wing tips under back; tie legs together.

4. Place breast side up on the rack of a roasting pan. Melt the remaining butter and brush some on the birds.

5. Roast for 55 minutes or until tender. Brush with butter twice as they bake.

Tarragon-Baked Cornish Game Hens

Serves 4

2	Cornish game hens
¼	cup dry white wine
2	tablespoons lemon juice
2	teaspoons vegetable oil
¼	teaspoon minced garlic
2	teaspoons dried tarragon, crushed
1¼	teaspoons salt
¼	teaspoon pepper

1. Have hens split in half at the meat market. Wash well. Place in one layer in a 7-by-11-inch or 9-by-12-inch baking pan.
2. Combine the wine, lemon juice, oil, garlic, tarragon, salt and pepper. Pour over the hens. Turn hens over in marinade to coat thoroughly and let stand, refrigerated, 1 hour or more, skin side down.
3. Preheat oven to 350°.
4. Turn the hens over and leave in the same pan. Bake uncovered for 30 minutes.
5. Turn the hens again, baste with pan juices and bake 30 minutes longer.
6. To complete browning, turn the hens over, skin side up, and broil about 6 inches from heat for 2 to 3 minutes, or until golden brown. Serve immediately.

Brandied Curried Chicken

Serves 4

½	cup dried apricots
½	cup hot water
2	tablespoons vegetable oil
1	cup chopped onion
2	cloves garlic, minced
2	teaspoons curry powder
½	teaspoon ground coriander
½	teaspoon salt
¼	teaspoon pepper

¼	teaspoon ground cumin
¼	teaspoon ground cinnamon
⅛	teaspoon ground cloves
2-2½	pounds chicken, cut in pieces
½	cup apricot brandy
½	cup chicken stock or broth
2	tablespoons lime juice
¼	cup ground almonds

1. In a small bowl, combine the apricots and hot water and let stand at least 1 hour.

2. In a large skillet, heat the oil and sauté the onion, garlic, curry powder, coriander, salt, pepper, cumin, cinnamon and cloves. Stir constantly until the onion is tender.

3. Add the chicken and brown on both sides. Stir in the apricot brandy, chicken stock and lime juice; spoon the mixture over the chicken. Cover and simmer 20 to 30 minutes or until chicken is tender. Remove the chicken to a warm serving platter.

4. Drain the apricots and discard the liquid. Add the apricots and ground almonds to the skillet and mix well. Simmer until the sauce is slightly thickened. Garnish the chicken with apricots. Spoon the almond sauce over chicken.

Roast Turkey

1. **Thaw the turkey in its original plastic wrap, either in the refrigerator or in the sink, covered entirely with cold water, according to the accompanying thawing chart, changing the water every ½ hour.**

2. **When ready to cook, remove the wrapping; remove the giblets and reserve for making broth. Wash the bird inside and out. Prepare the turkey stuffing and stuff the bird just before roasting, *never the night before*.**

3. **If stuffing is to be baked separately, season the inside of the turkey cavity with salt and pepper and add a chopped apple and chopped onion to the cavity. This will provide both moisture and flavor.**

4. **Tie the legs together with string and twist the wings behind its back "akimbo style," or tie close to the body with string.**

5. **Place the turkey in a shallow roasting pan and rub the bird lightly with oil. Insert a meat thermometer into the center of the thigh, next to the body, without touching bone. If cooking a stuffed turkey, a second thermometer should be placed in the center of the stuffing to ensure that the stuffing reaches 165°F.**

6. **Roast the turkey according to accompanying roasting timetable. After the bird has browned, cover with a loose tent of foil so the skin will not get too crisp.**

7. **When the turkey is done, the thigh thermometer should read 180° to 185°F. and the stuffing temperature should be 165°F. If no thermometer is available, the turkey is done when breast or thigh is pierced with a fork and the juices run clear instead of pink, and the leg twists easily.**

Approximate roasting times for stuffed turkey

Ready-to-cook	Approx. cooking time in 325° oven
6 to 8 pounds	3 to 3½ hours
8 to 12 pounds	3½ to 4½ hours
12 to 16 pounds	4½ to 5½ hours
16 to 20 pounds	5½ to 6½ hours
20 to 24 pounds	6½ to 7 hours

Unstuffed turkeys require about ½ to 1 hour less roasting time.
Note: Roasting time can only be approximate since conformation of turkey, accuracy of home ovens and degree to which turkey is thawed are all variable.

Mediterranean Turkey Breast

Serves 6 to 8

1	(4-6 pound) whole turkey breast
2	teaspoons salt
½	teaspoon pepper
2	cloves garlic, minced
½	cup olive oil
½	cup white-wine vinegar
2	medium tomatoes, chopped
2	medium green peppers, chopped
¼	cup chopped parsley
1	(2¼ ounce) can sliced ripe olives, drained

1. Rinse the turkey breast, drain and pat dry.

2. Mix the salt, pepper and garlic to a paste; rub thoroughly into turkey breast. Place turkey in a large, heavy-duty plastic cooking bag.

3. Combine the oil, vinegar, tomatoes, green peppers, parsley and olives and pour over the turkey breast. Close the bag securely and refrigerate several hours or overnight, turning occasionally.

4. Preheat oven to 325°.

5. Remove the turkey breast from the plastic bag, reserving marinade. Place turkey on a rack in a foil-lined roasting pan. Insert a meat thermometer into the thickest part of the turkey breast, making certain it does not touch bone. Pour the reserved marinade and vegetables over the turkey breast.

6. Roast 2 to 2½ hours, or until the thermometer registers 185°F., basting frequently with marinade.

7. Remove from oven and allow to stand 20 minutes before carving. Serve the cooked marinade from roasting pan as a sauce for turkey.

Frozen-turkey thawing timetable

Weight	In refrigerator	In water
8 to 12 pounds	1 to 2 days	4 to 6 hours
12 to 16 pounds	2 to 3 days	6 to 9 hours
16 to 20 pounds	3 to 4 days	9 to 11 hours

Refrigerate, if not cooked immediately. Refreezing is not recommended.

Roast Turkey with Vegetable Medley

Serves 6 to 8

1	(3-6 pound) turkey hindquarter roast
3	cups cooked rice
2	cups lightly steamed vegetables (a selection of sugar-snap peas, sliced carrots, asparagus, broccoli or zucchini)
½	cup oil
⅓	cup red-wine vinegar
2	tablespoons sliced green onion
2	cloves garlic, minced
1	tablespoon Dijon mustard
1	teaspoon honey
½	teaspoon dried oregano, crushed
½	teaspoon dried basil, crushed
½	teaspoon dried tarragon, crushed
	Salt and freshly ground pepper

1. Preheat oven to 325°.
2. Place the turkey hindquarter roast on a rack in a shallow roasting pan. Insert a meat thermometer into the thickest part of the thigh. Roast for 1½ to 2½ hours, depending on the size of the roast or until the meat thermometer registers 185°F.
3. During the last half hour of roasting, cook the rice according to package directions and lightly steam the vegetables. Keep both warm.
4. Combine the oil, vinegar, green onion, garlic, mustard, honey, oregano, basil, tarragon, salt and pepper. Heat through.
5. Baste the turkey roast with some of the oil-vinegar mixture. Combine the rest of the oil-vinegar mixture with the rice and vegetables.
6. Arrange the vegetables and rice on a platter and top with the turkey roast to serve.

Sausage-Chestnut Stuffing

Enough for a 16-pound turkey

	Giblets from turkey and neck
12	ounces mild sausage

12	ounces hot sausage
1	large onion, chopped
2	cups sliced celery
12	cups fresh bread cubes
3	eggs, slightly beaten
½	teaspoon dried thyme, crushed
¾	teaspoon poultry seasoning
¾-1	teaspoon salt
¼	teaspoon pepper
1	pound fresh chestnuts, shelled and cooked

1. Simmer the giblets (except liver) and neck in salted water to cover until almost tender, about 1½ hours. Add the liver and cook another 20 minutes. Drain, reserving the broth for gravy. Dice the meat and set aside.

2. In a large Dutch oven, cook the sausage over medium heat, breaking it up with a fork until it is cooked and lightly brown. Using a slotted spoon, remove sausage to a bowl.

3. Pour off drippings from the Dutch oven, reserving ¼ cup. Sauté the onion and celery in the reserved drippings over medium-low heat, 10 to 15 minutes or until tender, stirring occasionally.

4. Preheat oven to 325°.

5. Remove the Dutch oven from heat. Add reserved giblet meat and sausage, mixing well. Toss in the bread cubes. Add the beaten eggs and seasonings, blending gently but thoroughly. Mix in coarsely crumbled chestnuts.

6. Place the dressing in a buttered 2-quart casserole and bake for 1 hour and 15 minutes or use it to stuff a turkey.

Double Corn Dressing

Enough for a 12- to 14-pound turkey

6	cups corn bread (see index), cooled and crumbled
6	cups day-old bread cubes
1	large onion, chopped
2	cloves garlic, minced
½	cup butter
1	teaspoon dried basil, crushed
1	teaspoon dried thyme, crushed
½-¾	teaspoon salt
1	(12 ounce) can Mexican-style corn
	Chicken stock or broth
2	eggs, beaten

1. Preheat oven to 325°.
2. Combine the crumbled corn bread with bread cubes in a large bowl.
3. Sauté the onion and garlic in butter in a medium skillet. Add the basil, thyme and salt. Pour over the bread, tossing to mix well.
4. Drain the corn, reserving liquid, and add the corn to the bread mixture. Add enough broth to the reserved corn liquid to make 2 cups. Add to the bread mixture with beaten eggs.
5. Place the dressing in a buttered 2-quart casserole and bake for 1 hour and 15 minutes or use it to stuff a turkey.

Corn Bread Stuffing

Enough for a 12- to 14-pound turkey

6	cups crumbled corn bread (see index)
6	cups day-old bread cubes
1	large onion, chopped
2	cups chopped celery
½	cup butter
2	teaspoons salt
1	tablespoon sage
3	cups turkey broth, from simmering giblets and neck in water
2	eggs

1. Preheat oven to 325°.
2. Combine the crumbled corn bread and bread cubes in a large mixing bowl.
3. Sauté the chopped onion and celery in butter. Add the salt, sage and turkey broth to bread mixture. Mix till bread is moistened throughout. Add the sautéed onions and eggs; mix thoroughly.
4. Place the dressing in a buttered 2-quart casserole and bake for 1 hour and 15 minutes or use it to stuff a turkey.

Oyster Stuffing
Enough for a 12- to 14-pound turkey

1	(1 pound) loaf white bread
2	cups finely chopped celery
2	cups finely chopped onion
¾	cup butter
	Turkey broth
3	(8-10 ounce) jars fresh oysters, drained and cut up (reserve liquid)
1	teaspoon lemon juice
¼	teaspoon nutmeg
¾-1	teaspoon poultry seasoning
¼	teaspoon salt
¼	teaspoon pepper

1. Dry the bread slices on a rack in a 250° oven for 1 to 1½ hours or leave slices out in the air overnight.
2. In a skillet, sauté the celery and onion in butter until tender.
3. Preheat oven to 325°.
4. Tear the bread into ½-inch pieces, making about 11 cups, and place in large mixing bowl. Add enough turkey broth to oyster liquid to make ½ cup. Sprinkle the oyster liquid-broth mixture over the bread, tossing lightly. Add the onion-celery mixture and oysters to bread; toss to mix well. Sprinkle with the lemon juice, nutmeg, poultry seasoning, salt and pepper. Mix thoroughly.
5. Place the dressing in a buttered 2-quart casserole and bake for 1 hour and 15 minutes or use it to stuff a turkey.

Uncle Alfred's Dressing

Enough for a 14- to 16-pound turkey

1	medium onion, chopped
2	stalks celery, chopped
¼	cup butter
8	cups crumbled corn bread (see index), aged a day
1	teaspoon dried rosemary, crushed
1	teaspoon sage
1¼	teaspoons salt
½	teaspoon pepper
¼	pound dried peaches, diced
¼	pound dried apricots, diced
¼	pound golden raisins
¼	pound dried figs, diced
¼	pound currants
⅛	pound shelled pine nuts
1½	cups fruity white wine or fruit juice

1. Preheat oven to 325°.

2. Sauté the onion and celery in butter in a skillet until tender-crisp. Put the onion-celery mixture into a large bowl and add the corn bread, rosemary, sage, salt and pepper and toss lightly. Add the dried fruit and nuts and mix gently. Moisten with the wine and toss. The mixture should be crumbly.

3. Place the dressing in a buttered 2-quart casserole and bake for 1 hour and 15 minutes or use it to stuff a turkey.

This is the favorite creation of Alf Collins.

Macadamia Nut Stuffing

Enough for a 12-pound turkey

8	cups bread cubes
½	cup butter
1	cup chopped onion
½	clove garlic, minced
½	cup chopped celery

½	cup chopped celery leaves
½	teaspoon powdered sage
½	teaspoon dried thyme, crushed
½	teaspoon crushed dried bay leaf
1½	teaspoons salt
½	teaspoon pepper
1	egg, beaten
1	tablespoon brandy or dry sherry
1	cup chopped macadamia nuts

1. Preheat oven to 325°.
2. Place the bread cubes in a large bowl.
3. Melt the butter in a skillet, then sauté the onions, garlic, celery and celery leaves until tender.
4. Add the sautéed vegetables to the bread cubes and toss. Add the sage, thyme, bay leaf, salt, pepper, beaten egg, brandy and nuts. Toss together lightly. If the stuffing seems very dry, moisten slightly with liquid (melted butter, milk, chicken stock or water).
5. Place the dressing in a buttered 2-quart casserole and bake for 1 hour and 15 minutes or use it to stuff a turkey.

Pasta & Grains

Since running for fitness spread across the country from Eugene, Ore., Seattle has made it a mass participation activity. There are far more fun runs, 10Ks and marathons in this area than food events.

Physical-fitness buffs, with their "carbo-loading" before races, have taught us that "carbohydrate" wasn't a bad word after all. That has brought about a delightful change in the American diet and made pasta a versatile culinary standby.

Pasta, which was often just the unadorned "starch" of the meat-starch-vegetable meal regimen, has blossomed into a star and is often the centerpiece of the meal.

Eaten hot or cold, pasta welcomes healthful additions of vegetables and meats and can be cooked quickly to ensure proper nutrition for the athlete's rigid training program or a busy family's erratic eat-and-run schedule.

Whether as a sort of edible plate for interesting new ingredients or as an absorbent mound to trap sauces, almost anything teams with pasta, pizza, rice and grains.

Among the recipes that combine the best of the Northwest harvest with pasta or a pizza dough are our Seafood Fettuccine, the colorful Northwest Summer Pasta or the Parmesan Pesto Pizza.

Rice and pasta also combine perfectly with spicy foods. Take, for example, the mix of curry and Yakima fruit in Rice with Curried Fruit or the blending of Italian sausages, garlic and herbs in the Lasagne with Italian Sausage.

◇

Northwest Summer Pasta

Serves 8 to 10

1	bunch broccoli
2	large carrots, sliced
3	scallopini squash, cut lengthwise in quarters then sliced crosswise
1	cup green beans, cut in small pieces
1	cup shelled peas
1¼	cups thinly sliced mushrooms
6	green onions, chopped
6	cloves garlic, minced
½	cup butter
1¾	cups halved cherry tomatoes or chopped regular tomatoes
½	cup chopped parsley
¼	cup chopped fresh basil or 2½ teaspoons dried basil, crushed
3	tablespoons chicken stock or broth
1	cup whipping cream
1	cup freshly grated parmesan cheese plus extra for serving
	Salt and pepper
1	pound very thin spaghetti, broken in half and cooked until just tender
	Chopped pecans or walnuts

1. Wash the broccoli and cut the flowerettes off the stalks. Use only the flowerettes for this recipe, reserving the stalks for other uses.

2. Cook the broccoli flowerettes, carrots, scallopini squash, green beans and peas separately in boiling salted water until just barely tender. Rinse in cold water immediately to stop cooking. It is best to have the vegetables crisp. Drain well. Place the vegetables in plastic bags and keep refrigerated until ready to use.

3. When ready to prepare the pasta, place the cooked vegetables in a bowl and allow to come to room temperature. In a skillet, sauté the mushrooms, green onions and garlic in 3 tablespoons of the butter until wilted. Add the tomatoes and cook about 1 minute more, stirring. Add them to the bowl of vegetables. Then add the parsley and basil and gently mix together.

4. In a very large Dutch oven or kettle, melt the remaining butter. Stir in the chicken stock and whipping cream. Add the cheese and salt and pepper to taste. Whisk the mixture until smooth, but do not let it boil. Add the vegetables and let them heat through. Add the hot cooked spaghetti and stir gently to mix.

5. Place on a large warmed platter and sprinkle with more parmesan

cheese. Sprinkle top with the pecans. Pass extra parmesan cheese at the table.

◇

Pasta e Fagioli
Serves 6 to 8

1¼	cups dried navy beans
4	cups water
½	cup plus 1 tablespoon oil
1	bay leaf
3-4	cloves garlic
3	carrots, diced
2	stalks celery, sliced
1	onion, chopped
1	teaspoon dried oregano, crushed
1	teaspoon dried basil, crushed
6-7	tomatoes, peeled and chopped
1	teaspoon salt
½	teaspoon pepper
2	cups uncooked macaroni
	Parmesan cheese

1. Wash and sort the beans. Combine the beans, water, 6 tablespoons oil, bay leaf and 2 to 3 whole, peeled garlic cloves. Bring to a boil and boil 2 minutes. Remove from heat, cover and let stand 1 hour.

2. Bring to a boil again and simmer 2 hours or until beans are tender. Drain and reserve liquid, discarding the bay leaf and garlic cloves.

3. Cook the carrots, celery and onion in remaining 3 tablespoons oil until the onion is soft. Mince the remaining garlic clove and add to the carrot-celery mixture. Add the oregano and basil and simmer 30 minutes. Add the tomatoes and cook another 10 minutes. Season with the salt and pepper.

4. Cook the macaroni separately, according to package directions, until just tender. Combine the beans, vegetables and drained macaroni along with 1½ cups bean liquid. Cover and simmer another 10 minutes. Serve hot, in warm bowls, topped with parmesan cheese.

Note: For a heartier meal, 1½ pounds of smoked, fully cooked bone-in ham could be added when cooking the beans. When beans are done, remove ham, cut meat from the bone, dice and return to bean mixture.

Paella

Serves 8

½	pound chorizo sausage, cut in ½-inch slices
3	tablespoons olive oil
1	medium onion, sliced
1	large clove garlic, minced
4	chicken drumsticks
4	chicken thighs
¼	teaspoon ground oregano
	Salt and pepper
¼	teaspoon saffron
2½-3	cups hot chicken stock
1½	cups uncooked rice
1	sweet red pepper, white membranes removed, seeded and thinly sliced
1	green pepper, white membranes removed, seeded and thinly sliced
¼	cup chopped parsley
3	tomatoes, peeled, seeded and diced
1	cup shelled peas
1	pound medium raw shrimp, shelled and deveined
12-18	clams in shells
	Lemon wedges
	Parsley

1. In a 4-quart pan, brown the sausage in 1 tablespoon olive oil. Remove sausage from pan and set aside.

2. Sauté the onion and garlic in hot drippings until golden over medium-high heat. Add more olive oil to the pan and cook the chicken pieces until lightly brown on all sides. Season with the oregano and salt and pepper to taste.

3. Mix the saffron in ½ cup hot stock and add to the pan. Add ½ cup more hot stock; cover and simmer the chicken 15 minutes.

4. Add the rice and 1 cup more stock to the pan. Bring to a boil; reduce heat and simmer 15 minutes. If necessary, add more stock.

5. Add the sausage, peppers, parsley, tomatoes, peas and shrimp, then put the clams on top. Cover and simmer 10 minutes more or until the shrimp and clams are cooked and liquid is absorbed by rice. Discard any unopened clams. Garnish with lemon wedges and parsley.

Fettuccine with Artichokes and Sausage

Serves 6

4	mild Italian sausages (about ¾ pound total), casings removed and meat crumbled
1	large onion, chopped
2	cloves garlic, minced
3	(9 ounce) packages frozen artichoke hearts, thawed and drained
½	cup dry white wine
1	cup chicken stock or broth
2	tablespoons whipping cream
¾	pound fettuccine
½	stick unsalted butter, melted
	Salt and pepper
⅓	cup freshly grated parmesan cheese
2	tablespoons minced fresh parsley

1. In a large skillet, sauté the sausage over moderately high heat until browned. Add the onion and garlic and cook the mixture over moderate heat, stirring until onion is golden.

2. Add the artichoke hearts, wine and broth. Bring the liquid to a boil and simmer the mixture, covered, for 5 to 6 minutes or until artichoke hearts are just tender.

3. Remove the artichoke-meat mixture from the skillet and keep warm.

4. Reduce the liquid in the skillet until thickened. Add the whipping cream and heat through.

5. Return the artichoke-meat mixture to the skillet and mix together well.

6. Meanwhile, cook the fettuccine in boiling salted water until it is firm to the bite. Drain and transfer to a heated large bowl.

7. Toss the fettuccine with melted butter, artichoke mixture and salt and pepper to taste. Sprinkle with the parmesan cheese and parsley.

Seafood Fettuccine

Serves 8 to 10

1	cup white wine
1	teaspoon salt
6	peppercorns
1	bay leaf
1	large onion, sliced
12	ounces fresh shrimp, cleaned, peeled and deveined
2	pounds fresh boneless cod fillets, cut into small pieces
2	tablespoons chopped parsley
1	cup whipping cream
2	cloves garlic, minced
1	pound fettuccine
¼	cup butter, melted
½	cup grated romano or parmesan cheese plus extra for serving

1. Combine the wine, salt, peppercorns and bay leaf in a large skillet. Add the sliced onion and simmer gently 5 minutes. Discard the onion, bay leaf and peppercorns.

2. Add the shrimp to the flavored wine and simmer until fully cooked. Remove and reserve the shrimp.

3. Place three-fourths of the cod in the wine and simmer 10 minutes. Remove the fish and reserve the poaching liquid.

4. In a blender or food processor, purée the remaining raw fish with 3 tablespoons of the wine poaching liquid. Place the puréed fish in a saucepan with the parsley, cream and garlic. Simmer over low heat, stirring often, just until mixture thickens slightly.

5. Meanwhile, cook the fettuccine according to package directions and drain. Toss the fettuccine with the puréed fish mixture, melted butter and cheese, adding additional poaching liquid as needed. Add the shrimp and fish pieces and toss lightly. Serve with additional cheese.

Lasagne with Italian Sausage

Serves 8 to 10

1	pound Italian sausage, removed from casings if link
1	clove garlic, minced

1	tablespoon dried basil, crushed
1	tablespoon dried oregano, crushed
1½	teaspoons salt
1	(16 ounce) can diced tomatoes in purée
2	(6 ounce) cans tomato paste
2	tomato-paste cans of water
12	ounces lasagne noodles
3	eggs
4½	cups ricotta or cream-style cottage cheese
¾	cup grated parmesan cheese
¼	cup finely chopped parsley
1	teaspoon salt
½	teaspoon pepper
1	pound mozzarella cheese, sliced very thin or grated

1. Brown the sausage slowly; spoon off excess fat.
2. Add the garlic, basil, oregano, salt, tomatoes, tomato paste and water. Simmer, uncovered, 30 minutes, stirring occasionally and adding more water if necessary.
3. Cook the noodles according to package directions. Drain and rinse.
4. Preheat oven to 375°.
5. Beat the eggs; add the ricotta cheese, parmesan cheese, chopped parsley, salt and pepper.
6. Arrange successive layers of noodles, ricotta cheese mixture, mozzarella cheese and meat sauce in a greased 9-by-13-inch pan. End with a layer of mozzarella cheese. Cover with foil and bake for 30 minutes. Remove cover and bake 30 minutes longer. Let set 10 minutes before serving.

Pasta with Veal Filling

Serves 6 to 8

1	cup chopped onion
1	clove garlic, minced
2	tablespoons olive oil
1	(16 ounce) can diced tomatoes in purée
1	(16 ounce) can tomatoes, cut up
½	teaspoon dried thyme, crushed
½	teaspoon dried basil, crushed
½	teaspoon dried oregano, crushed
1	teaspoon Worcestershire sauce
1	pound ground veal
¼	cup milk
1	egg, slightly beaten
1	teaspoon salt
¼	teaspoon black pepper
6	ounces manicotti

1. Sauté ½ cup onion and the garlic in oil. Add the diced tomatoes, cut up tomatoes, thyme, basil, oregano and Worcestershire sauce. Bring to a boil. Reduce heat and simmer for 30 minutes.

2. Preheat oven to 375°.

3. Combine the veal, milk, egg, remaining ½ cup onion, salt and pepper. Mix well. Stuff the uncooked manicotti shells with the veal mixture.

4. Pour half the tomato sauce into an oblong baking dish. Arrange the shells in the dish. Pour remaining sauce over top. Cover and bake for 60 minutes.

Spinach Pasta Alfredo

Serves 8

¾	cup butter
2½	cups whipping cream
2	pounds fresh spinach pasta or 1 pound dried spinach pasta
4	cups parmesan cheese
	Salt and pepper
	Freshly grated nutmeg

1. Melt the butter in a large frying pan over high heat until lightly browned. Add 1 cup whipping cream and boil rapidly until large shiny bubbles form; stir occasionally.

2. Cook the pasta in plenty of boiling salted water, 1 or 2 minutes for fresh and according to package directions for dried. Drain pasta well.

3. Add the pasta to the sauce in the skillet and toss well with 2 forks. Add 2 cups of the cheese and remaining cream, a little at a time, in about 3 additions. The noodles should be kept moist, but not too liquid.

4. Season with salt, pepper and grated nutmeg to taste. Serve immediately with the remaining 2 cups of cheese on the side to sprinkle on individual servings.

Capellini Primavera
Serves 8 to 10

½	cup shelled peas
2	cups broccoli flowerettes
2	cups cauliflower flowerettes
½	cup zucchini, sliced
¾	cup asparagus, sliced in 1-inch lengths
1	cup sliced raw mushrooms
1	carrot, finely julienned
¼	cup pine nuts
2	tablespoons clarified butter
1	(10 ounce) package capellini (very fine soup noodles)
1½	cups whipping cream
	Parmesan cheese
	Salt and pepper
6	cherry tomatoes, halved

1. Blanch the peas, broccoli, cauliflower, zucchini, asparagus, mushrooms and carrots separately and set aside. Sauté the pine nuts in clarified butter, until the nuts are golden brown.

2. Meanwhile, cook the pasta in 4 quarts of boiling water until firm to the bite. Drain pasta quickly in a colander and rinse with very cold water, making sure all excess starch is removed.

3. In a large kettle, combine the pasta, vegetables, pine nuts, cream, cheese, and salt and pepper to taste. Add the tomatoes and toss. Serve.

Almond Linguine

Serves 4 to 6

¾	cup chopped onion
3	tablespoons butter
3	tablespoons vegetable oil
3	tablespoons flour
¾	teaspoon dried thyme, crushed
	Salt and pepper
2	cups beef stock or broth
¾	cup whipping cream
3	tablespoons Dijon mustard
½	pound cooked ham, cut into strips
¾	cup chopped parsley plus extra for garnish
¾	cup blanched slivered almonds, toasted, plus extra for garnish
½	pound linguine, cooked until firm to the bite
	Spinach leaves

1. In a skillet, sauté the onions in the butter and oil until limp. Blend in the flour, thyme, salt and pepper to taste; cook and stir over low heat until flour is well blended.

2. Gradually stir in the stock and cream and stir over medium heat until mixture thickens, about 5 minutes.

3. Stir in the mustard, ham, parsley and almonds. Toss the hot linguine with the sauce; serve on a bed of fresh spinach leaves. Garnish with additional chopped parsley and toasted slivered almonds. If serving for a buffet where people help themselves, you might wish to shred the spinach to make serving easier.

Parmesan Pesto Pizza

Makes one 15-inch pizza

Parmesan Crust:

	Butter
⅓	cup plus 2 tablespoons grated parmesan cheese
2⅔	cups flour
2½	teaspoons baking powder
1	teaspoon salt

¼	cup butter
5	tablespoons shortening
¾	cup milk

Filling:

2	cloves garlic, minced
¼	cup grated parmesan cheese
½	cup walnuts, crushed
2	teaspoons dried basil, crushed
¼	cup fresh parsley, chopped
½	teaspoon salt
¼	teaspoon pepper
2	tablespoons olive oil
6	medium tomatoes, thinly sliced and drained
¾	pound mushrooms, sliced
4	cups shredded fontina cheese

1. Preheat oven to 425°.
2. To prepare crust: Butter a 15-inch pizza pan and dust with 2 tablespoons grated parmesan cheese. In a large bowl, combine the flour, remaining ⅓ cup parmesan cheese, baking powder and salt. Use a pastry blender or 2 knives to cut the butter and shortening into the flour mixture. Gradually stir in the milk; beat by hand or with an electric mixer on low until mixture leaves the side of bowl. Knead the dough about 10 times in the bowl.
3. Turn the dough onto a lightly floured surface and roll out to fit a 15-inch pizza pan; transfer the dough to the pan. Crimp to make a slightly raised edge.
4. Bake 9 minutes, then cool 10 minutes on a wire rack.
5. To prepare filling: In a small bowl, combine the garlic, parmesan cheese, walnuts, basil, parsley, salt and pepper and set aside.
6. Spread the pre-baked crust with the olive oil. Spread half the tomatoes over the crust; add half the parmesan cheese mixture, half the mushrooms and half the fontina cheese. Repeat layering.
7. Return to the oven and bake 20 to 25 minutes or until crust is browned and filling is bubbling.

Vegetarian Pizza

Makes one 12- to 14-inch pizza

Crust:

1¼	cups flour
¾	cup enriched white corn meal
1	teaspoon baking powder
1	teaspoon salt
⅔	cup milk
¼	cup vegetable oil

Topping:

1	cup pizza sauce
1	medium onion, thinly sliced and separated into rings
1	medium zucchini, thinly sliced
1	medium green pepper, cut into thin rings
2	cups shredded mozzarella cheese
¼	cup grated parmesan cheese

1. Preheat oven to 425°.

2. To prepare crust: Combine the flour, corn meal, baking powder and salt in a mixing bowl. Add the milk and vegetable oil and stir with a large spoon until mixture forms a ball.

3. Turn out into a greased 12- to 14-inch round pizza pan and let stand 2 to 3 minutes. With the back of a large spoon, spread the dough into the pan, and flatten evenly. Shape the edge to form a rim. Bake about 15 minutes.

4. To prepare topping: Spread the pizza sauce over the partly baked crust. Top with onion, zucchini and green pepper. Sprinkle the mozzarella and parmesan on top. Return to the oven and bake for 20 minutes or until golden brown.

Hot Chili Pizza

Serves 6 to 8

1	tablespoon vegetable oil
1	cup chopped onion
1	clove garlic, minced

1	tablespoon plus 2 teaspoons chili powder
1	pound ground beef
1	(16 ounce) can cut up tomatoes, undrained
1¼	teaspoons salt
½	teaspoon celery seed
¼	teaspoon ground cumin
½	teaspoon Tabasco
	Favorite pizza crust to fit 12-by-15-inch jelly roll pan
1	avocado, peeled and sliced
1	red or Spanish onion, thinly sliced and separated into rings
1½-2	cups shredded Monterey jack cheese

1. Preheat oven to 450°.

2. In a large skillet, heat the oil, then sauté the onion, garlic and chili powder until the onion is soft. Add the ground beef; break up with a fork and cook until lightly browned. Drain off excess fat.

3. Add the tomatoes, salt, celery seed, cumin and Tabasco; simmer 5 minutes.

4. Pat, stretch or roll dough to fit a lightly greased 12-by-15-inch jelly roll pan. Spread the meat mixture over the dough. Bake for 10 minutes.

5. Remove from the oven. Arrange the avocado slices and onion rings over the top and sprinkle with cheese. Return to oven and bake 5 minutes longer or until crust is light brown and cheese is melted. Put under broiler to bubble and brown cheese lightly. Be careful not to overbrown crust.

Feijoada
Serves 8 to 10

1	pound dried black beans
	Water
4	slices bacon
1	pound beef stew meat, cut in 1-inch pieces
1	large onion, sliced
1½	pounds smoked ham hocks
1	tablespoon vegetable oil
4	cups chopped onion
4	cloves garlic, minced
1	fresh tomato, chopped
2	tablespoons chopped parsley
1	pound chorizo (Mexican sausage) or other smoked, garlic pork sausage
4	drops Tabasco
	Salt and pepper

Accompaniments:

	Hot cooked rice
4	oranges, peeled and sliced
4	bananas, halved and sautéed in butter
2	bunches spinach, washed, drained, steamed until wilted, then chopped

1. Sort over and wash the beans. Drain and place in a large bowl; cover with water and soak overnight. (For quick-soak method, place beans in a large saucepan and cover with 6 cups water. Heat to boiling; boil 2 minutes. Remove from heat. Cover and let stand 1 hour.)

2. Drain the beans, reserving soaking liquid, and set the beans aside. In a Dutch oven, sauté the bacon slices until crisp. Remove, crumble and set aside. Add the stew meat to the bacon drippings and brown well on all sides.

3. Stir in the sliced onion and sauté until soft. Add enough water to the reserved soaking liquid to make 4 cups. Then add the liquid, beans, ham hocks and bacon to Dutch oven; cover and simmer 2 hours.

4. Heat 1 tablespoon oil in a large skillet. Add the chopped onions, garlic, tomato and parsley and sauté 5 minutes, stirring occasionally. Remove 1 cup beans from the Dutch oven and add to the skillet, mashing them into the vegetable mixture. Stir the vegetables into the beans in the Dutch oven and simmer 30 minutes or until the beans are tender.

5. Meanwhile, cut the sausage into ½-inch slices. Sauté in a large skillet until browned, about 10 minutes. Drain and add to the beans and cook until heated through, about 5 minutes. Add the Tabasco and salt and pepper to taste. Transfer the beans to a large, warm, serving platter. Arrange accompaniments around beans.

Rice with Curried Fruit

Serves 6
½ cup chutney, finely chopped
2 cups melon balls (½ cantaloupe and ½ honeydew)
1 cup chunked fresh pineapple
1 banana, sliced
1 cup other fruit, such as peaches, pears, grapes, etc., cut in chunks
1 cup uncooked rice
2 cups chicken stock or broth
1 tablespoon cornstarch
1 tablespoon curry powder
½ cup slivered toasted almonds
¼ cup pistachio nuts, shelled and halved
¼ cup plumped raisins (cover with warm water and let stand a few hours, then drain)
Parsley, finely chopped

1. In a large bowl, combine the chutney, melon balls, pineapple, banana and other fruit. Cover and refrigerate until well chilled.

2. Prepare rice according the package directions.

3. Meanwhile, combine the chicken stock, cornstarch and curry powder in a saucepan and simmer until thickened. Add the nuts and raisins to the sauce, and heat through.

4. When ready to serve, place the hot rice on a heated platter and top with the chilled fruit, then cover the fruit and rice with the curry sauce. Sprinkle generously with chopped parsley.

Note: This dish is to be a contrast of flavors and textures. The rice should be piping-hot, the sauce should be at the boiling point, and the fruit chilled. Serve as a side dish with poultry, ham or pork.

Dirty Rice

Serves 8 to 10

3	cups water
½	teaspoon salt
2	teaspoons Worcestershire sauce
½	teaspoon red pepper
½	pound chicken gizzards
½	pound chicken livers
3	slices bacon, cut in small pieces
3	tablespoons bacon drippings, oil or butter
½	cup chopped celery
1	green pepper, finely chopped
1	bunch green onions, chopped
½	pound lean ground beef
1	pound hot bulk sausage
1	cup uncooked rice
	Chopped parsley

1. Combine the water, salt, Worcestershire sauce and pepper; bring to a boil and add the gizzards and livers. Cook about 30 minutes.

2. Remove the gizzards and livers, reserving the liquid; let the meat cool and then coarsely grind or finely mince it. Set aside.

3. In a large Dutch oven, sauté the bacon pieces until crisp. Drain on paper towels. Measure bacon drippings and add oil or butter to make 3 tablespoons. In the same Dutch oven, sauté the celery and green pepper until almost tender. Then add the green onions, and cook until tender.

4. In a separate skillet, brown the ground beef and sausage. Pour off the excess fat. Add the bacon, gizzards, livers and meats to the vegetables in the Dutch oven. Sauté slowly for 5 minutes.

5. Add 2 cups of the reserved liquid and simmer slowly for about 30 minutes. If it thickens too much, add a little more liquid. Turn off heat under the Dutch oven while cooking the rice.

6. Cook the rice according to package directions until tender and fluffy. When ready to serve, combine the rice with the meat mixture in the Dutch oven and heat through, about 10 minutes. To serve, heap on a warm platter and top with chopped parsley.

Rice with Vegetables
Serves 6

2	cups zucchini, cut in 1-inch strips
1	sweet red pepper, cut in 2-inch pieces
1	cup cut green beans
1	cup carrots, in julienne strips
1	cup cauliflower flowerettes
3	tablespoons olive oil
½	cup chopped onion
1	clove garlic, minced
1	(14½-16 ounce) can tomatoes
1½	cups chicken stock or broth
1	cup tomato sauce
½	teaspoon dried oregano, crushed
1	teaspoon Italian seasoning
½	teaspoon dried rosemary, crushed
½	teaspoon sugar
1	teaspoon salt
¼	teaspoon Tabasco
4½	cups hot, cooked rice
	Freshly ground black pepper
¾	cup grated parmesan cheese

1. Stir-fry the zucchini, pepper, green beans, carrots and cauliflower in 2 tablespoons olive oil until tender-crisp. Set aside.

2. In a 3-quart saucepan, cook the onion and garlic in remaining oil over medium-high heat until tender-crisp, about 3 minutes.

3. Add the tomatoes, stock, tomato sauce, oregano, Italian seasoning, rosemary, sugar, salt and Tabasco. Bring the mixture to a boil over high heat. Reduce heat to medium and cook 25 to 30 minutes, stirring occasionally.

4. Add the stir-fried vegetables and cook over low heat 10 minutes.

5. Serve over beds of fluffy rice. Top with freshly ground black pepper and parmesan cheese.

Vegetables

Vegetables are the color of cooking. Just seeing the vivid reds, oranges, greens, yellows and purples at their seasonal best sets up flavor associations with anticipation as vivid as the colors.

The seasons become a vibrant part of the Northwest cook's calendar, and the bounty comes steadily to market.

Where else can the shopper choose among Savoy, Napa or Cannonball cabbages to try in favorite recipes? Or to experiment with yellow Finns, purple Swedes or red new potatoes rather than the tried-and-true White Roses and Russets?

The appearance of fresh basil sets off a wave of pesto-making throughout the region that will make winter greener and more savory, and Skagit Valley cauliflower, Kent peas and Puyallup Valley salad greens keep avid followers among food buffs.

Whether grown in the back yard or picked by a farmer for sale at an open-air market, the first vegetables of the season dictate menus and generally overshadow whatever else is served with them.

As the seasons come to fullness and the novelty of each vegetable wears off, the cook's skill comes into play. Peak of the season means the lowest prices of the year, and a little ingenuity in the kitchen can add up to a lot of savings.

A sauce, a cheese, a seasoned butter can transform the simple, clear flavor of a fresh vegetable into something different. Vegetables baked or sautéed rather than steamed provide a chance to introduce seasonings. A mélange of vegetables chosen for complementary flavors can take on a complexity of its own.

Recipes in this chapter are designed to add variety and new dimensions to a vegetable repertoire. The subtle shadings of colors and flavors make these dishes as much a treat for the eye as for the palate.

Stuffed Artichokes Sicilian

Serves 4

4	medium artichokes
⅓	cup olive oil
1	medium onion, minced
1	clove garlic, minced
2	mild Italian sausages (about 6 ounces), casings removed
½	teaspoon dried rosemary, crushed
4	anchovies, chopped, or 2 teaspoons anchovy paste
1	tablespoon chopped capers
1	cup dry, coarse bread crumbs
½	cup grated romano cheese
1-1¼	cups chicken stock or broth

1. Cut off the stems from the artichokes evenly at the base to make them stand securely. Cut 1 inch off the top and trim remaining leaves with scissors.

2. Cut out the fuzzy choke and the prickly leaves around it with a melon baller or sharp spoon. This also may be done after the artichokes have been cooked.

3. Bring a large saucepan full of salted water to a boil. Add the artichokes, and weigh them down with a plate that just fits in the pan to keep them submerged in the water. Cook gently for 30 to 45 minutes or until bottoms are almost tender. Turn upside down to drain.

4. Prepare filling while artichokes are cooking. Heat ¼ cup olive oil in a skillet. Add the onion, garlic and sausages and sauté until the mixture begins to take on color, about 8 minutes. Add the rosemary, anchovies, capers, bread crumbs and half the cheese; stir to distribute ingredients evenly.

5. Preheat oven to 375°.

6. Stuff each artichoke center with filling and force any remaining filling between the outside leaves. Pour the stock in a baking pan just large enough to contain artichokes; place artichokes in pan. Sprinkle with remaining cheese and drizzle on remaining oil.

7. Cover tightly with aluminum foil and bake for 30 minutes. Serve immediately as an entrée.

Artichoke Hearts au Gratin

Serves 4

2	(9 ounce) packages frozen artichoke hearts
3	tablespoons butter
3	tablespoons flour
1	cup milk
½	cup half-and-half or whipping cream
½	cup grated Gruyère or Swiss cheese
	Salt and pepper
¼	cup dried bread crumbs
½	clove garlic, minced
	Butter

1. Cook the artichokes according to package directions. Drain artichokes well between layers of paper towels.

2. Preheat oven to 350°.

3. Melt the butter in a small saucepan and blend in the flour. Add the milk and cook over medium-low heat, stirring constantly, until sauce is thickened. Add the half-and-half or whipping cream, stirring constantly.

4. Add the Gruyère to the sauce a little at a time, stirring until cheese is melted. Season with salt and pepper to taste.

5. Place drained artichoke hearts in one layer in an oven-proof casserole. Pour the sauce over them evenly. Mix the bread crumbs with the minced garlic. Sprinkle on top of dish. Dot with butter. Bake for 20 minutes or until bubbly.

Artichokes Italiano

Serves 6

⅓	pound sausage, pepperoni, ham or prosciutto
6	tablespoons plus 1 teaspoon olive oil
1½	cups fresh bread crumbs
2	tablespoons chopped fresh parsley
2	cloves garlic, minced
3	eggs
¼	cup milk
	Salt and freshly ground pepper
6	large artichokes, cleaned, trimmed and prepared for stuffing
½	cup peeled, seeded, juiced and chopped tomatoes
4	cups water
2	whole cloves garlic, peeled

1. Cut the meat into small pieces or slices. Heat 1 teaspoon oil in a small skillet and cook the meat briefly, shaking the skillet and stirring. Drain and put in a mixing bowl. Add the bread crumbs, parsley and minced garlic. Toss well. Beat the eggs with the milk and 2 tablespoons olive oil. Add the egg mixture to the bread crumb mixture. Add salt and pepper to taste. Stir to blend.

2. Cut the stems from the artichokes evenly at the base to make them stand securely. Cut 1 inch off the top and trim remaining leaves with scissors. Cut out the fuzzy choke and prickly leaves around it with a sharp spoon.

3. Stuff the artichokes with the egg-bread crumb mixture, starting with the center of each artichoke, then stuffing between the leaves more or less at random, pushing the stuffing down.

4. Select a pan large enough to hold the artichokes snugly in one layer. Arrange them in the pan and spoon equal amounts of tomatoes on the top of each. Pour the water around the artichokes and add the whole garlic cloves to the water. Sprinkle the artichokes with the remaining ¼ cup of olive oil. Cover closely and bring to a boil. Reduce heat and simmer until the artichoke bottoms are tender, 45 to 60 minutes. To test for doneness, pull off an outside leaf; if it comes off easily, the artichokes are done.

Oven Asparagus Puff

Serves 4

¾-1	pound asparagus
4	tablespoons butter
3	tablespoons chopped green onions, including some green tops
½	teaspoon sugar
1	teaspoon salt
2	tablespoons water
6	eggs
⅓	cup whipping cream
	Freshly ground pepper
1½	cups grated Jarlsberg or Swiss cheese

1. Preheat oven to 425°.

2. Snap off and discard tough ends of the asparagus. Wash in cold water. Cut asparagus into 1-inch pieces. You should have 2 to 2½ cups.

3. Melt 2 tablespoons butter in a skillet and sauté the onion until soft and golden. Add the asparagus, sprinkle with sugar and ½ teaspoon salt, then toss for 1 minute. Add the water, cover and steam-cook for 1 to 2 minutes while shaking the pan. Remove the cover and cook until liquid has evaporated. Remove the asparagus from the pan and cool slightly.

4. Beat together the eggs, cream, ½ teaspoon salt and pepper to taste. Melt the remaining 2 tablespoons butter in a metal 10-by-10-inch baking dish or a large oven-proof skillet. Pour in the egg mixture and cook over medium heat until the bottom is set, about 3 minutes.

5. Arrange asparagus and onions in a single layer on top of the eggs. Bake for 5 minutes. Remove from oven, cover the asparagus with the grated cheese, then bake an additional 10 minutes. When the eggs have puffed and the cheese has lightly browned, it is ready to serve.

Asparagus Almondine

Serves 4

1½	pounds fresh asparagus
⅓	cup slivered almonds
6	tablespoons salad oil
¼	cup vinegar
¾	teaspoon dried tarragon, crushed
1	teaspoon sugar
¼	teaspoon salt
⅛	teaspoon pepper

1. Cut off the woody ends of the asparagus spears and wash carefully. Drop asparagus into a kettle with 2 or 3 inches of boiling salted water. Cover, return to a boil and cook gently about 5 minutes or until spears are tender-crisp. Drain and chill.

2. Sauté the almonds in 2 tablespoons salad oil in a skillet, stirring until roasted and golden brown in color.

3. Add the remaining salad oil, vinegar, tarragon, sugar, salt and pepper. Heat for 1 minute, then pour over the cold asparagus, turning asparagus to coat thoroughly.

4. Portion 3 to 6 spears onto each plate and "bundle" together by spooning a crosswise "strip" of almonds and a little additional dressing.

Asparagus with Sauce Nouvelle

Serves 4

1	pound fresh asparagus
¾	teaspoon salt
1	tablespoon vegetable oil
1	small onion, sliced
1	clove garlic, minced
2	tomatoes, peeled, seeded and chopped
¼	cup whipping cream
¼	cup chopped fresh parsley
¼	teaspoon dried basil, crushed
¼	teaspoon pepper

1. Break off each stalk of asparagus as far down as it snaps easily. Wash thoroughly, using a brush. Tie stalks of asparagus in a bundle with a string. Stand them upright in the bottom part of a double boiler. Sprinkle with ½ teaspoon salt. Add 1½ inches boiling water. Cover with top part of double boiler, inverted. Steam 10 to 15 minutes, depending upon the thickness of the stalks, or until just tender-crisp.

2. Meanwhile, in a small skillet, heat the oil and sauté the onion and garlic until tender. Add the tomatoes, whipping cream, parsley, basil, ¼ teaspoon salt and pepper. Bring to a boil. Simmer, uncovered, 5 minutes until sauce thickens slightly, stirring occasionally. Keep warm until ready to serve.

3. When the asparagus is cooked, lift it out of the pan by catching the string with tines of a fork. Drain. Cut the string. Arrange on a serving platter and pour warm sauce over center of the spears.

Bok Toy with Mushrooms

Serves 4 to 6

8	Chinese dried mushrooms
1	pound bok toy
2	tablespoons vegetable oil
1	teaspoon salt
½	cup sliced bamboo shoots
½	cup chicken stock or broth
1½	teaspoons cornstarch dissolved in 3 tablespoons chicken stock

1. Soak the mushrooms in hot water for 20 minutes. Cut off and discard the stems, then cut the mushrooms in quarters.

2. Wash the bok toy and cut the stalks and leaves into 1-inch pieces.

3. Heat the oil in a wok over high heat and add 1 teaspoon salt. Stir-fry the bok toy for about 1 minute. Add the mushrooms and bamboo-shoot slices. Mix well. Add ½ cup chicken stock and bring to a boil. Cover, turn to medium heat, and cook 4 to 5 minutes.

4. Remove cover and mix a few times. Stir the cornstarch mixture well and add to the wok. Stir well to thicken the sauce. Serve immediately.

Note: Do not remove the cover before the vegetables have simmered the full 4 to 5 minutes. The vegetables will turn yellow if the cover is removed and then put on again to cook.

Brussels Sprouts in Green Rice Ring

Serves 10 to 12

Rice Ring:

¾	cup minced spinach
½	cup minced green onions
¼	cup minced parsley
¼	cup butter
1¼	cups rice
2	cups chicken stock or broth
	Salt and white pepper
½	cup grated parmesan cheese

Brussels Sprouts:

1	pound brussels sprouts
3	tablespoons vegetable oil
3	cloves garlic, minced
1	tablespoon flour
1	teaspoon salt
¼	teaspoon nutmeg
1	cup whipping cream or half-and-half
1	(4 ounce) jar pimentos, drained

1. To prepare rice ring: Sauté the spinach, green onions and parsley in butter in a large saucepan for 3 to 4 minutes. Add the rice, chicken stock and salt and pepper to taste. Bring to a boil; reduce heat and cook, covered, until liquid is absorbed and rice is tender. Toss the parmesan cheese into rice.

2. While the rice is cooking, cut the brussels sprouts into quarters. Heat the oil in a large skillet. Add the garlic and cook 1 minute. Add the brussels sprouts; cook over medium heat, stirring frequently, until the brussels sprouts are tender-crisp, about 15 minutes.

3. Dissolve the flour, salt and nutmeg in the cream and stir into the skillet with brussels sprouts. Heat until sauce bubbles. Cook over medium heat, stirring constantly, until the mixture is thickened, about 5 minutes. Stir in the pimentos; heat through.

4. Spoon the hot rice into a 6-cup ring mold; let stand 2 to 3 minutes. Invert the ring onto a serving platter. Fill the center with the vegetable mixture.

Broccoli Soufflé

Serves 2 to 4

1	pound broccoli
	Butter
	Parmesan cheese
¼	cup butter
¼	cup flour
½	teaspoon salt
1	cup milk
4	eggs, separated
½	teaspoon cream of tartar
½	cup shredded Swiss cheese
1	teaspoon chicken flavor base

1. Wash the broccoli and separate it into flowerettes to make 1½ cups. Blanch them in boiling water, then drain and chop them finely.

2. Butter a 1½-quart soufflé dish or straight-sided casserole and dust with parmesan cheese. Add a collar, if necessary. Set aside.

3. In a medium saucepan over medium-high heat, melt ¼ cup butter. Blend in the flour and salt. Cook, stirring constantly, until mixture is smooth and bubbly.

4. Stir in the milk all at once. Cook and stir until mixture boils and is smooth and thickened. Set aside.

5. Preheat oven to 350°.

6. In a large mixing bowl, beat the egg whites with the cream of tartar at high speed until stiff but not dry.

7. Thoroughly blend the egg yolks, broccoli, cheese and chicken base into the reserved sauce.

8. Gently but thoroughly fold the yolk mixture into the whites. Carefully pour into the prepared soufflé dish or casserole.

9. Bake about 40 minutes until puffy and delicately browned. Carefully remove collar, if used. Serve immediately.

Cashew-Topped Broccoli

Serves 6

2	tablespoons butter
3	tablespoons minced fresh onion
1½	cups sour cream
2	teaspoons sugar
1	teaspoon white vinegar
½	teaspoon poppy seed
½	teaspoon paprika
½	teaspoon salt
	Dash cayenne
1½	pounds fresh broccoli
⅓	cup chopped cashews or toasted slivered almonds

1. Melt the butter in the top of a double boiler and sauté onion until golden. While the onion cooks, combine the sour cream, sugar, vinegar, poppy seed, paprika, salt and cayenne. Stir to mix well.

2. Remove the onion from heat and stir in the sour cream mixture. Keep the sauce warm over bottom of double boiler.

3. Wash, trim and cut the broccoli into serving pieces. Cook in a steamer until just tender-crisp.

4. When done, arrange broccoli on a warm serving platter and top with heated sauce. Sprinkle with the cashews or toasted almonds. Serve immediately.

Carrots à l'Orange

Serves 8 to 10

2	bunches carrots, peeled and cut into julienne strips
1½	cups orange juice
	Grated peel of 2 oranges
⅓	cup sugar or less
1	tablespoon butter
	Chopped parsley

1. Cook the carrots in a small amount of salted water until tender-crisp, about 7 to 8 minutes. Drain.

2. In a saucepan, combine the orange juice, peel, sugar to taste and butter, and bring to a boil.

3. Pour over hot carrots, garnish with chopped parsley and serve warm.

Sweet and Sour Cabbage

Serves 4

2	thin slices bacon, diced
1¼	cups thinly sliced red onion
1	teaspoon minced garlic
4	cups shredded red cabbage
1¼	cups chopped apple
½	cup apple cider or apple juice
3	tablespoons Italian herb red-wine vinegar
½	teaspoon salt
	Dash pepper
1	bay leaf

1. Put the bacon, onion and garlic into a large, heavy saucepan with a tight-fitting lid. Cover and cook about 10 minutes on medium heat until onion is tender.

2. Add the cabbage, apple, apple cider, vinegar, salt, pepper and bay leaf. Mix well, cover and cook about 20 minutes over low heat or until cabbage is tender.

3. Check once in a while and add more cider or water if the mixture seems dry, or if you want a moister dish.

4. Remove bay leaf and serve hot with a pork dinner.

Cauliflower Mousse with Mousseline Sauce

Serves 6

Mousse:

1	large cauliflower
1	pound potatoes
½	cup butter
4	eggs
	Salt and pepper

Mousseline Sauce:

¾	cup butter
3	egg yolks
1	tablespoon water
	Juice of 1 lemon
	Salt and pepper
½	cup whipping cream, whipped

1. To prepare mousse: Cut the cauliflower into flowerettes, discarding the center stalk, and wash in cold water.

2. In a large saucepan, bring 2 quarts water to a boil. Add the cauliflower and bring back to a boil over high heat. Lower the heat and simmer, uncovered, for 30 minutes.

3. Meanwhile, peel the potatoes and cook in salted water for 20 minutes or until soft. Purée through a sieve or food mill or process in a food processor until smooth.

4. Preheat oven to 450°.

5. Drain the cauliflower and run it under cold water. Return it to the saucepan with 6 tablespoons butter. Mash to a purée. Add the puréed potatoes. Add the eggs, 1 at a time, beating well. Season to taste with salt and pepper.

6. Butter a shallow glass dish. Spoon in the mousse. Dot the surface with the remaining 2 tablespoons butter. Place in a larger pan of hot water. Bake for 1 hour.

7. To prepare sauce: Place the butter in the top of a double boiler and place over barely simmering water to melt. Add the egg yolks, 1 at a time, mixing well. Add the water and lemon juice. Season with salt and pepper to taste and blend well. Cook, stirring constantly, until the sauce becomes thick and shiny. When the sauce has reached the consistency of mayonnaise, remove from heat and beat in the whipped cream. Serve with the mousse.

Baked Carrot Ring with Sour Cream Dill Sauce

Serves 8

Sour Cream Dill Sauce:

2	tablespoons butter
2	tablespoons flour
	White pepper
1	cup hot chicken stock or broth
½	teaspoon dill weed
¼	cup sour cream

Carrot Ring:

½	cup chopped onion
2	tablespoons butter
1	pound carrots, scraped and shredded
½	cup coarsely chopped celery
1½	cups soft bread crumbs
2	eggs, slightly beaten
1	cup milk
½	teaspoon dill weed
1½	teaspoons salt
	Pepper
	Buttered peas

1. Preheat oven to 325°.

2. To prepare sauce: In a saucepan, melt the butter until bubbly. Stir in the flour and pepper and cook, stirring constantly, 1 minute. Gradually add the hot stock, stirring constantly. Cook and stir until thickened and smooth. Remove from heat. Stir in the dill weed and sour cream until sauce is smooth.

3. To prepare carrot ring: Sauté the onion in butter until soft but not browned. In a large bowl, combine the cooked onion with the carrots, celery, bread crumbs, eggs, milk, dill weed, salt and pepper, stirring well to mix.

4. Turn the carrot mixture into a well-greased 4-cup ring mold. Bake 50 minutes or until a table knife inserted in the mold comes out clean.

5. Turn upside down onto a platter. Fill the center with buttered peas and serve with sour cream dill sauce.

Eggplant Lasagne

Serves 6 to 8

2	tablespoons olive oil
1	cup chopped onion
1	large green pepper, cut in slivers
2	cloves garlic, minced
4	cups peeled, diced and drained tomatoes
2	teaspoons dried oregano, crushed
1	tablespoon chopped fresh basil or 1 teaspoon dried basil, crushed
1	teaspoon salt
¼	teaspoon pepper
4	eggs
1	large eggplant, unpeeled, sliced ½-inch thick
⅔	cup seasoned dry bread crumbs
2	cups ricotta cheese
¼	cup grated parmesan cheese
8	ounces Monterey jack cheese, shredded or thinly sliced

1. In a large saucepan, heat the oil and sauté the onion, green pepper and garlic until tender. Stir in the tomatoes, oregano, basil, salt and pepper. Cover and simmer 35 to 40 minutes, stirring occasionally.

2. Preheat oven to 350°.

3. In a shallow dish, beat 2 eggs until foamy. Dip the eggplant slices in the eggs, then in bread crumbs. Arrange slices on a lightly oiled baking sheet. Bake 20 to 25 minutes or until tender. Remove and reset oven to 375°.

4. Spread about 1 cup of the tomato sauce in a 9-by-13-inch baking dish. Cover with half the eggplant slices.

5. In a small bowl, lightly beat the remaining 2 eggs; stir in the ricotta cheese. Spoon half the cheese mixture over the eggplant; sprinkle with 2 tablespoons parmesan cheese, half the jack cheese and 1 cup of the tomato sauce. Repeat layers, ending with jack cheese on top. Bake 30 to 35 minutes until hot and bubbly. Let stand 10 minutes before serving.

Stuffed Eggplant à la Grecque

Serves 4

2	medium eggplants
	Salt
½	cup vegetable oil
3	small tomatoes, peeled, chopped and drained
1	cup chopped onion
1	clove garlic, minced
¼	cup chopped parsley
¼	cup chopped green onions
1	cup cooked rice
1	(8 ounce) carton small-curd cottage cheese or feta cheese
	Pepper
½	teaspoon dried oregano, crushed
½	teaspoon dried thyme, crushed
¼	cup seasoned dry bread crumbs

1. Cut the eggplants in half lengthwise; remove the centers, leaving ½-inch thick shells. Dice the pulp.

2. Lightly salt the eggplant interiors and drain cut side down on paper towels for 30 minutes. Also lightly salt the diced pulp and allow to drain for 30 minutes.

3. Preheat oven to 350°.

4. In a large skillet, heat the oil and sauté the pulp until soft. Add the tomatoes, onion, garlic, parsley and green onions. Heat, stirring, until vegetables are tender, 5 minutes. Stir in the cooked rice, cheese and seasonings.

5. Stuff the eggplant shells with the mixture. Sprinkle tops with seasoned bread crumbs.

6. Place the stuffed shells in a shallow baking pan with just enough water to cover the bottom of the pan. Bake 45 to 50 minutes.

Note: The eggplants can be stuffed and refrigerated up to 24 hours before baking. Bring to room temperature before baking.

Eggplant with Miso Sauce

Serves 4 to 6

2	medium eggplants, washed
4	tablespoons vegetable oil
½	cup miso paste (paste from fermented cooked soy beans)
1	tablespoon shoyu (Japanese soy sauce)
1	tablespoon sugar
2	tablespoons mirin (sweet rice wine)
1	teaspoon freshly grated ginger

1. Cut the eggplants in half, then cut crosswise into ½-inch slices. Soak in water in a bowl for 10 minutes. Drain and pat dry between paper towels.
2. Brush the eggplant slices with vegetable oil. Broil until golden brown, about 20 minutes.
3. Mix the miso paste, shoyu, sugar, mirin and ginger in a small saucepan. Cook over low heat until thoroughly blended. Remove from heat and serve with the eggplant.

Belgian Endive au Gratin

Serves 6

12	heads Belgian endive
1	teaspoon salt
¼	cup butter
3	tablespoons flour
1⅓	cups milk
¼-½	cup whipping cream
¼	teaspoon white pepper
¼	cup grated Gruyère or Swiss cheese
6	tablespoons grated parmesan cheese

1. Wash the endive and place in a Dutch oven. Pour boiling water to a depth of 1 inch over the endive and add ½ teaspoon salt. Cover and cook until tender, about 20 minutes.
2. Drain the endive thoroughly by standing it in a strainer, then pressing it with toweling to remove all excess moisture. Arrange the endive

in a shallow greased baking dish. Preheat broiler.

3. Meanwhile, melt the butter in a saucepan, add the flour and stir with a wire whisk until blended. Bring the milk to a boil. Add all at once to the butter-flour mixture, stirring vigorously with the whisk until the sauce is thick and smooth. Remove from heat and thin out with the whipping cream, as desired. Season with ½ teaspoon salt and the pepper. Add the Gruyère cheese and half the parmesan; stir until the cheese has melted. Pour over the endive.

4. Sprinkle with the remaining parmesan cheese, adding more to taste so the endive is completely coated. Broil until the sauce is bubbly and lightly browned.

Green Beans with Macadamia-Lemon Butter

Serves 4

1	pound green beans
½	cup butter
½	cup coarsely chopped macadamia nuts
2	tablespoons lemon juice
	Salt and pepper

1. Wash and trim or snap ends from the green beans. Cook whole in a small amount of boiling salted water until tender-crisp, about 8 to 10 minutes.

2. Meanwhile, melt the butter until foamy. Add the nuts and stir until nicely browned. Add the lemon juice and season to taste with salt and pepper.

3. Pour sauce over the drained, cooked green beans and serve immediately.

Haricots Verts à la Lyonnaise

Serves 6

1½	pounds fresh green beans
¼	cup butter
1	medium onion, thinly sliced
½	teaspoon salt
	Dash pepper
¼	teaspoon nutmeg
1	teaspoon wine vinegar
1	tablespoon minced parsley

1. Snap the stems off each end of the green beans. Then wash and French cut them. Cook in boiling, salted water until just tender, about 15 minutes. Drain well.

2. Meanwhile, melt the butter in a skillet; add the onion and cook over medium heat until the onion is transparent and tender. Add the green beans, salt, pepper, nutmeg and vinegar. Cook, stirring for 5 minutes. Add the parsley, toss and serve immediately.

Sautéed Chanterelles

Serves 3 to 4

1	tablespoon oil
3	tablespoons unsalted butter
½	pound chanterelles, sliced
1	clove garlic, minced
3-4	tablespoons dry vermouth
	Chopped parsley

1. Heat the oil and butter over medium-high heat until sizzling. Add the chanterelles and garlic and sauté 1 to 2 minutes or until just cooked through. Do not overcook. Remove to a hot platter and keep warm.

2. Deglaze the pan by adding the vermouth to the remaining hot mushroom juices. Let reduce by about one-half.

3. Pour the reduced vermouth over the chanterelles and serve immediately, garnished with parsley if desired.

Ratatouille Provençale

Serves 6 to 8

2	medium eggplants
	Salt
2	green peppers
3	large zucchini
3	large tomatoes, peeled
5	tablespoons olive oil
2	onions, chopped
2	cloves garlic, peeled and minced
1	bay leaf
1	teaspoon dried thyme, crushed
	Pepper
¼	cup dry white wine
½	cup chopped fresh basil or parsley

1. Peel the eggplants and cut into 1-inch cubes. Place in a colander, sprinkle with salt and let stand 30 minutes. Blot the eggplant on paper towels, squeezing to remove extra water. Reserve.

2. Wash and seed the green peppers and cut into ½-inch strips. Wash and stem the zucchini and cut into ½-inch slices. Cut the tomatoes in eighths and squeeze gently to extract excess water and seeds.

3. Heat 2 tablespoons oil in a large Dutch oven over medium heat. Add the eggplant and sauté for 5 minutes. Remove to a large bowl.

4. Add 1 tablespoon oil to the Dutch oven. Add the pepper strips and sauté for 5 minutes. Put in the bowl with the eggplant.

5. Add 1 tablespoon oil to the Dutch oven and sauté the zucchini for 10 minutes. Remove to the bowl with the eggplant.

6. Add 1 tablespoon oil to Dutch oven and sauté the onions for a few minutes. Add the tomatoes, garlic, bay leaf and thyme. Cook for 15 minutes or until tomatoes and onions are soft and start forming a sauce.

7. Add all the vegetables to the sauce. Season with salt and pepper to taste and add the wine. Cover and simmer for 1 hour. Uncover and simmer 15 to 20 minutes to reduce juice.

8. Remove the bay leaf. Place the ratatouille in a serving bowl and sprinkle with chopped basil or parsley.

Jerusalem Artichokes à la Crème
Serves 4

6	medium Jerusalem artichokes
2	tablespoons sweet butter
	Salt
¾	cup whipping cream
	Freshly ground black pepper
2	tablespoons finely chopped parsley

1. Wash the artichokes.

2. In a large saucepan, bring salted water to a boil. Add the artichokes and cook, covered, over medium heat until tender when pierced with a fork. This takes about 25 minutes. Drain well, then peel with a vegetable peeler and slice.

3. In a large skillet, melt the butter. Add the artichokes and sauté for 2 minutes, constantly shaking the pan to coat the artichokes evenly with butter. Season with salt.

4. Add the whipping cream and continue cooking until the cream sauce reduces by half.

5. Sprinkle with black pepper and garnish with parsley. Serve immediately.

Mélange of Mushrooms
Serves 4

1	cup chicken stock or broth
⅓	cup dried wild mushrooms
5	tablespoons unsalted butter
3	cups sliced fresh chanterelles
1	cup sliced button mushrooms
3	green onions, white part only, minced
1	clove garlic, minced
	Salt and pepper
2	tablespoons zinfandel
2	tablespoons whipping cream
2	tablespoons minced parsley

1. Bring the chicken stock to a boil. Add the wild mushrooms and let soak for about 30 minutes. Slice if they're large; strain the broth and set aside.

2. Melt 3 tablespoons butter in a heavy saucepan over medium-high heat. Sauté the dried soaked mushrooms for about 1 minute, then add the chanterelles and cultivated mushrooms and continue to sauté about 1 minute more. Add the green onions and garlic and season with salt and pepper to taste.

3. Add the zinfandel and chicken stock and bring to a boil. Add 2 tablespoons butter and whipping cream. Remove from heat and adjust the seasonings. Serve immediately, garnished with parsley.

Note: The mushrooms can be served on slices of toasted French bread that have been rubbed with garlic.

Florentine Mushroom-Topped Potatoes

Serves 4

6	tablespoons butter, melted
2	tablespoons oil
1	pound mushrooms, sliced
1-2	cloves garlic, minced
2	pounds spinach, washed, drained, finely chopped and dried
2	cups whipping cream
	Salt and freshly ground pepper
	Nutmeg
4	large baked potatoes

1. Heat 3 tablespoons butter and oil in a large skillet until sizzling. Sauté the mushrooms until nicely browned. Remove from skillet and set aside.

2. Heat the remaining butter in the same skillet until brown. Add the garlic and spinach and sauté together.

3. Add the cream and let it reduce until slightly thickened. Add the mushrooms and heat through. Season to taste with the salt, pepper and nutmeg.

4. Serve immediately over the hot, slit baked potatoes.

Walla Walla Onion Pie in Caraway Pastry

Serves 6

Caraway Pastry:

1⅓	cups flour
½	teaspoon salt
½	cup shortening
1	tablespoon caraway seeds
3-4	tablespoons cold water

Filling:

4	cups sliced Walla Walla sweet onions
2½	tablespoons flour
1½	teaspoons salt
¼	teaspoon paprika
½	cup grated parmesan cheese
3	eggs, slightly beaten
1½	cups milk
4	slices bacon, diced and crisply cooked

1. Preheat oven to 400°.

2. To prepare pastry: Measure the flour and salt into a bowl, then cut in the shortening thoroughly. Add the caraway seeds. Sprinkle with the water 1 tablespoon at a time, mixing until all the flour is moistened and dough almost cleans the sides of the bowl.

3. Gather the dough into a ball; shape into a flattened round on a lightly floured cloth-covered board. Roll out the dough into a 12-inch circle. Fit pastry into a 10-inch pie pan. Trim overhanging pastry edge about 1 inch from rim of pan. Fold and roll the pastry under, even with the pan. Flute the edge.

4. Partly bake the crust, about 10 minutes.

5. To prepare filling: Cook the onions, covered, in a kettle over low heat until tender-crisp. Drain well to remove excess liquid. Line the partly baked pie shell with the onions.

6. In a mixing bowl, combine the flour, salt, paprika and parmesan cheese. Add the eggs and milk and mix well. Pour into the shell. Bake 35 to 40 minutes. If the edge of the pastry gets too brown, place a strip of foil over it. Garnish with crisp diced bacon. Serve warm or cold.

Walla Walla Sweets en Casserole

Serves 6 to 8

3	cups Walla Walla sweet onions, cut in ¾-inch wedges
2	tablespoons butter
2	tablespoons flour
1	cup chicken stock or broth
¼	cup half-and-half
½	teaspoon salt
¼	teaspoon pepper
1	tablespoon white wine
1	teaspoon Dijon mustard
1½	stalks celery, finely chopped
⅓	cup sliced almonds, toasted
½	cup fine dry unseasoned bread crumbs
⅓	cup grated cheddar cheese
	Chopped parsley

1. Preheat oven to 350°.

2. Parboil the onions in a small amount of water or steam until tender-crisp. Drain well, if needed.

3. Melt the butter in a saucepan, then blend in the flour. Add the chicken stock, half-and-half, salt, pepper, wine and Dijon mustard. Cook, stirring constantly until a smooth sauce forms.

4. Place onions in a buttered 8-by-8-inch baking dish or a 9-inch quiche pan. Combine the sauce with the celery and almonds. Pour the sauce over the onions.

5. Bake the onion dish in a pan of hot water for 35 to 45 minutes or until the onions are as tender as desired.

6. Combine the bread crumbs and cheese. Remove the onion dish and water from oven. Sprinkle the top with cheese-bread crumb mixture and place under the broiler to brown. Watch carefully so it doesn't burn. Sprinkle with parsley just before serving.

Potatoes and Prawns Normande
Serves 4

2	tablespoons oil
2	tablespoons butter
1	pound fresh medium prawns, shelled and deveined
1	green pepper, sliced in 2-by-¼-inch strips
1	red pepper, sliced in 2-by-¼-inch strips
2-3	tablespoons lemon juice
4	large baked potatoes
1	cup sour cream

1. Heat the oil and butter together in a large skillet. Sauté the prawns with all the pepper strips until the prawns are just cooked and the peppers are tender-crisp.
2. Sprinkle the lemon juice over the prawns and peppers and toss lightly.
3. Top each hot, slit baked potato with ¼ cup sour cream. Add the prawn-pepper mixture. Serve immediately.

Jansson's Temptation
Swedish Potatoes with Anchovies
Serves 6

2	yellow onions, sliced
3	tablespoons butter
4-5	medium potatoes
20	whole, flat anchovy fillets
1½	cups whipping cream

1. Preheat oven to 400°.
2. Sauté the sliced onions in 2 tablespoons butter until golden. Set aside.
3. Meanwhile, peel the potatoes and cut in julienne strips.
4. Butter a deep 9-inch round oven-to-table baking dish. Place half the potatoes in the bottom of the dish. Then top with all the onions and anchovy fillets. Cover with a layer of the remaining potatoes. Pour a little of the juice from the anchovy can over the top. Dot the top with the remaining 1 tablespoon butter.

5. Bake 10 minutes. Add half the cream. Return to oven and bake 10 minutes more. Add the remaining cream; reduce heat to 300° and bake 20 to 40 minutes longer, depending on size of potatoes. Serve immediately.

This recipe is from Marianne Forssblad.

Parmesan Potato Sticks

Serves 6

2	pounds russet potatoes
½	cup butter, melted
½	cup fine dry bread crumbs
½	cup grated parmesan cheese
½	teaspoon salt
⅛	teaspoon garlic powder
⅛	teaspoon pepper

1. Preheat oven to 400°.
2. Peel the potatoes and cut lengthwise into quarters. Cut each quarter into 3 strips. Roll the strips in melted butter, then in a mixture of the bread crumbs, cheese, salt, garlic powder and pepper.
3. Place the coated potatoes in a single layer in a shallow baking dish. Pour any remaining melted butter over the potatoes.
4. Bake 30 to 35 minutes, or until potatoes are tender. Turn half way through cooking time.

Sausage-Topped Sweet Potatoes
Serves 4

1	pound seasoned pork sausage
2	golden Delicious apples, peeled and diced
½	teaspoon freshly grated nutmeg
4	tablespoons butter
4	baked sweet potatoes or yams
2	tablespoons finely chopped green onions

1. Brown the sausage in a lightly oiled large skillet over medium heat for a couple of minutes. Add the apples and cook together until sausage is cooked through and apples are tender. Sprinkle with nutmeg.

2. Put 1 tablespoon of butter into each slit potato. Top each potato with the sausage-apple mixture.

3. Garnish with finely chopped green onions and serve immediately.

Gratin Savoyard
Serves 6 to 8

6	medium potatoes
	Salt and pepper
½	teaspoon ground nutmeg
¼	pound Gruyère cheese, grated
1	cup chicken stock or broth
1½	tablespoons butter

1. Preheat oven to 350°.

2. Peel and slice the potatoes very thinly into cold water. Drain thoroughly and dry between paper towels.

3. Butter a 2-quart baking dish generously. Layer the potatoes, salt, pepper, nutmeg and Gruyère cheese, reserving some cheese for the top layer. Pour the stock over all. Top with the reserved cheese and dot with butter.

4. Bake 1½ hours or until done and the top is golden.

Mediterranean Stuffed Peppers

Serves 8

4	large green peppers
1	pound lean ground beef
¼	pound bulk sausage
⅓	cup chopped onion
1	(16 ounce) can whole tomatoes, undrained
1	clove garlic, minced
1½	cups cooked rice
⅓	cup chopped walnuts
1	teaspoon dried basil, crushed
½	teaspoon dried oregano, crushed
½	teaspoon salt
¼	teaspoon ground cinnamon
⅓	cup dark seedless raisins
	Grated cheddar cheese

1. Wash the peppers, then cut them in half lengthwise to make boat shapes. Remove seeds. Drop the peppers in a large pot of boiling salted water for 3 minutes. Remove and drain.

2. In a large skillet, cook the beef and sausage just until pink color disappears; transfer to a large mixing bowl. Add the onion to the skillet and sauté 3 minutes, then add to mixing bowl also.

3. Add the tomatoes and garlic to the same skillet and simmer 10 minutes, breaking up the tomatoes.

4. Preheat oven to 350°.

5. Meanwhile, add the rice, walnuts, basil, oregano, salt and cinnamon to the meat mixture. Add ½ cup of the tomatoes and mix well. Stir in the raisins.

6. Spoon the mixture into the green pepper halves. Arrange the peppers in an oven-proof casserole. Spoon the remaining tomato sauce over peppers. Top each with 2 tablespoons grated cheddar cheese. Cover and bake 35 to 40 minutes or until peppers are tender.

Spinach Pie

Serves 12

3	pounds fresh spinach
1	onion, finely chopped
¼	cup butter
3	eggs
½	pound feta cheese, crumbled
¼	cup chopped parsley
1½	teaspoons dried dill weed
1	teaspoon salt
	Generous dash pepper
¾-1	cup clarified butter
16	sheets phyllo dough

1. Wash the spinach, then blanch in boiling water 1½ to 2 minutes. Drain, chop and squeeze dry.

2. Sauté the onion in ¼ cup butter until golden. Add the well-drained spinach and mix thoroughly.

3. Beat the eggs until foamy. Add the cheese, parsley, dill weed and spinach mixture. Season with salt and pepper.

4. Preheat oven to 350°.

5. Brush a 9-by-13-inch pan with clarified butter. Place 1 sheet of phyllo in the buttered pan, leaving the excess standing up on the sides of the pan. Brush the phyllo with butter.

6. Continue layering and brushing the dough until you have 8 sheets of dough in the pan. Try to work quickly so the dough doesn't dry out.

7. Spread the spinach mixture evenly on top of the phyllo layers.

8. Repeat the process by placing the last 8 sheets of phyllo the same as the first, brushing each sheet with melted butter.

9. When finished, take the excess dough on the edge of the pan and roll it all under, making an even roll around the edge of the pan.

10. Make slash marks on top of the dough in a diamond shape. Bake about 35 minutes or until puffy and golden.

Note: To make ahead, do not slash the dough. Just place foil over the top of the pan and cover with a damp towel. Refrigerate until ready to bake. Remove the towel and foil and make slash marks in the dough. Place in a preheated 350° oven and bake 50 minutes or until puffy and golden.

Italian Stuffed Tomatoes

Serves 4

4	large, firm tomatoes
	Salt and pepper
2	tablespoons butter
1	large onion, chopped
1	clove garlic, minced
½	pound mild Italian sausage, removed from casing and crumbled
¼	cup grated parmesan cheese
¼	cup chopped parsley, packed
½	cup crushed seasoned white-bread dressing mix
	Extra finely chopped parsley
	Extra parmesan cheese

1. Slice the tops from the tomatoes and cut the centers out, leaving about a ¼-inch shell. A grapefruit knife is good for this; otherwise, use a small paring knife. Season lightly with salt and pepper to taste. Reserve shells.

2. Discard the seeds and juice from the pulp removed from the centers. Chop the pulp and set aside.

3. Preheat oven to 350°.

4. In a skillet, heat the butter and sauté the onion, garlic and sausage until brown and crumbly. Stir in the tomato pulp and simmer for 10 to 15 minutes or until thickened.

5. Stir in the cheese, parsley and stuffing mix. Spoon the mixture into the reserved tomato shells.

6. Place the stuffed tomatoes in a greased shallow casserole. Bake 30 minutes or until lightly browned.

7. Sprinkle with additional parmesan cheese and finely chopped parsley, and serve.

Tomatoes filled with Orzo

Serves 8

¼	pound orzo pasta
8	medium tomatoes
	Salt and pepper
1	cup whipping cream
1	cup half-and-half
3	tablespoons fresh basil, chopped
½	teaspoon salt
⅛	teaspoon white pepper
	Freshly grated parmesan cheese

1. Cook the orzo in boiling salted water, according to package directions, until firm to the bite. Drain well.

2. Cut the tops off the tomatoes and scoop out the insides. (Reserve pulp for other use.) Season the insides of the shells with salt and pepper. Stand the tomatoes upside down on paper towels to drain.

3. Preheat oven to 350°.

4. Heat the whipping cream and half-and-half in a medium saucepan. Season with the basil, salt and white pepper. Add the drained orzo and simmer gently until all liquid is absorbed, about 15 minutes, stirring often to prevent sticking. Add more salt, if necessary.

5. Meanwhile, place the tomatoes in an ungreased, shallow baking dish and bake 5 minutes or until heated through.

6. Fill the shells with the orzo mixture and sprinkle tops with cheese. Return the tomatoes to the oven and bake 8 to 10 minutes more.

Deep-Fried Green Tomatoes

Serves 6 to 8

1	cup flour
2	tablespoons cornstarch
1	teaspoon salt
1	tablespoon baking powder
2	eggs
1	cup cold water
2	pounds green tomatoes, cut in thin slices or chunks

Salt and pepper
Seasoning salt
Oil for deep frying
Lemon wedges

1. Mix the flour, cornstarch, salt and baking powder together and sift into a bowl. Add the whole eggs and mix well to a smooth batter.

2. Add the cold water until it is a smooth batter that is quite thin. (It should be a little thicker than the consistency of whipping cream.) Season the tomatoes with salt, pepper and seasoning salt and add them to the batter.

3. Heat the oil in a heavy deep pan or in a deep-fat fryer to 375°. Using tongs, lower the tomatoes into the oil and fry to a light golden brown. Remove with a slotted spoon and drain on absorbent towels. Serve hot with a lemon wedge.

◇

Spaghetti Squash with Feta Cheese

Serves 8

1	medium spaghetti squash
1	(16 ounce) can stewed tomatoes, broken up
1	cup tomato sauce (see index)
1	tablespoon lemon juice
1	teaspoon dried mint, crushed
¼	teaspoon dried oregano, crushed
	Pinch cinnamon
	Pinch nutmeg
2	ounces feta cheese, crumbled

1. Preheat oven to 375°.

2. Cut the squash in half and scoop out the seeds. Place the squash halves cut side down on a nonstick baking pan. Bake 30 to 40 minutes, or until tender.

3. Meanwhile, combine the tomatoes, tomato sauce, lemon juice, mint, oregano, cinnamon and nutmeg in a saucepan. Cover and simmer 20 minutes.

4. When the squash is cooked, scoop strands from the shell and fluff with a fork. Top with the sauce and sprinkle with feta cheese.

Zucchini with Meatballs

Serves 8 to 10

2	pounds lean ground beef
	Salt and pepper
2	tablespoons salad oil
⅓	pound fresh mushrooms, sliced
2	ribs celery, thinly sliced
1	large onion, chopped
1	medium green pepper, seeded and diced
1	clove garlic, minced
3	medium zucchini, thinly sliced
1	(28 ounce) can whole tomatoes, broken up
2	tablespoons fresh lime juice
½	teaspoon dried basil, crushed
½	teaspoon ground cumin
1	teaspoon dried oregano, crushed
3	teaspoons cornstarch dissolved in ¼ cup cold water
	Hot cooked rice or pasta

1. Season the ground beef with salt and pepper. Shape into tiny meatballs, using 1 tablespoon meat for each. Brown quickly over high heat in the oil in a large skillet. Set aside.

2. Discard all but 2 tablespoons of the pan drippings. In the same skillet, sauté the mushrooms until browned. Set aside.

3. In the same skillet, sauté the celery, onion, green pepper and garlic, adding more oil if necessary. Cook over medium heat until onion is limp.

4. Add the zucchini, tomatoes and their liquid, lime juice, basil, cumin, oregano and salt and pepper to taste.

5. Add the meatballs and mushrooms and bring to a boil; reduce heat, cover and simmer for 5 minutes or until the zucchini is just tender. Do not overcook the zucchini.

6. Stir the cornstarch mixture into the sauce and cook until slightly thickened. Serve over hot rice or pasta.

Zucchini with Italian Sausage

Serves 8

4	small to medium zucchini
3	sweet Italian sausages, removed from casings
1	medium onion, diced
½	clove garlic, minced
2	medium tomatoes, peeled, seeded, chopped and drained
2	tablespoons chopped parsley
	Salt and pepper
⅓	cup grated parmesan or romano cheese
	Butter

1. Preheat oven to 350°.

2. Cut the zucchini in half lengthwise and spoon out most of the pulp, leaving a ¼-inch shell. Drain the pulp on paper towels.

3. Cook the sausage meat in a skillet until crumbled and brown. Pour off most of the fat. Add the onion and garlic and sauté a few minutes. Add the tomatoes, parsley, drained zucchini pulp and salt and pepper to taste.

4. Spoon the mixture into the zucchini shells. Top with the parmesan or romano cheese and dot generously with butter.

5. Place the zucchini in a baking dish and add about 1 inch of boiling water. Bake 30 minutes. If desired, brown the top under the broiler for a few minutes.

Salads

We North-westerners have taken a leap beyond lettuce and tomato salads. Not only are the fertile fields of the Puyallup Valley bringing us new greens such as bok toy, arugula and mustard greens, but experienced chefs also are working with gatherers far from intrusive pesticide sprays to use wild greens such as shephard's purse, ethnic specialities such as chrysanthemum leaves and flown-in exotics such as mache. This new arsenal of flavors is waking up our palates and demanding a new approach to salads.

What we used to think of as "just a salad" is being expanded to include meats, seafoods, potatoes, pasta and rice. It takes on new status as a main dish, and the time-honored parental call to "eat your greens" takes on a whole new meaning.

The new kind of salad fits the way we live — on the go and informally — and complements the array of ingredients that growers are bringing to market.

Serving several substantial salads— perhaps Soy-Anise-Chicken, New Potato and Pea, Wilted Romaine Hazelnut and Melon-Ginger—would yield a whole dinner menu which guests can proportion to their own tastes.

The recipes in this chapter should help bring exciting combinations of ingredients together and develop satisfying lunch or dinner entrées.

Salads also can be a low-cost solution to stretching a dinner or used as a showcase for something new from the produce section.

◇

Greek Vegetable Salad

Serves 8

Salad:

8	plum tomatoes, chopped
2	green peppers, diced
1	small red onion, diced
1	small unpeeled cucumber, diced
½	cup chopped fresh parsley
½	cup chopped Greek olives
¼	pound feta cheese, crumbled

Dressing:

¾	cup olive oil
3	tablespoons lemon juice
3	tablespoons wine vinegar
2	teaspoons Dijon mustard
1	large clove garlic, minced
	Salt and pepper

Garnish:

	Lettuce leaves
	Additional Greek olives

1. To prepare salad: Combine the tomatoes, green peppers, onion, cucumber, parsley, olives and feta cheese in a large serving bowl.

2. To prepare dressing: Combine the oil, lemon juice, vinegar, mustard, garlic and salt and pepper to taste in a blender and mix well.

3. Pour the dressing over the salad. Let the salad marinate for at least 30 minutes. Serve on lettuce leaves and garnish with olives.

Wilted Romaine Hazelnut Salad

Serves 6

6	slices bacon
1	medium head romaine
½	cup hazelnuts, finely chopped

¼	cup bacon drippings
⅓	cup cider vinegar
1	tablespoon sugar
1	tablespoon water
½	teaspoon salt
¼	teaspoon dry mustard
¼	teaspoon pepper

1. Cook the bacon until crisp. Reserve ¼ cup of the drippings for the dressing.

2. Toss the romaine, torn into bite-sized pieces, with the hazelnuts in a large salad bowl. Refrigerate until ready to serve.

3. Mix the bacon drippings, vinegar, sugar, water, salt, mustard and pepper. Cook until the mixture starts to boil, stirring to dissolve the sugar.

4. Pour the dressing over the salad greens and hazelnuts, tossing to coat. Crumble the bacon and sprinkle over the top. Serve immediately.

◇

Brussels Sprouts Vinaigrette
Serves 6

1½	pounds fresh brussels sprouts
1	cup oil
⅓	cup herb-flavored red-wine vinegar
1	teaspoon dried oregano, crushed
1	teaspoon salt
½	teaspoon dry mustard
2	cloves garlic, minced
2-3	tomatoes
	Fresh parsley, chopped

1. Trim and wash the brussels sprouts. Cook in boiling salted water until tender-crisp. Drain and put in a bowl.

2. Mix together the oil, vinegar, oregano, salt, mustard and garlic in a jar. Cover tightly and shake well. Pour over the sprouts. Chill 2 to 3 hours.

3. Drain, reserving the marinade. Place the sprouts in a serving dish. Cut the tomatoes into wedges and toss with the brussels sprouts. Garnish with parsley, if desired. The reserved marinade can be drizzled over the salad.

Wilted Spinach Salad

Serves 4 to 6

½	cup red-wine vinegar
1	teaspoon salt
1	tablespoon sugar
½	teaspoon dry mustard
1	teaspoon sweet-pickle relish
1	teaspoon finely chopped capers
1½	cups vegetable oil
1½	teaspoons olive oil
2	hard-cooked eggs
3	bunches spinach
¼	pound bacon, minced
½	onion, minced
¼	pound mushrooms, sliced

1. Blend together the vinegar, salt, sugar, mustard, pickle relish and capers. Stir in the vegetable and olive oils. Set aside. Finely chop the eggs, cover and set aside.

2. Clean the spinach, removing the tough stems. Drain the leaves well and place in a large bowl.

3. In a skillet, sauté the bacon until crisp. Remove the bacon from the drippings and sprinkle bacon over the spinach. Add the onion and mushrooms to drippings in skillet. Sauté until tender.

4. Stir in 1 cup of the reserved dressing. Bring to a boil. Pour over the spinach and toss. Garnish with the reserved chopped eggs and serve with additional dressing, if needed.

Mushroom-Spinach Salad

Serves 6

Salad:

1	bunch fresh spinach
½	pound mushrooms
½	medium purple onion
4	strips bacon

Dressing:

½	cup olive oil
2	tablespoons lemon juice
2	tablespoons white-wine vinegar
¼	teaspoon salt
⅛	teaspoon pepper
¼	teaspoon dry mustard
¼	teaspoon dried sweet basil, crushed
¼	teaspoon dried tarragon, crushed

1. Trim and thoroughly wash the spinach. Dry and break into bite-sized pieces. Chill in the refrigerator until just before the salad is served.

2. Clean and slice the mushrooms. Peel and thinly slice the purple onion.

3. Fry and crumble the bacon strips.

4. To prepare dressing: Combine the olive oil, lemon juice, wine vinegar, salt, pepper, dry mustard, sweet basil and tarragon in a blender jar and blend at low speed for about 5 seconds.

5. Pour the dressing into the bottom of a salad bowl, add the sliced onion and let marinate about 20 minutes.

6. Add the spinach, mushrooms and bacon just before serving. Toss gently and serve.

Caesar Salad

Serves 4 to 5

2	cloves garlic
¼	cup olive oil
2	cups bread cubes
3	quarts (pressed down) lettuce greens, ½ curly endive and ½ romaine
¼	cup grated parmesan cheese
¼	cup crumbled blue cheese
½	cup salad oil
1	tablespoon Worcestershire sauce
¾	teaspoon salt
¼	teaspoon freshly ground black pepper
1	egg
¼	cup fresh lemon juice
6	anchovy fillets, cut up

1. Slice the cloves of garlic into quarters and let stand in olive oil for 1 to several days.

2. Preheat oven to 225°.

3. To make croutons, sprinkle the oil over the bread cubes which have been spread on a baking sheet. Heat for a couple of hours, raising the heat to 300° if necessary to make them golden.

4. Wash the greens. Tear them into generous bite-size pieces in a wooden salad bowl. Sprinkle the cheeses on top. Combine the salad oil, Worcestershire, salt and pepper and drizzle over the salad greens. Toss gently until every leaf glistens.

5. Break the egg onto the greens; sprinkle on the lemon juice and toss again until all specks of egg disappear. Add the anchovies and croutons and give one last quick toss.

Asparagus-Walnut Salad

Serves 6

2	pounds fresh asparagus
¼	cup soy sauce
3	tablespoons white vinegar
2	tablespoons vegetable oil

1	tablespoon sugar
¼	teaspoon pepper
1½	tablespoons grated fresh ginger
1	clove garlic, minced
⅓	cup walnuts, chopped

1. Wash the asparagus. Snap off the tough ends. Cut into 1-inch pieces. Cook in salted boiling water until tender-crisp. Drain and chill.

2. In a large bowl, combine the soy sauce, vinegar, oil, sugar, pepper, ginger and garlic.

3. Add the asparagus and toss thoroughly. Cover and chill 1 to 2 hours. Sprinkle with the walnuts before serving.

Marinated Fresh Green Bean Salad

Serves 8 to 10

1	pound fresh green beans cut in 1-inch pieces, cooked and drained
1	(15½ ounce) can garbanzo beans, drained
1	(14 ounce) can white hominy, drained
¾	cup cider vinegar
½-¾	cup sugar
1	small white onion, thinly sliced
¼	cup diced green pepper
2	tablespoons chopped pimento
1	tablespoon soy sauce
1	teaspoon celery salt
½	teaspoon salt
½	teaspoon black pepper
2	tablespoons salad oil
2	tablespoons olive oil
	Salad greens

1. In a large shallow bowl, combine the green beans, garbanzo beans and hominy. Add the vinegar, sugar, onion, green pepper, chopped pimento, soy sauce, celery salt, salt and black pepper. Cover and marinate overnight in the refrigerator.

2. Just before serving, drain well. Toss with the oils and serve on salad greens.

Asparagus-Shrimp Vinaigrette Salad

Serves 6

1	hard-cooked egg
2	green onions, including tops, minced
1	tablespoon minced parsley
¼	teaspoon salt
⅛	teaspoon pepper
3	tablespoons rice-wine vinegar
3	tablespoons white-wine vinegar
¾	cup olive oil
½	pound small cooked shrimp
18-24	asparagus spears (at least 1 pound)
	Bibb lettuce leaves

1. In a bowl, mash the egg. Add the onions, parsley, salt, pepper, both vinegars and oil, then blend well. Add the shrimp; cover and chill until ready to use.

2. Snap off and discard the tough ends of the asparagus. Wash the spears in cold water. Lay the spears parallel in a large frying pan. Pour boiling water over them just to cover. Cook over high heat, uncovered, until stems are tender-crisp, about 6 to 8 minutes. Drain asparagus and immediately immerse in cold water; drain again. Cover and chill.

3. Just before serving, arrange several bibb lettuce leaves on each of 6 individual salad plates. Arrange an equal amount of asparagus spears on each lettuce-lined plate. Spoon some shrimp mixture over each serving.

Orzo-Seafood Salad

Serves 18-20

24	ounces orzo pasta
5	stalks celery and leaves from the heart, finely diced
1	(7 ounce) jar stuffed olives, sliced (save some whole for garnish)
2	(4½ ounce) cans chopped ripe olives
6	hard-cooked eggs (4 finely chopped, 2 cut into wedges)

3	whole crabs (pick from the shell and save larger whole leg meat for garnish) or 4½ cups crab meat
½	pound tiny shrimp
2	cups cooked salad dressing (see index)
¼	cup ketchup
3-4	tablespoons milk
¾	cup finely chopped sweet pickle
½	cup chopped pimento
	Salt and pepper
	Whole pitted ripe olives
	Parsley
1	tomato, cut in wedges
	Whole or sliced pimento

1. Cook the orzo according to package directions until done. Rinse with cold water and drain well. Place in a large bowl in the refrigerator.

2. In a small bowl, mix the celery, stuffed olives, chopped ripe olives and chopped eggs. Stir into the chilled orzo along with crab meat and shrimp.

3. In another bowl, mix the salad dressing, ketchup and enough milk to thin to proper consistency. Beat with a hand beater until very smooth and whipped.

4. Add the sweet pickle and chopped pimento. Mix the dressing into the salad. Season to taste with salt and pepper.

5. Mound the salad onto a large round platter and decorate the top of it with crab legs. Garnish around the edges with the egg wedges, whole ripe and stuffed olives, parsley sprigs and tomato wedges.

6. Cut thin strips of pimento and use them to decorate top of salad.

Vegetable Pasta Salad

Serves 4

	Grated peel of ½ orange
	Juice of 1 orange
3	tablespoons salad oil
1	teaspoon seasoned salt
¾	teaspoon dill weed
2	cups curly or spiral pasta, cooked and drained
2	oranges, peeled, seeded and segmented
2	cups broccoli flowerettes, parboiled just until tender-crisp
½	cup sliced celery
⅓	cup sliced green onions
	Pepper

1. In a large bowl, combine the orange peel, orange juice, oil, seasoned salt and dill.
2. Add the pasta, oranges, broccoli, celery, green onions and pepper to taste. Toss gently. Taste and correct the seasonings, adding more seasoned salt and pepper, if needed. Chill until ready to serve.

Spaghetti Squash Vinaigrette

Serves 6 to 8

⅓	cup vinegar
½	teaspoon sugar
1	teaspoon salt
	Dash cayenne
1	clove garlic, minced
½	cup oil
2	tablespoons finely chopped parsley
2	tablespoons finely chopped green onions
5	cups cooked spaghetti squash, separated into strands
1	small carrot, cut into fine julienne strips
½	green pepper, cut into fine julienne strips
2	hard-cooked eggs, chopped

1. In a cruet or screw-top jar, combine the vinegar, sugar, salt, cayenne, garlic, oil, parsley and green onion. Mix well by shaking vigorously.

2. In a medium bowl, place the squash, carrot and green pepper strips. Pour the dressing over the vegetables. Toss lightly and refrigerate until thoroughly chilled. Garnish with the chopped eggs before serving.

Swedish Mimosa Salad
Serves 6

1	head cauliflower
1	pound fresh asparagus spears
2	pounds fresh peas
1	apple
1	hard-cooked egg, yolk and white separated
½-¾	cup mayonnaise
	Whipping cream
	Curry powder
	Tomato wedges

1. Cook the whole cauliflower in boiling salted water until tender-crisp. Drain, cool and cut into flowerettes.

2. Snap off the tough ends of the asparagus. Wash. Cook the spears in boiling salted water until tender-crisp. Drain, cool and cut into 2-inch lengths.

3. Shell the peas, then cook in boiling salted water until tender-crisp. Drain and cool.

4. Dice the apple and egg white. Combine the cauliflower with the apples, egg white, asparagus and peas.

5. Mix the mayonnaise and cream until it is of the desired consistency. Season to taste with curry powder. Spoon the dressing over the salad to cover the top. Press the egg yolk through a sieve and sprinkle over the dressing. Garnish the salad with tomatoes around the edges. Mix the dressing into the salad at the table.

This recipe is from Marianne Forssblad.

French Potato Salad

Serves 6

Tarragon-Mustard Salad Dressing:

2	tablespoons white-wine vinegar
6	tablespoons olive oil
2	teaspoons Dijon mustard
½	teaspoon dried tarragon, crushed
½	teaspoon salt
¼	teaspoon freshly ground pepper

Salad:

6	medium boiling potatoes (about 1½ pounds)
¼	cup dry white wine
3	tablespoons chopped red onion
3	tablespoons chopped fresh parsley
2	medium tomatoes, cut in wedges
12	whole pitted black olives
2	hard-cooked eggs, quartered
6	cornichons

1. To prepare dressing: Combine the vinegar, oil, mustard, tarragon, salt and pepper in a small bowl or jar. Mix well, cover and refrigerate until ready to serve.

2. To prepare salad: In a medium saucepan, bring some salted water to a boil. Add the whole unpeeled potatoes and cook 15 to 20 minutes. Potatoes should be tender when pierced with a knife. Drain well and cool slightly.

3. Peel, quarter and slice the potatoes ¼-inch thick. Place the slices in a large bowl and pour the wine over them. Mix gently, then cool 10 minutes.

4. Pour the dressing over the potatoes and mix lightly. Gently stir in the onion. Sprinkle the salad with the parsley.

5. Serve chilled or at room temperature. Serve on a platter garnished with the tomato wedges, olives, eggs and cornichons.

New Potato-and-Pea Salad

Serves 6

Salad:

2	pounds very small new red-skinned potatoes (1½-2 inches in diameter)
1	cup fresh shelled peas
1	pound fresh asparagus
1	small red pepper cut in 2-inch strips

Dressing:

2	tablespoons red-wine vinegar
2	tablespoons rice-wine vinegar
1	heaping teaspoon Dijon mustard
1	teaspoon dried summer savory, crushed
	Salt and freshly ground pepper
¾	cup salad or olive oil

1. To prepare salad: Cook the whole, unpeeled potatoes in boiling water until tender, about 10 minutes. Drain and cut in half or quarters.

2. Blanch the fresh peas about 3 or 4 minutes until just tender-crisp.

3. Break off the tough ends of the asparagus, then cut asparagus into ¾-inch lengths. Blanch for about 5 minutes or until tender-crisp. Immediately, cool under cold running water to stop cooking.

4. To prepare dressing: Mix the vinegars, mustard, savory, salt and pepper to taste. Add the oil very slowly, beating well until dressing is smooth. Taste for seasonings.

5. Mix the warm vegetables and red pepper with the dressing and refrigerate until chilled but not cold.

Sugar Snap Pea Salad

Serves 6

Dressing:

1	clove garlic, cut in half
1	hard-cooked egg
¼	teaspoon dry mustard
⅛	teaspoon mild chili powder
½	teaspoon salt
2½	teaspoons sugar
¼	cup Italian herb-flavored red-wine vinegar
½	cup salad oil

Salad:

1	small Walla Walla sweet onion, sliced and divided into rings
½	large bunch young spinach
½	head crisp lettuce
1½-2	cups sugar snap peas, broken into pieces
½	cup diced salami
½	cup diced Danish havarti cheese

1. To prepare dressing: Rub a small bowl generously with the cut clove of garlic. Separate the egg yolk and white. Place the yolk in the garlic-rubbed bowl. Sliver or dice the white and reserve for salad.

2. Add the mustard, chili powder, salt and sugar to the yolk. Blend together with a fork. Whip in the vinegar and oil.

3. To prepare salad: Combine the onion, washed and torn spinach leaves and bite-sized chunks of lettuce in a large salad bowl. Add the sugar peas and egg white. Toss until all is well mixed.

4. Keep in the refrigerator until serving time. Just before serving, pour most of the dressing on the salad, tossing to mix well. Serve the remaining dressing at table.

5. Combine the salami and cheese in a small bowl and pass as a garnish for the salad.

Seasoned-Rice Salad

Serves 6 to 8

Lemon-Dill Dressing:

1	cup vegetable oil
⅔	cup lemon juice
1	tablespoon Dijon mustard
2½	teaspoons dried dill, crushed
2	cloves garlic, minced
½	teaspoon salt
½	teaspoon dried tarragon, crushed
¼	teaspoon paprika
¼	teaspoon pepper

Salad:

3	cups hot cooked rice
½	pound fresh mushrooms, sliced
3	medium fresh tomatoes, cut in wedges
6	slices bacon, cooked crisp and crumbled
⅓	cup sliced green onions
	Spinach leaves

1. To prepare dressing: Combine the oil, lemon juice, mustard, dill, garlic, salt, tarragon, paprika and pepper in a jar with a tight-fitting lid. Cover and shake well. Set aside.

2. To prepare salad: Toss the hot cooked rice with half of the dressing. Stir in the mushrooms and tomatoes. Cover and chill several hours or overnight.

3. Stir in the bacon and green onions.

4. Arrange the spinach on a serving plate and pour on the remaining dressing. Spoon the tomato-rice mixture onto the beds of spinach.

Ham Aspic

Serves 8 to 10

3	cups chopped cooked ham
⅔	cup chopped celery
⅔	cup chopped green pepper
⅔	cup chopped green onions
¼	cup chopped pimento
1	tablespoon minced parsley
1	tablespoon lemon juice
1	teaspoon salt
⅛	teaspoon white pepper
	Dash cayenne
2	envelopes unflavored gelatin
½	cup cold water
1	cup milk
1	cup chicken stock or broth
2	tablespoons white wine
2	teaspoons Dijon mustard
2	eggs yolks, beaten
½	cup whipping cream

1. Combine the ham, celery, green peppers, green onions, pimento, parsley, lemon juice, salt, pepper and cayenne. Set aside.

2. Soften the gelatin in ¼ cup cold water in the top of a double boiler. Add the remaining water, milk, chicken stock and wine. Place over hot water and cook until the gelatin is dissolved.

3. Add the mustard and egg yolks, stirring well. Cook and stir over boiling water for several minutes. Let cool to room temperature.

4. Combine the gelatin-mustard mixture with the meat-vegetable mixture; chill until it attains the consistency of unbeaten egg whites.

5. Whip the cream until stiff and fold into the gelatin mixture. Pour into a well-oiled 9- to 10-cup ring mold and refrigerate. Chill at least 3 hours or until firm.

6. Unmold by dipping the bottom of the mold into a pan of warm water for 20 to 30 seconds. Then cover with a serving plate and invert. Molded salad should slide out easily.

Note: The mold can be prepared a day ahead and kept refrigerated, covered with plastic wrap.

24-Hour Ham-Pasta Salad

Serves 6

1	cup salad macaroni, tiny shells or alphabet noodles
3	cups loosely packed shredded lettuce
	Salt and pepper
2	large hard-cooked eggs, sliced
1	cup cooked ham, cut in julienne strips
1	cup fresh peas, blanched 3 to 4 minutes in boiling water
⅔	cup shredded Swiss cheese
1	small tomato, chopped fine
½	cup mayonnaise
⅓	cup sour cream
3	green onions, chopped
1	teaspoon prepared mustard
	Dash Tabasco
	Paprika
	Chopped parsley

1. Cook the pasta in boiling salted water, according to package directions, until tender. Drain and rinse in cold water and drain again. Cool.

2. Place the lettuce in the bottom of a 2-quart casserole or 7-by-11-inch glass dish. Sprinkle with salt and pepper to taste.

3. Cover evenly with cooled pasta. Sprinkle the egg slices with salt to taste and layer on top of pasta. Top the egg layer with a layer of ham strips, then a layer of peas. Cover with cheese and top with the chopped tomatoes.

4. Combine the mayonnaise, sour cream, green onions, mustard and Tabasco. Spread this evenly over the top, covering the whole salad. Sprinkle with paprika and finally the chopped parsley.

5. Cover the dish and refrigerate overnight. To serve, use a large serving spoon, making sure to include all layers.

Seafood Pasta Salad

Serves 4

Fresh Basil-Dill Dressing:

1	egg
¼	cup wine vinegar
½	teaspoon salt
¼	teaspoon pepper
1	clove garlic, peeled and cut-up
½	teaspoon sugar
2	tablespoons fresh parsley leaves
2	tablespoons fresh dill weed or 2-3 teaspoons dried dill weed
6-8	fresh basil leaves, washed
1	cup salad oil

Salad:

1	cup combined fresh crab meat and tiny shrimp
½	pound spiral macaroni
¼	pound fresh snow peas, washed and blanched
1½	cups fresh broccoli flowerettes, chopped fine and blanched
1	cup cherry tomatoes, washed and halved
⅓	cup sliced water chestnuts

1. To prepare dressing: Place the egg, vinegar, salt, pepper, garlic, sugar, parsley, dill and basil in a blender container. Blend on high until smooth. With the motor running, add the oil in a pencil-thin stream until the mixture thickens. Once it thickens, the remaining oil may be added more rapidly. Set aside.

2. To prepare salad: Pick over the fresh crab for cartilage and rinse the shrimp.

3. Cook the macaroni according to package directions. When tender, drain well and mix while still warm with some of the basil-dill dressing and place in a bowl.

4. Add the vegetables to the macaroni along with the seafood. Toss to combine well. Add more dressing to moisten salad to taste.

5. Chill at least 1 hour before serving.

Chicken Pasta Salad Primavera

Serves 8

Oil and Vinegar Dressing:

¾	cup olive oil
¼	cup tarragon white-wine vinegar
1	teaspoon Dijon mustard
¾-1	teaspoon dried tarragon, crushed
	Salt and freshly ground pepper

Salad:

8	ounces pasta shells or macaroni, cooked and drained
2	cups cubed cooked chicken
⅓	cup mayonnaise
1	cup sliced fresh mushrooms
½	cup peas, cooked tender-crisp
1	green or red pepper, diced
¼	cup sliced green onions
2	tablespoons minced parsley
2	medium tomatoes, cut in wedges

1. To prepare dressing: In a jar with a tight-fitting lid, mix together the oil, vinegar, mustard, tarragon and salt and pepper to taste. Shake well to blend.

2. To prepare salad: Toss the hot pasta with the salad dressing. Cover and chill for 2 hours.

3. Combine the chicken and mayonnaise. Toss with the pasta, mushrooms, peas, pepper and onions. Turn into a serving bowl. Sprinkle with the parsley and garnish with tomato wedges.

Soy-Anise Chicken

Serves 4

Soy-Anise Dressing:

½	cup oil
⅓	cup rice vinegar
1	tablespoon soy sauce
1	tablespoon brown sugar
¼	teaspoon ground ginger
	Pinch anise seed, crushed

Salad:

1	head crisp lettuce
2	chicken breasts, boned and skinned
1	tablespoon flour
	Pinch paprika
1	tablespoon salad oil
½	cup pea pods, blanched for 30 seconds
½	cup sliced water chestnuts
½	cup sliced fresh mushrooms
½	cup halved cherry tomatoes
¼	cup alfalfa sprouts
2	tablespoons sliced green onion

1. To prepare dressing: In a jar, measure the oil, rice vinegar, soy sauce, brown sugar, ginger and anise seed. Cover tightly and shake well to blend. Set aside.

2. To prepare salad: Core, rinse and drain the lettuce. Chill in a disposable plastic bag or plastic crisper.

3. Cut the chicken into 1-inch strips. Dust with a mixture of flour and paprika. Heat the oil in a skillet, add the chicken and sauté until browned, stirring frequently.

4. Remove the chicken from the skillet and transfer to a bowl. Shake the dressing well and add ½ cup to the chicken. Marinate in the refrigerator 1 hour or longer.

5. Just before serving, add the pea pods, water chestnuts, mushrooms, tomatoes, alfalfa sprouts and green onion to the chicken.

6. Slice the lettuce crosswise into four 1-inch slices. Place each on an individual salad plate. Top the lettuce "rafts" with the chicken mixture and serve at once, passing remaining dressing.

West Coast Summer Salad

Serves 6 to 8

Chunky Avocado Dressing:

2	ripe avocados, peeled and seeded
4	tablespoons freshly squeezed lime or lemon juice
1	cup plain yogurt
2	teaspoons minced onion
½	teaspoon salt
½	teaspoon sugar

Salad:

1	pound fresh spinach
4	cups cooked chicken or ham, cut into thin strips (about 1½ pounds)
2	tomatoes, sliced
¼	pound mushrooms, sliced
1	cucumber, sliced

1. To prepare dressing: Cut 1 avocado into ½-inch chunks and toss with 2 tablespoons lime or lemon juice. Set aside.

2. In the container of an electric blender or food processor, combine the remaining avocado, 2 tablespoons lime or lemon juice, yogurt, onion, salt and sugar. Process on high speed until smooth. Spoon into a serving bowl. Stir in the avocado chunks.

3. To prepare salad: Wash, drain and remove stems from the spinach. Tear the leaves into bite-size pieces.

4. Arrange the spinach, chicken, tomatoes, mushrooms and cucumber slices on luncheon plates. Serve with chunky avocado dressing.

Mediterranean Beef Salad

Serves 6

3	pounds sirloin tip roast
6	tablespoons red-wine vinegar
1½	tablespoons Dijon mustard
1	tablespoon dried tarragon, crushed
	Salt and pepper
¾	cup olive oil
¾	cup salad oil
1	(9 ounce) package frozen artichoke hearts or ½ pound Belgian endive
1	head romaine lettuce
6	ounces goat cheese, crumbled
1	pint cherry tomatoes

1. Preheat oven to 425°.

2. Place the roast on a rack in a roasting pan. Place in the oven and reduce heat to 325°. Roast 20 minutes per pound or until thermometer registers 160°F. Cool and refrigerate overnight.

3. The next day, slice the beef into thin strips.

4. Put the vinegar, mustard, tarragon and salt and pepper in a large bowl. Slowly mix in the olive and salad oils until the mixture is smooth and well blended.

5. If using artichoke hearts, steam for 4 minutes, then cool. If using endive, wash, dry and cut in half crosswise. Wash the romaine, dry and cut the leaves in half lengthwise.

6. Marinate the meat and artichoke hearts or endive in ½ cup of the dressing in the refrigerator for 2 hours.

7. To serve, line a platter with the romaine. Arrange the marinated meat and artichokes or endive on salad greens. Sprinkle the goat cheese over the meat and vegetables. Garnish with the tomatoes. Drizzle the remaining dressing over all.

Scandinavian Salad

Serves 6

Salad:

	Meat from 2 cooked lobsters
24	mussels, steamed until shells open, then removed, discard any unopened mussels
½	pound cooked tiny shrimp
¼	pound fresh mushrooms
2	tomatoes
	Whole lettuce leaves

Vinaigrette:

2	tablespoons rice-wine vinegar
2	tablespoons wine vinegar
1	teaspoon Dijon mustard
¾	cup olive oil
	Salt and pepper

	Tomato wedges
	Hard-cooked egg wedges

1. To prepare salad: Cut the lobster meat into bite-size pieces. Leave the mussels and shrimp whole. Clean and slice the mushrooms. Cut the tomatoes in small pieces. Line the salad bowl with lettuce leaves. Refrigerate all salad ingredients until ready to serve.

2. To prepare vinaigrette: Combine the vinegars and mustard. Slowly add the olive oil and whisk until well mixed. Add salt and pepper to taste.

3. When ready to serve, toss the lobster meat, mussels, shrimp, mushrooms and tomatoes with the vinaigrette. Place into the lettuce-lined bowl. Garnish with tomato and egg wedges.

This recipe is from Marianne Forssblad.

Lobster Salad

Serves 6

2	chicken breasts, boned and skinned
1	tablespoon butter
2	tablespoons water
6	ounces sliced cooked ham, cut into julienne strips
2	tablespoons capers
3-4	cornichons or small pickles, cut into julienne strips
½	cup dry white wine
1	shallot, finely chopped
¼	cup sherry vinegar
1	tablespoon brown seedless mustard
1	clove garlic, minced
	Pinch dried tarragon, crushed
	Pinch dried chervil, crushed
¼	teaspoon dried chives
1½	tablespoons lemon juice
	Salt and freshly ground pepper
¾	cup olive oil
1	head romaine
½	head curly endive
½	head red-leaf lettuce
1¼	pounds cooked lobster meat, sliced
1	cup thinly sliced mushrooms
¼	cup chopped parsley

1. Lightly sauté the chicken breasts in the butter; add the water and simmer just until tender, 10 to 15 minutes. Remove from the pan, cool and slice into julienne strips.

2. Marinate the chicken, ham, capers and cornichons in white wine for 30 minutes, then drain.

3. In a bowl, combine the shallot, vinegar, mustard, garlic, tarragon, chervil, chives and lemon juice; season with salt and pepper to taste. Add the olive oil slowly in a steady stream, whisking until thoroughly blended.

4. Wash the lettuces, discarding the outer leaves, and gently pat dry. Tear into large pieces and place in a salad bowl. Add the drained, marinated chicken mixture and the lobster. Toss lightly with the herb dressing. Sprinkle with the sliced mushrooms and parsley.

Fresh Salmon Salad
Serves 6

1⅔	cups cooked flaked salmon
1	tablespoon vegetable oil
¼	cup plus 1 tablespoon cold water
2	teaspoons unflavored gelatin
¼	cup wine vinegar (tarragon-flavored if desired)
1½	teaspoons dry mustard
1	teaspoon sugar
1	teaspoon salt
2	egg yolks
2	tablespoons unsalted butter, cut into ¼-inch pieces
¾	cup milk

1. Be sure all bones are removed from the salmon flakes. With a pastry brush, spread the oil evenly over the bottom of six 4-ounce molds.

2. Pour ¼ cup water into a small bowl, sprinkle the gelatin on top and let soften.

3. Combine the wine vinegar, dry mustard, sugar and salt in a 1-quart enameled or stainless-steel saucepan. Stir until the dry ingredients are dissolved, then boil briskly to reduce the mixture to about 3 tablespoons. Remove from heat and add 1 tablespoon water.

4. Add the egg yolks, stirring constantly. Return to heat and cook over lowest heat, stirring with a wire whisk constantly for 1 minute, or until it thickens slightly. Do not let the mixture get too hot or it will curdle. Immediately remove the pan from the heat and whisk in the butter pieces.

5. In a separate small saucepan, heat the milk over moderate heat until bubbles begin to appear around the edges. Add the gelatin to the milk and stir until it dissolves completely.

6. Add the gelatin-milk mixture to the vinegar mixture, stirring with a whisk. Stir in the flaked salmon. Adjust seasonings.

7. Pour the mixture into the oiled molds, spreading it and smoothing the top with a spatula. Refrigerate at least 4 hours, or until firm.

Italian Sausage Salad
Serves 6

5	Italian-style sweet link sausages
½	pound elbow macaroni or twists
4	green peppers, peeled and cut into strips
1	red onion, thinly sliced
2	(15½ ounce) cans kidney beans, drained
2	cups chopped celery
3	hard-cooked eggs, quartered
1	carrot, finely chopped
3	tablespoons chopped parsley
⅔	cup olive oil
3	tablespoons white-wine vinegar
1	clove garlic, minced
½	teaspoon salt
	Freshly ground black pepper
	Pinch oregano

1. To cook the sausages, pierce the skins with a fork; put the sausages in a skillet with water to cover, bring to a boil, reduce heat, and poach for 1 minute.

2. Drain off the water, remove the skins, if desired, and slice the sausages into ½-inch lengths. Fry over medium heat in a dry skillet until browned.

3. Cook and drain the macaroni. Combine the sausage, peppers, onion, macaroni, kidney beans, celery, eggs, carrot and parsley in a bowl.

4. In a second bowl, combine the olive oil, vinegar, garlic, salt, pepper and oregano. Beat vigorously with a fork and pour the dressing over the salad, tossing gently to mix. Chill in the refrigerator a few hours to develop the flavors.

Honeydew Cups
Serves 4

2	small honeydew melons
1½	cups fully cooked ham or chicken, cut into julienne strips
2	large peaches, peeled, pitted and sliced

1	cup pitted dark sweet cherries
¼	cup chopped celery
½	cup peach yogurt

1. Cut the melons into halves. If you wish, make a zig-zag edge with a sharp knife. Remove the seeds.
2. In a large bowl, combine the ham, peaches, cherries and celery. Toss to mix. Spoon the fruit-ham mixture into the melon halves.
3. In a small bowl, stir the peach yogurt until smooth. Spoon the yogurt evenly over the fruit mixture. Serve a melon half on each of 4 individual plates.

Melon-Ginger Salad

Serves 4

1	cantaloupe
⅔	cup whipping cream
1	teaspoon lemon juice
3	tablespoons finely chopped sugar ginger or crystallized ginger
½	cup chopped, toasted almonds
	Pinch salt
	Pinch cayenne pepper

1. Cut the melon in half and remove the seeds. Peel and cut into cubes. Set aside.
2. Whisk the whipping cream with the lemon juice until it is thick but not stiff. Add the chopped ginger and most of the almonds. Season to taste with salt and cayenne pepper.
3. Pour the dressing over the melon and garnish with the remaining almonds.

Salad Dressings

Salad bars are perhaps the most visible aspect of our changing eating preferences. On the home-entertaining scene, a selection of salads has become the highlight, if not the entire menu, of many parties.

And with the appearance of more substantial ingredients, such as meats, seafoods and sharp, bitter, pungent greens to counterpoint more bland salad vegetables, salads have earned expanded attention in our dining.

Salad makers have more complexity to play with, and a whole range of dressings to bring it all together. They can choose from heavy, creamy versions that overcome contrasts, such as a Curry-Mustard Dressing, or they might prefer sharp vinaigrettes, perhaps a Northwestern specialty such as a raspberry dressing, that emphasize them.

But putting together greens and dressing doesn't need to be such a serious business. In most households, the traditional green salad still reigns supreme — and with it the same old dressings. The selection of dressings in this chapter should keep lettuce-and-tomato standards bright enough to make even the most finicky salad eater take a fresh look at what's on the plate.

◇

Cooked Salad Dressing

Makes 1¼ cups

2	tablespoons flour
1	tablespoon sugar
1	teaspoon dry mustard
1	teaspoon salt
	Dash cayenne
3	egg yolks
¾	cup milk
2	tablespoons butter
¼	cup vinegar
1	tablespoon lemon juice
2	tablespoons half-and-half

1. Mix together the flour, sugar, dry mustard, salt and cayenne.

2. Beat the egg yolks with ¼ cup milk and mix with the dry ingredients to make a smooth paste.

3. Put the mixture in the top of a double boiler, add the butter and stir constantly while adding the remaining ½ cup milk alternately with the vinegar and lemon juice. Cook over boiling water, stirring constantly until thick.

4. Remove from heat and let cool, then thin with the half-and-half until the desired consistency is reached.

Curry-Mustard Dressing

Makes about 1 cup

1	(8 ounce) carton low-fat plain yogurt
2	teaspoons Dijon mustard
⅛	teaspoon salt
¼	teaspoon freshly ground black pepper
¼	teaspoon curry powder

Mix the yogurt, mustard, salt, pepper and curry powder until well blended. Chill a few hours to blend. Serve over a combination of fresh spinach greens, diced avocados and mandarin oranges. Refrigerate unused portion.

Mustard-Egg Dressing
Makes ¾ cup

1	tablespoon Dijon mustard
2	tablespoons freshly squeezed lemon juice
2	tablespoons cider vinegar
¼	cup plus 2 tablespoons olive oil
¼	cup plus 2 tablespoons salad oil
1	hard-cooked egg, finely chopped
¼	cup loosely packed chopped parsley
	Salt and pepper

1. In a medium bowl, place the mustard, lemon juice, vinegar and olive and salad oils. Beat for 1 minute with a wire whisk.

2. Add the egg and parsley. Season to taste with salt and pepper. Store in a glass jar in the refrigerator and shake well before using. Use within 5 days.

French Mustard Dressing
Makes about 1¾ cups

¾	cup olive oil
½	cup red-wine vinegar
1½	teaspoons Dijon mustard
¼	teaspoon salt
½	teaspoon freshly ground black pepper
½	teaspoon sugar
1	clove garlic, minced
	Dash cayenne pepper
½	cup crumbled blue cheese

1. Combine the oil, vinegar, mustard, salt, pepper, sugar, garlic, cayenne pepper and blue cheese, and blend well. Cover and chill to allow flavors to blend.

2. Serve over tossed greens or combination salads. Refrigerate unused portion.

Basic Quick Mayonnaise

Makes 1 cup

1	large egg at room temperature
5	teaspoons lemon juice
1	teaspoon Dijon mustard
¼	teaspoon salt
¼	teaspoon white pepper
½	cup extra virgin olive oil
½	cup vegetable oil

1. Using a food processor fitted with the steel blade or a blender with the motor on high, blend the egg, lemon juice, mustard, salt and pepper.

2. Add the olive and vegetable oils in a slow stream and blend for 3½ minutes or until the mayonnaise is thickened.

Note: For a richer flavor, eliminate the vegetable oil and use 1 cup olive oil. Mayonnaise will keep up to 1 week in the refrigerator.

Lemon-Mustard Salad Dressing

Makes ⅔ cup

2	cloves garlic
½	teaspoon grated lemon peel
¼	teaspoon salt
1½	teaspoons Dijon mustard
1¾	tablespoons lemon juice
½	cup vegetable oil
	Freshly ground pepper

1. Place the garlic, lemon peel and salt in a blender container and whirl until it is a pasty mixture.

2. Add the mustard and lemon juice and whirl again to make a thick mixture.

3. Through the opening in the blender cover, add the oil very slowly, running blender on low until the mixture emulsifies. Add freshly ground black pepper to taste. (If the mixture separates, stir it together before serving.)

Shallot Dressing
Makes 4 to 5 cups

6	shallots, peeled
2	cloves garlic, peeled
2	teaspoons salt
1	teaspoon freshly ground black pepper
1	tablespoon sugar
1½	teaspoons Dijon mustard
1½	teaspoons water
¼	cup plus 2 tablespoons shallot vinegar
2	cups olive oil

1. Place the shallots, garlic, salt, pepper, sugar, mustard, water and vinegar in the container of a blender. Blend for about 1 minute.

2. Add the olive oil and blend well. This can be stored indefinitely in a jar in the refrigerator.

Poppy Seed Dressing
Makes 1⅔ cups

¾	cup sugar
1	teaspoon dry mustard
1	teaspoon salt
⅓	cup cider vinegar
1	tablespoon onion juice
1	cup salad oil
1½	tablespoons poppy seeds

1. In a medium bowl, combine the sugar, mustard, salt, vinegar and onion juice.

2. Using an electric mixer, gradually beat in the oil until the mixture is thick and smooth. Stir in the poppy seeds.

3. Store, covered, in the refrigerator. This dressing is good with any fruit salad, and on salad greens.

Sherry Wine Dressing

Makes 5½ to 6 cups

1	egg
2	teaspoons sugar
2½	teaspoons salt
2	cups olive oil
2	cups salad oil
½	cup vinegar
½	cup dry sherry
3	cloves garlic, peeled

1. In a very large bowl, beat the egg, sugar and salt together. Slowly add the oils and vinegar alternately, in small amounts, beating slowly until all is added. This forms an emulsion almost as thick as mayonnaise.

2. Slowly drip in the sherry while beating. This will thin the mixture to a consistency similar to whipping cream. Crush the garlic cloves and stir into the dressing.

3. Store in glass jars with tight lids in the refrigerator until needed. Use within 5 days.

Herb-Cheese Dressing

Makes about 2½ cups

½	cup mayonnaise
1	cup sour cream
2	teaspoons fresh lemon juice
¼	teaspoon dried tarragon, crushed
¼	cup minced parsley
2	tablespoons minced green onion
1	cup crumbled blue cheese

1. Combine the mayonnaise, sour cream, lemon juice, tarragon, parsley, green onion and blue cheese, and blend well. Cover and chill to allow flavors to blend.

2. Serve over tossed greens or combination salads. Refrigerate unused portion.

Raspberry Salad Dressing

Makes 1⅔ cups

¾	cup sugar
½	teaspoon salt
⅓	cup raspberry vinegar or white vinegar
½-1	teaspoon raspberry flavoring
1	cup salad oil

1. In the medium bowl of a mixer, combine the sugar, salt, vinegar and raspberry flavoring. Gradually beat in the salad oil until the dressing is thick and smooth.

2. Serve on tossed greens or fruit salads. Refrigerate unused portion.

Mint Dressing

Makes about 2 cups

1	cup mint leaves
2	green onions
1	egg plus 1 egg yolk
2	teaspoons Dijon mustard
2	tablespoons lemon juice
1¼	cups olive oil
½	teaspoon salt

1. Chop the mint and green onions in a food processor. Add the egg, egg yolk, mustard and lemon juice; blend well.

2. Slowly add the olive oil until a mayonnaise consistency is reached. Season with salt. This is particularly good on poultry salad.

Sauces

The Northwest is particularly well-suited to the growing of most herbs and fruits and to the production of dairy products. That gives us the basic ingredients for sauces and condiments that can make our dining rich and sophisticated.

Having the best ingredients doesn't guarantee success, but it does eliminate some risks. A sure sense of proportion and a great deal of imagination are needed to know where you are headed before combining the ingredients.

Most sauces and condiments in this chapter are masterly blends of strong or subtle flavors, but the key to success is skillful cooking.

The blend of ingredients must be subtle yet give the palate a hint of each distinctive flavor. Then it must add refinement to the accompanying food without taking over.

The effectiveness of a sauce is revealed by what it does for the delectable flavors of top-quality foods — fresh vegetables, meats and seafoods. A sauce used as a mask usually will unmask its creator.

After a sauce is mastered comes the best part of all — finding something to put it on. This is where culinary inhibitions have to be released. It was a truly imaginative cook who first used anchovy butter on a steak.

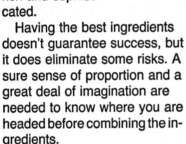

Rhubarb Chutney

Makes 2 to 3 pints

4	cups chopped rhubarb
2½	cups sliced onions
¾	cup raisins
3½	cups firmly packed light brown sugar
2	cups cider vinegar
1	tablespoon salt
1	teaspoon cinnamon
1	tablespoon grated fresh ginger
½	teaspoon ground cloves
1	tablespoon mustard seeds
	Dash cayenne pepper

1. Combine the rhubarb, onions, raisins, brown sugar, vinegar, salt, cinnamon, ginger, cloves, mustard seeds and cayenne pepper in a heavy Dutch oven. Bring to a boil and simmer gently until thick, 50 to 60 minutes. Stir often to prevent sticking.

2. Cool and pour into pint jars. Keep refrigerated and use within 2 months.

Gooseberry Chutney

Makes 1½ pints

3	cups fresh gooseberries
1	large onion, chopped
1½	cups firmly packed light brown sugar
¾	cup cider vinegar
¾	cup white-wine vinegar
½	cup raisins
1	teaspoon dry mustard
½	teaspoon ground ginger
½	teaspoon turmeric
½	teaspoon cayenne pepper
	Salt

1. Remove the stems and blossom ends from the gooseberries, and wash.
2. Working with small amounts, coarsely chop the gooseberries in a food processor or blender.
3. Combine the gooseberries with the onion, brown sugar, vinegar, raisins, dry mustard, ginger, turmeric, cayenne pepper and salt to taste in a large saucepan. Cook on medium heat for 2 hours or until thick and glossy.
4. Cool and pour into pint jars. Keep refrigerated and use within 2 months.

Anchovy Butter

Makes ¼ pound

1½	teaspoons anchovy paste
1	tablespoon lemon juice
2	teaspoons capers
1	clove garlic, minced
½	cup unsalted butter, cut into ½-inch slices and softened

1. Place the anchovy paste, lemon juice, capers and garlic in a food processor and whirl until almost smooth.
2. Add the butter bit by bit very quickly. Process just long enough to incorporate thoroughly.
3. Place the compound butter in a line on a sheet of parchment or wax paper and roll into a tube, twisting the ends to secure.
4. Chill in the refrigerator until firm, at least 45 minutes. It may be stored in the refrigerator up to 2 weeks. Serve on sautéed veal.

Mustard Butter

Makes ¼ pound

1½	tablespoons finely chopped parsley
2	teaspoons lemon juice
2½	tablespoons Dijon mustard
½	cup unsalted butter, cut into ½-inch slices and softened

1. Place the parsley, lemon juice and mustard in a food processor and whirl until well combined.
2. Add the butter bit by bit very quickly. Process just long enough to incorporate thoroughly.
3. Place the compound butter in a line on a sheet of parchment or wax paper and roll into a tube, twisting the ends to secure.
4. Chill in the refrigerator until firm, at least 45 minutes. It may be stored in the refrigerator up to 2 weeks. Serve on roasted lamb or broiled lamb chops or steaks.

Dill Butter

Makes ¼ pound

2	tablespoons finely chopped dill
1	teaspoon finely shredded lemon peel
2	teaspoons lemon juice
¼	teaspoon salt
	Pinch white pepper
½	cup unsalted butter, cut into ½-inch slices and softened

1. Place the dill, lemon peel and juice, salt and pepper in a food processor and whirl until well combined.
2. Add the butter bit by bit very quickly. Process just long enough to incorporate thoroughly.
3. Place the compound butter in a line on a sheet of parchment or wax paper and roll into a tube, twisting the ends to secure.
4. Chill in the refrigerator until firm, at least 45 minutes. It may be stored in the refrigerator up to 2 weeks. Serve on baked fish or vegetables.

Pesto Butter

Makes ¼ pound

2	tablespoons chopped fresh basil
1	tablespoon finely grated parmesan cheese
1	small clove garlic, minced
	Pinch salt
	Pinch white pepper
½	cup unsalted butter, cut into ½-inch slices and softened

1. Place the basil, parmesan cheese, garlic, salt and pepper in a food processor and whirl until well combined.
2. Add the butter bit by bit very quickly. Process just long enough to incorporate thoroughly.
3. Place the compound butter in a line on a sheet of parchment or wax paper and roll into a tube, twisting the ends to secure.
4. Chill in the refrigerator until firm, at least 45 minutes. It may be stored in the refrigerator up to 2 weeks. Serve on vegetables or baked fish.

Tarragon-Shallot Butter

Makes ¼ pound

2	tablespoons fresh tarragon
2	tablespoons coarsely chopped shallots
½	cup unsalted butter, cut into ½-inch slices and softened

1. Place the tarragon and shallots in a food processor and whirl until finely chopped.
2. Add the butter bit by bit very quickly. Process just long enough to incorporate thoroughly.
3. Place the compound butter in a line on a sheet of parchment or wax paper and roll into a tube, twisting the ends to secure.
4. Chill in the refrigerator until firm, at least 45 minutes. It may be stored in the refrigerator up to 2 weeks. Serve on broiled steak or baked fish.

Lime-Cilantro Butter

Makes ¼ pound

2	tablespoons chopped cilantro
½-1	teaspoon shredded lime peel
4	teaspoons lime juice
¼	teaspoon salt
	Pinch white pepper
½	cup unsalted butter, cut into ½-inch slices and softened

1. Place the cilantro, lime peel, lime juice, salt and pepper in a food processor and whirl until well combined.

2. Add the butter bit by bit very quickly. Process just long enough to incorporate thoroughly.

3. Place the compound butter in a line on a sheet of parchment or wax paper and roll into a tube, twisting the ends to secure.

4. Chill in the refrigerator until firm, at least 45 minutes. The roll may be stored in the refrigerator for up to 2 weeks. Serve on sautéed scallops or baked white fish.

Pesto

Makes 1½ cups

2	cups packed fresh basil leaves, washed and well drained
1	cup freshly grated parmesan cheese
2	cloves garlic, minced
2	tablespoons coarsely chopped pine nuts
½	cup olive oil

1. Put the basil, cheese, garlic and nuts in a food processor or blender and whirl together until smooth.

2. Add the oil to the mixture and continue to whirl until well combined. Pesto will keep in the refrigerator up to a week.

Note: To freeze: Pour pesto into double muffin-cup paper liners, allowing a generous ⅓ cup for each. Place pesto-filled paper cups on a tray and freeze until firm. Remove from tray and pack pesto-filled cups into plastic bags or freezer containers. Freeze up to 1 year.

Champagne Mustard

Makes 1⅓ pints

⅔	cup dry mustard
1	cup sugar
3	eggs
⅔	cup champagne vinegar

1. Mix the mustard and sugar well, in the top of a double boiler. Place over boiling water.
2. Add the eggs, one at a time, beating until well mixed and smooth.
3. Gradually add the vinegar, while continuing to beat and cook for 8 to 10 minutes until the mixture becomes thick.
4. Remove from the double boiler and pour into jars with tight-fitting lids. When cool, store in the refrigerator for up to 2 months.

Herb-Flavored Tartar Sauce

Makes 2¼ cups

4	gherkins, minced
3	shallots, minced
1	hard-cooked egg yolk, finely chopped
1	tablespoon minced capers
1	tablespoon minced parsley
1	tablespoon grated onion
1	tablespoon minced fresh tarragon or 1 teaspoon dried
1	tablespoon minced fresh chervil or 1 teaspoon dried
1	teaspoon Dijon mustard
1	teaspoon lemon juice
1	teaspoon sugar
1½	cups homemade mayonnaise (see index)
	Salt and white pepper

Fold the gherkins, shallots, egg yolk, capers, parsley, onion, tarragon, chervil, mustard, lemon juice and sugar into the mayonnaise. Season to taste with salt and pepper. Serve with seafood.

Cranberry-Pineapple Relish

Makes 8 to 9 cups

1	fresh pineapple
2	cups liquid (juice from pineapple and water)
2	cups sugar
1	(12 ounce) package cranberries
½	cup seedless raisins
	Grated peel of 1 orange
	Chopped pulp of 2 oranges
½	cup chopped almonds or walnuts

1. Cut the pineapple in fourths. Remove the flesh and cut it into chunks. Process in a food processor until crushed. Drain the juice and add enough water to it to measure 2 cups. Reserve. Measure 1½ cups crushed pineapple and set aside.

2. Combine the pineapple liquid with the sugar and heat until sugar is dissolved.

3. Add the cranberries, bring to a boil and cook 5 minutes. Add the crushed pineapple, raisins, orange peel and pulp; cook about 10 minutes or until thick. Add the nuts. Refrigerate 24 hours before serving.

Whole Cranberry Orange Sauce

Makes 3 cups

1	(12 ounce) package cranberries
1	cup orange juice
1	tablespoon grated orange peel
1⅓	cups sugar

1. Wash the cranberries and remove any stems still clinging to the berries. Drain.

2. In a large saucepan, mix the cranberries with the orange juice and peel and sugar. Blend well and let stand 5 minutes.

3. Cook over medium heat for 5 minutes, stirring once in a while. Remove from heat and let stand 5 minutes.

4. Return to medium heat and cook another 5 minutes, again stirring once in a while. Remove from heat and let stand 5 minutes.

5. Pour into a bowl and allow to cool. Cover and refrigerate overnight to allow juice to thicken.

Cranberries in Wine
Makes 4 cups

1½	cups sugar
¼	cup burgundy
	Grated peel of 1 orange
	Juice of 1 orange
4	cups cranberries
1	tablespoon currant jelly

1. In a saucepan, combine the sugar, wine, orange peel and orange juice; bring to a boil. Add the cranberries and simmer, shaking pan frequently, until the berries begin to burst.

2. Stir in the currant jelly and simmer the cranberries for a minute or so longer. Pour the mixture into a bowl and chill thoroughly. Serve with cold meats and poultry.

Crème Fraîche
Makes 2 cups

2	tablespoons buttermilk or sour cream
2	cups whipping cream

Add buttermilk or sour cream to the whipping cream. Mix and let sit at room temperature 6 to 8 hours. Cover and refrigerate at least 24 hours before using.

Note: It will keep a couple of weeks in the refrigerator.

Plum Sauce

Makes 2 cups

1	red bell pepper
1	pound plums, pitted and sliced
½	pound nectarines, pitted and sliced
1	cup cider vinegar
½	cup water
¼	cup sugar
½	cup firmly packed brown sugar
3	tablespoons light corn syrup
1	onion, chopped
2	cloves garlic, minced
1	tablespoon chopped fresh ginger
1	dried hot red pepper, seeded and crushed
½	cinnamon stick
½	teaspoon salt
½	teaspoon Szechuan peppercorns
2	teaspoons honey mustard

1. Cut the red pepper in half and place cut side down on a baking sheet. Broil the pepper until the skin blackens; remove the pepper halves to a plastic bag, close and set aside for 15 minutes. Remove the blackened skins from the pepper and chop the pepper.

2. Simmer the plums and nectarines with the vinegar and the water for 15 minutes. Add the red pepper, sugar, brown sugar, corn syrup, onion, garlic, ginger, hot red pepper, cinnamon stick, salt and peppercorns and simmer 15 minutes longer. Cool the mixture slightly; remove cinnamon stick. Purée in a food processor or blender. Stir in the mustard.

Note: This sauce is good served hot as an accompaniment to poultry or meats.

Raspberry Glaze for Poultry or Meat
Makes 1 cup

1 tablespoon chopped shallots
1 tablespoon butter
2 cups chicken stock (see index)
¾ cup seedless raspberry purée (about 3 cups of fresh berries)

1. Sauté the shallots in the butter until golden. Add the stock and reduce until syrupy.
2. Purée the raspberries in a food mill. Add the purée to the reduced stock and bring to a boil. The glaze is done when it coats a spoon. Serve over chicken, veal or other lightly flavored meat.

Note: Use fresh stock. Canned stock, when reduced, is salty.

Ginger Sauce for Fish
Makes about ¾ cup

1 green onion, thinly sliced
2 tablespoons chopped fresh ginger
¼ cup white wine
¼ cup clam juice
1 tablespoon rice-wine vinegar
1 clove garlic, minced
½ cup whipping cream
½ teaspoon soy sauce
6 tablespoons butter

1. Combine the green onion, ginger, white wine, clam juice, vinegar and garlic in a small saucepan. Bring to a boil and reduce the mixture to 2 tablespoons.
2. Add the cream and soy sauce and reduce by half. Add the butter, 1 tablespoon at a time, over medium-low heat, whisking until sauce has thickened. Serve over white fish.

Fresh Marinara Sauce

Makes 1½ to 2 quarts

6	pounds ripe tomatoes
⅓	cup olive oil
6	cloves garlic, minced
2	large onions, chopped
3-4	large carrots, finely chopped
2	tablespoons dried basil, crushed
1	tablespoon dried oregano, crushed
1½	teaspoons salt
¾	teaspoon pepper

1. Immerse the tomatoes, a few at a time, in boiling water for about 1 minute. Lift them out and immediately plunge them into cold water. Peel off and discard the skins. Coarsely chop the tomatoes to make 11 to 12 cups total.

2. Heat the oil in a 5-quart Dutch oven over medium heat. Cook the garlic, onions and carrots until soft, stirring occasionally.

3. Stir in the tomatoes, basil, oregano, salt and pepper. Bring to a boil. Reduce heat and simmer rapidly, uncovered, stirring occasionally for about 1½ hours or until the sauce is very thick and reduced by about half.

4. Cool quickly. Pour into freezer containers; cover, label and freeze for up to 4 months.

Savory Tomato Sauce

Makes 3½ cups

1	cup finely chopped celery, including leaves
1	large clove garlic, minced
2-3	carrots, finely minced
½	onion, finely minced
⅛	lemon, peel included, very finely chopped
1	small green pepper, finely chopped
½	cup finely chopped parsley
4	tablespoons butter
2	(16 ounce) cans diced tomatoes in purée

½	cup red wine
½	cup beef stock or broth
1	teaspoon sugar
½	teaspoon dried oregano, crushed
½	teaspoon dried basil, crushed
	Salt and pepper

1. Sauté the celery, garlic, carrots, onion, lemon, green pepper and parsley in butter over low heat until vegetables are soft but not brown.

2. Add the tomatoes, wine, beef stock, sugar, oregano, basil and salt and pepper to taste. Simmer, leaving cover partly ajar, 2 to 3 hours to allow flavors to develop and some of the liquid to evaporate. Stir often to prevent sticking. If the sauce becomes too thick, add a little more stock. The sauce will be rich and fairly thick. Taste and adjust seasonings.

3. Cool quickly. Pour into freezer containers; cover, label and freeze for up to 4 months

Barbecue Sauce
Makes 2 cups

2	tablespoons butter
1	onion, finely chopped
2	cloves garlic, minced
2	cups water
¼	teaspoon salt
1	teaspoon mild chili powder (or more to taste)
4	tablespoons firmly packed brown sugar
3	tablespoons vinegar
4	tablespoons Worcestershire sauce
1	cup ketchup
10	drops Tabasco

1. Melt the butter in a saucepan. Add the onion and garlic and sauté until the onion is soft.

2. Add the water, salt, chili powder, brown sugar, vinegar, Worcestershire sauce, ketchup and Tabasco, stirring until well mixed.

3. Simmer, uncovered, over low heat 30 minutes. The sauce will keep refrigerated for a week.

Desserts

We Americans find ourselves cutting back on fattening foods for dinner but sometimes rewarding ourselves with richer desserts. It's a contradiction that has puzzled more than one marketing expert, but, fortunately, Northwest fruit has a root in both camps.

Our pears, apples, berries and peaches provide a natural sweet for those who eat it straight, and a starting point for some rich, flavorful desserts. Perhaps, because we Northwesterners have such a wonderful stock of fresh fruits to work with, desserts such as the raspberry-jam-laced Linzer Torte, Gorgonzola Pears and Strawberry Sabayon have been consistent reader favorites over the years.

Fruit is the ideal ingredient for dessert. It brings most of its own sugar, a pleasant flavor and plenty of juices. The cook considering such a dessert has a choice of textures, degrees of acidities and methods of cooking, from baking to poaching.

Fruit-based desserts fit naturally into a well-coordinated menu, especially with the popularity of "new American" cooking and its emphasis on fruit-based sauces. The recipes in this chapter are not all Northwest and do reflect the national preoccupation with chocolate desserts, but our regional bent for baking shows itself in the list of cakes and tortes.

◇

Red Raspberry Soufflé

Serves 6

	Butter
	Sugar
4-5	**cups fresh raspberries**
¼	**cup water**
6	**eggs, separated**
¼	**teaspoon salt**
2	**envelopes unflavored gelatin**
¾	**teaspoon cream of tartar**
1½	**cups sugar**
1	**teaspoon vanilla**
1	**cup whipping cream, whipped**
	Mint leaves

1. Make a foil collar, then lightly butter one side and sprinkle with sugar. Wrap it around the outside of a 1½-quart soufflé dish with sugared side in. Fasten with tape or paper clips. The collar should extend 2 inches above the rim of the dish. Set aside.

2. Reserve 3 berries for garnish. Press the remaining berries through a sieve into a medium saucepan. Pour the water over the seeds and press again. Discard the seeds.

3. Stir the egg yolks and salt into the raspberry juice and pulp. Sprinkle with the gelatin and let stand 1 minute. Cook over medium heat, stirring until gelatin is dissolved, about 5 minutes.

4. Chill, stirring occasionally, until the mixture mounds slightly when dropped from a spoon.

5. In a large mixing bowl, beat the egg whites and cream of tartar at high speed until foamy. Add the sugar, 2 tablespoons at a time, beating constantly until sugar is dissolved and whites are glossy and stand in soft peaks. (Rub a bit of meringue between thumb and forefinger to feel whether the sugar has dissolved.) Beat in the vanilla.

6. Gently but thoroughly fold the chilled gelatin mixture and whipped cream into the egg whites. Carefully pour into the prepared dish. Chill until firm, several hours or overnight.

7. Just before serving, carefully remove the foil collar. Garnish with reserved berries and mint leaves, if desired.

Grand Marnier Soufflé

Serves 4 to 6

	Butter
	Sugar
3	tablespoons butter
3	tablespoons flour
¼	teaspoon salt
½	cup milk
4	eggs, separated
½	teaspoon cream of tartar
½	cup sugar
¼	cup Grand Marnier
	Grated peel of 1 orange
	Powdered sugar
	Whipped cream

1. Preheat oven to 350°.

2. Butter a 1½- or 2-quart soufflé dish or casserole. Dust with sugar. Set aside.

3. In a medium saucepan over medium-high heat, melt the butter. Blend in the flour and salt. Cook, stirring constantly, until the mixture is smooth and bubbly.

4. Stir in the milk all at once. Cook and stir until the mixture boils and is smooth and thickened. Set aside.

5. In a large mixing bowl, beat the egg whites and cream of tartar until foamy. Add the sugar, 2 tablespoons at a time, beating constantly until it is dissolved and the whites are glossy and stand in soft peaks. (Rub a bit of meringue between thumb and forefinger to feel whether the sugar has dissolved.)

6. Thoroughly blend the egg yolks, liqueur and orange peel into the reserved sauce. Gently but thoroughly fold the yolk mixture into the whites. Carefully pour into the prepared dish.

7. Bake 45 to 50 minutes or until puffy and delicately browned. Dust with powdered sugar. Serve immediately with whipped cream.

Cold Lemon Soufflé
Serves 10

Soufflé:

2	envelopes unflavored gelatin
¾	cup cold water
4-5	lemons
8	eggs, separated
½	teaspoon salt
2	cups sugar
¼	teaspoon nutmeg
¼	teaspoon cinnamon
¼	teaspoon mace
1	teaspoon almond extract
2	tablespoons Grand Marnier or ¾ teaspoon orange extract
2	cups whipping cream
½	cup powdered sugar

Spiced Whipped Cream:

1	cup whipping cream
6	tablespoons powdered sugar
1	teaspoon vanilla
⅛	teaspoon cinnamon
⅛	teaspoon nutmeg
⅛	teaspoon mace

Candied Lemon Shreds:

¼	cup lemon shreds
¼	cup sugar
¼	cup water
1	tablespoon Grand Marnier
1	whole allspice
1	(1-inch) piece vanilla bean

1. To prepare soufflé: Fold a 30-inch strip of foil in half lengthwise. Tie it around the outside of a 6 cup soufflé dish to make a collar which stands about 5 inches above the rim of the dish.
2. Soften the gelatin in cold water.
3. Cut ¼ cup long shreds of lemon peel from fresh lemon and set aside. Squeeze the lemons to obtain 1 cup juice.

4. Combine the egg yolks, lemon juice, salt, 1 cup sugar, nutmeg, cinnamon and mace in a heavy saucepan. Cook on low heat, stirring constantly, until slightly thickened. Stir in the gelatin until dissolved and ½ teaspoon almond extract. Pour into a large bowl. Cool. Stir in the Grand Marnier.

5. Beat the egg whites until foamy. Gradually add 1 cup sugar and beat until stiff peaks form. Whip the cream with the powdered sugar and ½ teaspoon almond extract. Fold the egg whites and cream into the gelatin mixture. Pour into the soufflé dish. Chill 6 hours or overnight.

6. To prepare spiced whipped cream: Whip the cream with the sugar until stiff. Fold in the vanilla, cinnamon, nutmeg and mace.

7. To prepare lemon shreds: Combine the lemon shreds, sugar, water, Grand Marnier, allspice and vanilla bean in a saucepan and simmer until peel is transparent. Remove the allspice and vanilla bean. Drain the lemon shreds on a cake rack.

8. To serve the soufflé, cut the string and carefully remove the foil collar. Decorate top of soufflé with spice whipped cream pressed through a pastry bag with a large star tip. Garnish the center with the candied lemon shreds.

This recipe is one of Maxine Jeffery's favorites.

Pumpkin Torte with Rum-Butter Cream

Makes one 9-inch round cake

Torte:

1½	cups flour
1	teaspoon baking soda
½	teaspoon salt
¼	teaspoon baking powder
1	teaspoon cocoa
1	teaspoon ground cinnamon
1	teaspoon ground nutmeg
½	teaspoon ground cloves
¼	teaspoon ground ginger
1	cup sugar
⅓	cup vegetable oil
2	eggs
1	cup pumpkin

Rum-Butter Cream:

⅔	cup sugar
3	tablespoons water
1	egg
3	egg yolks
1	cup unsalted butter, softened
3	tablespoons rum

1. Preheat oven to 325°.
2. To prepare torte: Combine the flour, baking soda, salt, baking powder, cocoa and spices in a medium bowl. Beat the sugar and vegetable oil in a large mixer bowl on medium speed until smooth, about 5 minutes.
3. Add the eggs one at a time to the sugar-oil mixture, beating until light and fluffy. Beat in the flour mixture alternately with the pumpkin at low speed.
4. Pour the batter into a lightly greased 9-inch round cake pan, lined with wax paper. Bake about 45 minutes, or until a wooden pick inserted in the center comes out clean. Cool in the pan 10 minutes; remove from the pan. Remove wax paper. Cool completely on a wire rack.
5. To prepare rum-butter cream: Boil the sugar and water in a small, heavy saucepan over low heat until a drop of the mixture forms a

soft ball in cold water. (The mixture will be 234° to 236°F. on a candy thermometer.)

6. Beat the egg and egg yolks slightly in the top of a double boiler. Pour the boiling sugar syrup in a slow, steady stream into the beaten eggs, while beating at high speed.

7. Place the top of the double boiler over simmering water on low to medium heat. (Do not let the bottom of the double boiler touch the water in the lower part.) Beat until the mixture is light and fluffy, about 6 minutes.

8. Place the top of the double boiler in a large bowl filled with ice. Continue beating on high speed until the mixture is cold, about 10 minutes. Spoon the mixture into a large mixer bowl.

9. Beat in ¾ cup of the butter, 1 tablespoon at a time, on high speed, until thick and creamy. Beat in the rum and remaining butter alternately, 1 tablespoon at a time; beat until smooth. Refrigerate covered, 30 minutes.

10. Slice the cake horizontally into 2 layers. Spread about ½ cup frosting between the layers. Spread the side and top of the cake with the remaining frosting. Refrigerate. Remove from refrigerator 30 minutes before serving.

Note: When using fresh pumpkin, cook down the mashed pulp over low heat until it is a very thick purée.

Easy Pots de Crème

Serves 4

½	cup hot milk
1	(6 ounce) package semisweet chocolate chips
1	egg at room temperature

1. Heat the milk almost to the boiling point.

2. Combine the milk, chocolate chips, and egg in a blender container and whirl until smooth. Pour the chocolate mixture into four demitasse cups.

3. Chill for 2 hours or more.

Linzer Torte

Makes one 9-inch torte

Almond Pastry:

1½	cups flour
1	cup ground almonds
¼	cup sugar
½	cup butter
1	egg, beaten

Apple Filling:

3	cups pared, cored and sliced golden Delicious apples, tossed in 1 tablespoon fresh lemon juice
2	tablespoons flour
¼	teaspoon ground cinnamon
¾	cup orange marmalade, or apricot preserves
2	tablespoons butter
¼	teaspoon almond extract

1. To prepare pastry: Combine the flour, ground almonds and sugar. Cut in the butter until mixture resembles coarse crumbs. Stir in the beaten egg, mixing ingredients thoroughly to hold them together.

2. Reserve ½ cup dough for a lattice top. Press the remaining dough into the bottom and sides of a 9-inch pie pan or fluted flan pan and refrigerate until the apple mixture is prepared.

3. Preheat oven to 350°.

4. To prepare filling: Combine the apples with the flour, cinnamon and ½ cup marmalade or apricot preserves. Place the apple mixture in the pastry-lined pan and dot with butter.

5. Roll the remaining pastry in a 9-inch round and cut into ¾-inch strips. Weave a lattice over the apples with pastry strips and trim the edges even with the pan.

6. Bake 40 minutes or until the apples are tender. Cool for 15 minutes.

7. Melt the remaining ¼ cup marmalade or apricot preserves, stir in the almond extract and spoon over the filling between lattice strips.

Strawberry Cheese Torte

Serves 10 to 12

2	cups graham cracker crumbs
½	cup butter, melted
2	pints fresh strawberries, washed and stemmed
½	cup hot water
2	envelopes unflavored gelatin
2	tablespoons fresh lemon juice
2	teaspoons grated lemon peel
⅔	cup sugar
2	(8 ounce) packages cream cheese, cut into chunks and softened
½	cup sour cream
1	cup ice cubes (see note)
	Sweetened whipped cream

1. In a small bowl, combine the graham cracker crumbs and butter; toss with a fork to mix thoroughly. Pat half of the crumb mixture into the bottom of an oiled 9-by-3-inch springform pan. Chill. Set aside the remaining crumb mixture.

2. Stem and slice the berries, reserving 12 whole berries for garnish.

3. In the container of an electric blender, combine the water, gelatin, lemon juice and peel. Blend until frothy. Scrape down the sides. Add 2 cups of the sliced berries and the sugar. Blend until smooth. Add the cream cheese, sour cream and ice. Blend until smooth. Chill about 15 minutes until slightly thickened.

4. Spoon half of the cheese mixture into the prepared pan. Layer the remaining crumb mixture and the remaining sliced berries over the cheese mixture. Top with the remaining cheese mixture and smooth out. Chill overnight.

5. To serve, cut into wedges. Dollop each with whipped cream and garnish with reserved whole berries.

Note: To measure ice cubes, pour 1 cup cold water into a 2-cup measuring cup. Add enough ice cubes to make 2 cups. Drain water and add ice to mixture immediately.

Black Forest Cherry Torte

Makes one 9-inch 2-layer torte

Cherry Layer:

2 (15-16 ounce) cans pitted sweet dark cherries

¾ cup kirsch

Cake:

1 cup firmly packed brown sugar

1 cup sugar

½ cup butter, softened

2 eggs, slightly beaten

2 ounces unsweetened chocolate, melted

2 cups flour

½ teaspoon salt

1½ teaspoons lemon juice

Milk

1 teaspoon vanilla

1 cup boiling water

1 teaspoon baking soda

Whipped Cream Layer:

2½ cups whipping cream

⅔ cup sugar

½ teaspoon vanilla

Frosting:

1 cup powdered sugar

1 ounce unsweetened chocolate, melted

¼ cup butter, melted

Garnish:

Maraschino cherries

1. To prepare cherry layer: Drain the cherries, reserving ½ cup liquid. Soak the cherries overnight in the kirsch in a tightly covered bowl in the refrigerator. Also refrigerate the reserved cherry liquid.

2. Preheat oven to 350°.

3. To prepare cake: Cream the sugars and butter together until fluffy. Add the eggs and melted chocolate.

4. Combine the flour and salt and add to the creamed mixture. Put the lemon juice in a measuring cup and add milk to make ½ cup. Add this to the creamed mixture and beat until smooth. Add the vanilla.

5. Combine the boiling water and baking soda. Add slowly to the cake batter, mixing 1 to 2 minutes or until smooth.

6. Pour the batter into 2 greased and floured 9-inch cake pans. Bake 25 minutes or until done. Let pans stand 10 minutes before removing the cakes to wire racks to complete cooling.

7. To prepare whipped cream layer: Beat the cold cream in a chilled bowl until soft peaks form. Slowly add the sugar and beat until stiffer peaks form. Beat in the vanilla and set aside.

8. To prepare frosting: Combine the powdered sugar, chocolate and butter, mixing until smooth. If too thick, add a few drops of milk.

9. To assemble: Cut the cakes into 4 layers. Place 1 layer on a serving platter. Perforate with a fork. Cover with one-third of the reserved juice and one-third of the cherry-kirsch mixture. Spread with one-fourth of the whipped cream. Continue in this manner until all cake layers are used. Do not cover the top layer and save remaining whipped cream for garnish.

10. Spread the top carefully with the frosting, then pipe the remaining whipped cream in a border around the edge with a cake decorator. Garnish the edge with maraschino cherries.

This recipe is from Melinda Bargreen.

Italian Cream Cake

Makes one 8-inch 3-layer cake

Cake:

½ cup butter, softened

½ cup shortening

2 cups sugar

5 eggs, separated

2 cups flour

1 teaspoon baking soda

¼ teaspoon salt

1 cup buttermilk

1 teaspoon vanilla

1 cup flaked coconut

1 cup chopped walnuts

Cream-Cheese Frosting:

1 (8 ounce) package cream cheese, softened

¼ cup butter, softened

1 pound powdered sugar

1 teaspoon vanilla

Extra chopped walnuts

1. Preheat oven to 350°.

2. To prepare cake: Cream the butter and shortening, then add the sugar and beat until smooth. Add the egg yolks and beat well.

3. Combine the flour, baking soda and salt and add to the creamed mixture alternately with the buttermilk. Add the vanilla, coconut and nuts.

4. Beat the egg whites until stiff. Then gently fold them into the batter.

5. Pour batter into 3 greased and floured 8-inch cake pans. Bake 25 to 30 minutes or until a toothpick inserted near the center comes out clean.

6. Remove the pans from the oven and cool for about 8 minutes; then remove the cakes from the pans to wire racks. Let cool completely.

7. To prepare frosting: Beat the cream cheese and butter until fluffy. Add the sugar slowly while beating and beat until smooth and fluffy. Add vanilla and beat to combine.

8. Spread the frosting between each layer and over the top and sides of the cake. Sprinkle frosting with the extra chopped walnuts. Cut in thin pieces since the cake is rich.

◇

Bittersweet Chocolate Cake

Makes one 8-inch cake

	Butter
	Sugar
7	ounces semisweet chocolate (the darkest you can find)
½	cup plus 6 tablespoons butter, softened
6	eggs, separated
1	cup sugar
1½	tablespoons amaretto
⅛	teaspoon almond extract
½	cup flour, sifted
	Powdered sugar

1. Butter and sugar an 8-inch springform pan and tap out any extra sugar.

2. Preheat oven to 325°.

3. Grate or break the chocolate into small pieces. Place the chocolate and butter in the top part of a double boiler over hot, not boiling, water and stir until blended. Let cool slightly.

4. Beat the egg yolks with the sugar until they are thick and pale yellow and form a ribbon when they fall from the beater. Add the amaretto and almond extract. Fold in the warm chocolate and butter. Fold in the sifted flour. Mix all thoroughly but gently.

5. Beat the egg whites until stiff. Stir a large spoonful of the chocolate mixture into the beaten egg whites. Mix well. Pour this mixture back into the chocolate mixture. Fold together gently, incorporating the whites completely. Pour the batter into the springform pan. Bake 1 hour and 10 minutes, or until cake tester inserted in center comes out clean.

6. Cool on a rack for 15 minutes, then remove the outer rim of the pan. When completely cool, refrigerate. Just before serving sprinkle with powdered sugar. Serve cold.

Full-of-Fruit Fruitcake

Makes 1 tube cake

1	pound pitted dates
½	pound candied cherries (save 6 for garnish)
½	pound candied sliced pineapple
1	pound coarsely chopped pecans or walnuts (save 12 halves for garnish)
1	cup sugar
1	cup flour
2	teaspoons baking powder
½	teaspoon salt
1	teaspoon ground nutmeg
4	eggs
1	teaspoon vanilla
	Candied sliced pineapple for garnish

1. Preheat oven to 250°.
2. Cut the dates, cherries and pineapple into small pieces; mix with the nuts.
3. Sift the sugar, flour, baking powder, salt and nutmeg together. Mix with the fruits and nuts.
4. Beat the eggs with the vanilla and pour over the fruit-flour mixture. Mix well.
5. Pack the batter into a well-greased angel-food cake pan and bake 2 to 2½ hours.
6. The top of the fruitcake may be decorated by removing the cake from the oven after 1 hour and garnishing with the pineapple slices, halved cherries and pecan halves; return to the oven to complete baking time.

Fyrstekake

Makes one 9-inch round cake

Cake:

2	cups flour
¾	cup butter
2	teaspoons baking powder

¾	cup sugar
1	egg yolk
2	tablespoons milk

Filling:

1¼	cups almonds
½	cup powdered sugar
¼	teaspoon almond extract
½	teaspoon ground cardamom
½	teaspoon ground cinnamon
1	egg, separated
6	tablespoons water

1. To prepare cake: Mix the flour and butter with a pastry blender until the mixture resembles bread crumbs. Mix the baking powder and sugar and add to the flour mixture.

2. Combine the egg yolk and milk. Sprinkle over the flour mixture. Mix well and form the dough into a ball.

3. Roll out two-thirds of the dough into a ¼-inch-thick layer. Cut a strip to fill the inside rim of the pan. Place the remaining dough in a 9-inch round cake pan with removable bottom. Fit the inside rim of the pan with the strip, pressing the two edges together along the base.

4. Preheat oven to 350°.

5. To prepare filling: Grind the almonds until they are the size of bread crumbs. Mix well with the powdered sugar, almond extract, ground cardamom, cinnamon, slightly beaten egg white and water. Spread evenly in the pastry-lined pan.

6. Roll out the remaining dough ¼-inch thick. Cut in 6 strips, each 1¼ inches wide. Place on top of the filling in a lattice fashion. Any remaining dough may be placed around the edge. Brush the top with beaten egg yolk. Bake on the lowest rack of the oven for 45 minutes. Cool in the pan on a wire cake rack.

This recipe is from Ingeborg Hansen.

Orange Buttermilk Cake

Makes one 9-inch-square cake

1	orange
1½	cups sugar
½	cup butter
2	eggs
2	cups sifted cake flour
¼	teaspoon baking soda
1½	teaspoons baking powder
¼	teaspoon salt
1	cup buttermilk
	Whipped cream or ice cream

1. Preheat oven to 350°.

2. Grate the peel of the orange on a coarse grater or fine shredder. Then cut the orange in half and extract the juice. Add ½ cup sugar to the juice and stir to dissolve the sugar. Set aside.

3. Cream the butter until light and fluffy, then add 1 cup sugar and continue to beat until light and creamy. Add the eggs and beat until fluffy. Stir the grated orange peel into the creamed mixture.

4. Sift together the cake flour, baking soda, baking powder and salt. Add the dry ingredients to the creamed mixture alternately with buttermilk, beginning and ending with the flour. Beat only enough to blend thoroughly.

5. Pour into a lightly greased and floured 7-by-11-inch or 9-inch-square pan. Bake 30 to 35 minutes or until a cake tester inserted in the center comes out clean.

6. Cool on a cake rack for 15 minutes. Poke holes in the top of the cake with a fork or skewer and spoon orange juice mixture over it.

7. Serve plain or with whipped cream or ice cream as a topping.

Orange-Poached Pears

Serves 6

1	cup sugar
1	cup freshly squeezed orange juice
½	cup freshly squeezed lemon juice

1	cinnamon stick
6	large fresh Bartlett pears
24	whole cloves
1	orange, washed and thinly sliced, unpeeled
1	cup seedless green grapes

1. In a large saucepan, combine the sugar, orange juice, lemon juice and cinnamon stick and bring to a boil. Stir until sugar is dissolved.

2. Peel the whole pears, leaving stems attached. Remove ½ inch of the core from the center of the broad end of each pear. Stud the opening with 4 whole cloves.

3. Place the pears carefully into the syrup and simmer covered 10 to 15 minutes, or until just tender. Turn occasionally to cook evenly. Remove cloves when done.

4. Remove the pears to a serving bowl. Bring the syrup to a full boil and cook until reduced to one third. Add the orange slices and grapes to the syrup. Pour the mixture over the pears and chill at least 2 hours before serving.

Danish Lemon Cloud

Serves 4

4	eggs, separated
½	cup sugar
	Juice of 2 lemons
	Grated peel of 1 lemon
1	envelope unflavored gelatin
¼	cup cold water

1. Beat the egg yolks. Add the sugar gradually, continuing to beat until thick and lemon colored. Add the lemon juice and peel.

2. Soften the gelatin in the cold water, then heat over hot water, stirring until dissolved.

3. Beat the egg whites to foamy peaks (not stiff). Fold the gelatin into the egg yolk mixture, then fold in the egg whites. Pour into a mold and chill until set.

This recipe is from Marianne Forssblad.

Chocolate Dipping Sauce for Cherries

Makes 1¼ cups

8	ounces semisweet chocolate
1	tablespoon butter
½	cup whipping cream
1	teaspoon kirsch or cherry-flavored liqueur
4-6	cups sweet cherries with stems, chilled

1. Melt the chocolate and butter in the top of a double boiler over simmering water, stirring constantly until smooth, about 8 to 10 minutes.
2. Leaving the mixture over the heat, gradually stir in the cream. Add kirsch or liqueur.
3. Serve warm in a chafing dish as a dipping sauce for the chilled cherries.

Chocolat à l'Orange

Serves 8

1	envelope unflavored gelatin
6	tablespoons sugar
2	eggs, separated
1	cup milk
6	ounces semisweet chocolate
2	tablespoons orange liqueur
1	cup whipping cream, whipped
1	(3 ounce) package ladyfingers, split, or 22 (1 by 3 inches) strips of pound cake
	Additional whipped cream
	Orange sections dipped in dipping chocolate, melted

1. In a medium saucepan, mix the unflavored gelatin with 4 tablespoons sugar. Beat the egg yolks and milk and blend into the gelatin. Let stand 1 minute. Stir over low heat until gelatin is completely dissolved, about 5 minutes.
2. Add the chocolate and continue cooking, stirring constantly, until chocolate is melted. With a wire whisk or rotary beater, beat the

mixture until chocolate is blended. Stir in the liqueur. Pour into a large bowl and chill, stirring occasionally, until the mixture mounds slightly when dropped from a spoon.

3. In another large bowl, beat the egg whites until soft peaks form. Gradually add the remaining sugar and beat until stiff. Fold the egg whites, then whipped cream into the gelatin mixture.

4. Place the ladyfingers, rounded side out, against the sides of a 9-by-5-by-3-inch loaf pan. Turn the gelatin mixture into pan and chill until firm.

5. To serve, unmold onto a serving platter and garnish with additional whipped cream and orange sections dipped in chocolate.

Strawberries and Molded Devonshire Cream

Serves 8

1	envelope unflavored gelatin
¾	cup cold water
1	cup sour cream at room temperature
1	cup whipping cream
½	cup sugar
1	teaspoon vanilla
2	pints fresh strawberries, sliced

1. In a saucepan, sprinkle the gelatin over the water, then dissolve over low heat. Stir into the sour cream, whisking lightly to smooth out lumps. Set aside.

2. In a mixing bowl, beat the cream, gradually adding the sugar, until soft peaks form. Stir in the vanilla and sour cream-gelatin mixture.

3. Rinse a 1-quart mold with cold water. Pour the cream mixture into the mold and chill until firm.

4. Unmold on a serving plate. Surround with the sliced berries, sweetened to taste. Slice the mold to serve and top each serving with berries.

Strawberries in Raspberry Purée

Serves 4 to 6

2	pints fresh strawberries
½	cup sugar
1	(10 ounce) package frozen red raspberries, thawed
3	tablespoons raspberry- or blackberry- flavored brandy
	Slivered toasted almonds
	Assorted cookies

1. Wash the strawberries gently and drain. Remove the stems and slice strawberries in half. Toss lightly in a bowl with ¼ cup sugar. Cover and chill for 1 hour.

2. Run defrosted raspberries through a food mill, or process in a blender and strain to remove the seeds.

3. Mix the raspberry purée with ¼ cup sugar, blending well. Add flavored brandy. Pour over the strawberries and chill for 2 to 3 hours.

4. To serve, place the strawberries and the sauce in individual serving dishes. Sprinkle with some almonds. Accompany with cookies.

Strawberry Sabayon

Serves 4 to 6

1½	pints strawberries, washed and hulled
3	tablespoons powdered sugar
1	(187 ml) split champagne
4	egg yolks
⅓	cup sugar
2	tablespoons cornstarch
1½	teaspoons vanilla
1	cup milk, scalded
¾	cup whipping cream

1. Combine the strawberries and powdered sugar in a bowl and mix well. Pour the champagne over the strawberries. Refrigerate, covered, at least 2 hours.

2. Beat the egg yolks with ⅓ cup sugar and cornstarch until light and fluffy. Beat in the vanilla and gradually add the milk. Cook in the top

of a double boiler over hot, not boiling, water until thick. Remove from heat and let stand to cool.

3. Whip the cream until thick and then fold into the custard. Spoon two-thirds of the custard into individual dessert dishes. Drain the strawberries and press one at a time into the custard. Spread remaining custard over the top. Refrigerate at least 2 hours.

Blackberry Puff

Makes one 9-inch puff

1⅓	cups flour
10	tablespoons butter at room temperature
2	tablespoons sugar
⅔	cup water
3	eggs
1	cup whipping cream
	Sugar
4	cups blackberries, cleaned and sugared

1. In a bowl, combine ⅔ cup flour, 5 tablespoons butter and 2 tablespoons sugar. Work the mixture together until smooth. Press the dough evenly into a 9-inch springform pan to make a smooth, even layer.

2. Preheat oven to 375°.

3. In a saucepan, combine the water and remaining 5 tablespoons butter. Bring to a boil, stirring to melt butter. Add remaining ⅔ cup flour all at once. Remove the pan from the heat and beat well until the mixture is smooth. Beat in the eggs, one at a time, until the mixture is smooth and glossy.

4. Spread the mixture over the dough in the pan. Bake 45 to 50 minutes, or until puff is browned. It will be irregular in shape.

5. Turn off the heat but leave the puff in the oven with the door closed for 10 minutes longer to dry. Remove pan rim and let the puff cool. It will settle slightly.

6. To serve, whip the cream until stiff and sweeten with sugar to taste. Spread in the depression of the puff, then pile slightly sweetened berries onto the cream and some around the edges. Cut in wedges to serve.

Gorgonzola Pears

Serves 4

3	ounces gorgonzola cheese
1	tablespoon brandy
4	ripe pears
2	tablespoons lemon juice
1	(3 ounce) package cream cheese at room temperature
⅓	cup sour cream
4	tablespoons coarsely chopped pecans
4	whole cloves
4	sprigs fresh mint

1. In a small bowl, use a fork to blend the gorgonzola cheese and brandy until smooth. Set aside 15 minutes.

2. Peel the pears, cut in half and core. Brush all surfaces of the pear halves with lemon juice and set aside.

3. Beat the cream cheese into the gorgonzola cheese mixture until smooth, then fold in the sour cream.

4. Spread one quarter of the cheese mixture on each of 4 pear halves. Top with remaining pear halves. The filling will push out around the edges.

5. Press the chopped pecans into the filling. Stand the pears, large end down, on a serving dish. Top each pear with a whole clove to represent the stem and a mint sprig to represent leaves. Serve at once or cover with plastic wrap and refrigerate no longer than 3 hours before serving.

Poached Pears with Crème Anglaise

Serves 8

8	pears (Bosc or Anjou) not too ripe
1	tablespoon plus additional lemon juice
4	cups water
2	cups sugar
1	teaspoon grated lemon peel
1	cinnamon stick
3	whole cloves

Crème Anglaise:

1	**cup milk**
½	**cup whipping cream**
1	**teaspoon vanilla extract**
6	**tablespoons sugar**
5	**large egg yolks**
2	**teaspoons cornstarch**

1. Peel the pears and drop them into cold water containing some lemon juice. This will keep the pears from turning dark. In a large pot or Dutch oven, bring 4 cups water, the sugar, 1 tablespoon lemon juice and lemon peel to a boil. Add the cinnamon stick, cloves and pears. Cover and simmer for 30 minutes.

2. Transfer the pears to a flat-bottomed dish. Stand them up so they keep their shape. Pour a little of the poaching syrup over them, cover and chill for several hours.

3. To prepare crème Anglaise: Combine the milk, cream and vanilla in a saucepan. Bring to a boil, remove from heat and let stand for 10 minutes.

4. Gradually beat the sugar into the egg yolks and continue beating for about 3 minutes until the mixture is pale yellow and creamy. Beat in the cornstarch. Stir the milk and cream mixture into the yolks, beating vigorously with a wire whisk.

5. Return the mixture to the saucepan and cook over very low heat, stirring with a wooden spoon until it is quite thick. This will take about 15 minutes. Do not let the mixture boil.

6. Remove the sauce from the heat and cool, stirring frequently. Chill thoroughly and spoon over pears.

Brandied Prunes
Makes 1 quart

1	pound dried prunes, pitted
	Grated peel of 1 orange
1	cinnamon stick, crushed
1	tablespoon honey
2	cups water
½	cup brandy

1. Wash the prunes in cold water and dry thoroughly. Pack the prunes loosely with the orange peel and crushed cinnamon in a 1-quart wide-mouth glass jar.

2. Dissolve the honey in the water over low heat, then pour it over the prunes. Add the brandy until the prunes are completely submerged. Cover the jar tightly and shake well. Leave in a cool place or refrigerate for at least 6 weeks. As the prunes swell, add more brandy if needed to ensure that all the fruit remains covered.

Deep-Dish Pear Pastry
Makes one 9-inch-square pastry

1½	cups sifted flour
⅓	cup sugar
¼	teaspoon salt
½	cup butter
1	egg yolk
4	tablespoons milk
½	cup cornflake or branflake crumbs
3	medium ripe pears
¼	teaspoon ground cinnamon
⅛	teaspoon ground nutmeg

Powdered Sugar Glaze:

½	cup sifted powdered sugar
1	tablespoon lemon juice

1. Stir together the flour, 2 tablespoons sugar and salt. Cut in the butter until the mixture forms fine crumbs. Beat the egg yolk lightly with a fork and add to the flour mixture. Add the milk, 1 tablespoon at a time, to make a stiff dough.

2. Divide the dough in two, with one part slightly larger than the other. Pat the larger portion over the bottom and about 1 inch up the sides of a greased 9-inch-square baking pan. Sprinkle the cereal crumbs over the dough.

3. Preheat oven to 375°.

4. Pare and thinly slice the pears to measure 3 cups and arrange over the crumbs. Combine the remaining sugar with the cinnamon and nutmeg and sprinkle it over the pears.

5. Roll the smaller portion of the dough on a sheet of wax paper to a 9-inch square. Invert the dough over the pears and gently loosen it from the paper. Pinch the pieces of dough together and cut a few slits in the top.

6. Bake 30 to 45 minutes until nicely brown.

7. To make glaze: Combine the sifted powdered sugar and lemon juice, mixing until smooth. Brush it over the top of the pastry while it is still warm. To serve, cut into squares when cool.

Minted Pots de Crème

Serves 6

6	ounces semisweet chocolate
¼	cup water
1	tablespoon butter
¼	cup green crème de menthe
3	eggs, separated
	Whipping cream, whipped

1. In a small saucepan, combine the chocolate and water and stir over medium heat until smooth. Cool slightly, then stir in the butter.

2. In a medium bowl, beat the crème de menthe and egg yolks. Beat in the chocolate mixture.

3. Beat the egg whites until stiff, then fold into the chocolate mixture. Spoon into small dessert dishes. Chill at least 3 hours. Serve with a dollop of whipped cream.

Rhubarb Meringue Dessert

Serves 12

1	cup butter, softened
2¼	cups flour
2¼	cups sugar
6	eggs, separated
¼	teaspoon salt
5	cups chopped rhubarb (¼-inch pieces)
2	teaspoons vanilla

1. Preheat oven to 350°.
2. Cream the softened butter with a large spoon until smooth. Combine 2 cups flour and 2 tablespoons sugar, then slowly blend into the softened butter, creaming until well mixed and smooth.
3. Pat the dough out into a 9-by-13-inch pan, making it as smooth and even as possible. Bake 10 minutes.
4. Beat the egg yolks with a wire whisk. Combine 2 cups sugar, remaining 4 tablespoons flour and salt. Add slowly to the egg yolks, combining thoroughly with the wire whisk. Stir in the rhubarb.
5. Pour this mixture over the baked crust, spreading evenly. Return it to oven and bake for 45 minutes.
6. Beat the egg whites until soft peaks form. Slowly add the remaining 2 tablespoons sugar and beat until stiff. Add the vanilla.
7. Spread the meringue over the top of the dessert, swirling attractively and covering the top completely. Return it to oven and bake 10 minutes more, or until golden brown.

Chocolate Mousse

Serves 6

1	(8 ounce) package cream cheese at room temperature
1	cup sugar
⅓	cup unsweetened cocoa
1	teaspoon vanilla or almond extract
1	cup whipping cream

1. Place the softened cream cheese in the large bowl of an electric mixer. Add the sugar gradually, while beating. Beat well. Add the cocoa and vanilla, beating until well mixed.

2. Pour the whipping cream into the small chilled bowl of the mixer and beat until stiff. Fold the whipped cream into the chocolate mixture and pour into 1 large mold or 6 individual small molds. Chill until serving time.

Chocolate Amaretto Mousse

Serves 4 to 6

1 (6 ounce) package semisweet chocolate chips
3 tablespoons water
3 large eggs at room temperature, separated
1 tablespoon amaretto

1. Place the chocolate chips and water in a heavy saucepan. Keeping the heat at simmer, or as low as possible, let the chips melt, while stirring to a smooth consistency.

2. Beat the egg yolks just until well mixed. When the chocolate chip mixture is melted and smooth, remove from heat and slowly add to the egg yolks, mixing until smooth.

3. Beat the egg whites until stiff peaks form. Quickly fold the chocolate mixture into the whites until smooth and well combined. Stir in the amaretto.

4. Pour the mixture into small clear glasses or small dessert dishes. Cover each one with plastic wrap and refrigerate until ready to serve.

Steamed Plum Pudding
Serves 16

Pudding:

1⅓	cups dry bread crumbs
2	cups chopped suet or 1 cup butter at room temperature
1	cup sifted flour
½	teaspoon ground allspice
½	teaspoon ground nutmeg
½	teaspoon salt
½	teaspoon ground cinnamon
½	teaspoon ground ginger
2	cups finely cut apples
	Grated peel of 1 lemon
¾	cup candied orange peel
⅓	cup finely cut citron
½	cup finely cut blanched almonds
1½	cups currants
1½	cups dark raisins
1⅓	cups firmly packed brown sugar
⅓	cup molasses
4	eggs

Brandy Sauce:

⅔	cup sugar
2	teaspoons flour
¼	teaspoon ground nutmeg
⅛	teaspoon salt
1	cup water
2	tablespoons butter
2	tablespoons brandy

Hard Sauce:

1	cup powdered sugar
⅓	cup butter, softened
1	teaspoon brandy

1. To prepare pudding: Mix the bread crumbs and chopped suet. Add the flour, allspice, nutmeg, salt, cinnamon and ginger. Combine and then add the apples, lemon peel, orange peel, citron, almonds, currants, raisins, sugar, molasses and eggs. Blend thoroughly.

2. Pour the batter into a well-greased 2-quart mold about two-thirds full. (Or use two 1-quart molds.) Cover with the lid, if the mold has one, or cover with foil, sealing around the edge tightly.

3. Place a rack with legs in the bottom of a large kettle. Add about 1 inch of water in the bottom or almost to the top of the rack. Place the pudding on the rack, cover the kettle with the lid and bring to a boil over high heat until steam begins to come out around the edge of the lid. Lower heat and continue steaming slowly for 2 hours for smaller molds and about 4 hours for the larger mold. Check water level in the kettle from time to time. Test for doneness as you would a cake. When a toothpick inserted in the center comes out clean, it's done.

4. If you wish to flame the pudding, heat 2 tablespoons brandy slightly in a small metal container. Ignite with a match and, while flaming, pour over the pudding. Serve with brandy sauce or hard sauce.

5. To prepare brandy sauce: Combine the sugar, flour, nutmeg, salt, water and butter in a small saucepan, and cook until clear. Add the brandy and heat. Serve hot, over the pudding.

6. To prepare hard sauce: Sift the sugar. Cream the butter thoroughly and beat in the sugar gradually, continuing to beat until the mixture is very smooth and fluffy. Add the brandy, drop-by-drop, to keep the mixture from separating. If using an electric mixer, scrape down the sides of the bowl once or twice while beating. Chill or serve at room temperature.

Note: This pudding can be made ahead and reheated before serving. Remove the cooled pudding from the mold, wrap tightly with plastic wrap and foil; refrigerate. To reheat, unwrap the pudding and place it in the same mold. Cover with foil and place back in the kettle to steam for about 1 hour.

Pastries

While "movable feast" means different things to different people, it makes a wonderful definition of pies and pastries. The idea of being able to heap ingredients on an edible crust obviously comes to us from before there were table implements because pies could be picked up and transferred to the mouth with a minimum of mess.

Although table manners have improved a great deal, crust-based desserts haven't lost any of their popularity.

The crusts for pastries in this chapter are made of meringue, ground almonds, shortbread, chocolate cookies and even pretzels, as well as the standard pie crust, and are designed to rate equal flavor billing with the filling.

Pies and pastries are a wonderful way of dealing with seasonal bounty here in the Northwest.

A pie can embrace a bountiful picking of local blackberries; several boxes of lush, red-ripe strawberries, as in the Strawberry Tart or Strawberry Angel Pie. Eastern Washington-grown peaches star in our Peach Chantilly Pie and French Peach Custard Tart, while Northwest Purple Plums are spotlighted in the Purple Plum Cheese Tart.

Standard Pastry

Makes 1 one- or two-crust pie shell

For an 8- or 9-inch one-crust pie:

1	cup flour
½	teaspoon salt
⅓	cup plus 1 tablespoon vegetable shortening
2-3	tablespoons iced water

For an 8- or 9-inch two-crust pie:

2	cups flour
1	teaspoon salt
⅔	cup plus 2 tablespoons vegetable shortening
4-5	tablespoons iced water

1. For both crusts, measure the flour and salt into a bowl. Cut in the shortening with a pastry blender until the mixture resembles coarse corn meal. Add the water, a few drops at a time, mixing until all the flour is moistened. Gather the dough into a ball.

2. For a one-crust pie, shape the dough into a flattened round on a lightly floured board. Roll it out with a floured rolling pin until it is 2 inches larger in diameter than the pie pan. Ease the pastry into the pie pan. Fold it under even with the pan. Flute the edges. Fill and bake as directed in recipe.

3. For a two-crust pie, divide the dough in half. Roll out one portion of the dough with a floured rolling pin until it is 2 inches larger in diameter than the pie pan. Ease the pastry into the pie pan. Fill with desired filling. Trim the overhanging edge of pastry ½ inch from the rim of the pan. Roll the second portion of the dough in the same fashion and place over the filling. Trim overhanging edge of pastry 1 inch from the rim of the pan. Fold and roll the top edge under the lower edge, pressing on the rim to seal. Flute the edges. Bake as directed in recipe.

4. For recipes calling for baked pie shell: Pierce the bottom and sides of the pie shell thoroughly with the tines of a fork. Bake in preheated 475° oven for 8 to 10 minutes. Cool on a wire rack before filling.

Lemon Velvet Pie

Makes one 9-inch pie

1⅓	cups sugar
6	tablespoons cornstarch
½	teaspoon salt
1¾	cups cold water
2	eggs, separated
2	tablespoons butter
⅓	cup lemon juice
1	teaspoon grated lemon peel
1	teaspoon vanilla
1	envelope unflavored gelatin
1	cup half-and-half
1	(9-inch) pie shell, baked (see previous page)
1	cup whipping cream, whipped

1. Combine the sugar, cornstarch and salt in a 2-quart saucepan. Gradually stir in 1½ cups cold water. Cook over medium heat, stirring constantly, until the mixture thickens and mounds when dropped from a spoon.

2. Slightly beat the egg yolks, using a fork. Stir a small amount of the hot mixture into the egg yolks. Immediately pour back into remaining hot mixture, blending thoroughly.

3. Cook over low heat 2 more minutes, stirring constantly. Remove from heat. Gently stir in the butter, lemon juice, lemon peel and vanilla. Remove 1 cup of this cornstarch mixture; cool and reserve.

4. Soften the gelatin in remaining ¼ cup cold water 5 minutes. Add the gelatin mixture to remaining hot cornstarch mixture and stir until dissolved.

5. Gradually stir in half-and-half. Chill until it begins to thicken.

6. Beat the egg whites until stiff, then fold into the chilled cornstarch-gelatin mixture.

7. Pour the mixture into the baked pie shell. Chill in the refrigerator 15 minutes.

8. Carefully spread the reserved 1 cup cooled cornstarch mixture on top. Chill in the refrigerator until set. Decorate top with puffs of whipped cream.

Bananas Foster Chiffon Pie

Makes one 9-inch pie

Flaky Pastry Shell:

1	cup flour
¼	teaspoon salt
¼	cup vegetable shortening
¼	cup butter, softened slightly
2	tablespoons very cold water
1-1½	cups dried beans or pie weights

Filling:

4	eggs, separated
1	cup milk
1	cup sugar
¼	teaspoon salt
1	envelope unflavored gelatin
¼	cup light or dark rum
2	tablespoons banana liqueur
2	medium, firm bananas, peeled and sliced
1	cup whipping cream

1. To prepare shell: Combine the flour and salt in a large bowl. Add the shortening and butter and cut in with a pastry blender until the size of peas.

2. Add water, a few drops at a time, tossing and stirring with 2 forks until mixture is moistened.

3. Gather the dough together into a ball, wrap in plastic wrap and refrigerate at least 45 minutes.

4. Preheat oven to 475°.

5. Roll out the pastry on a well-floured board with a floured rolling pin and carefully transfer to a 9-inch pie plate. Trim the edge to a 1-inch overhang, fold under and flute. Pierce the crust with a fork.

6. Fit a 12-inch piece of foil into the shell. Pour dried beans or pie weights evenly onto the foil. Bake for 8 minutes. Remove the foil and beans, lower heat to 400° and bake crust 8 to 10 minutes longer, or until golden brown. Remove from oven and place on a rack to cool.

7. To prepare filling: In a saucepan, combine the egg yolks, milk, ½ cup sugar and salt. Cook over medium heat, stirring, until slightly thickened and mixture coats a spoon. Remove from heat.

8. Combine the gelatin, rum and liqueur, stirring until gelatin softens. Add to the hot filling, stirring well until the gelatin dissolves. Cool.

9. Beat the egg whites until foamy. Gradually beat in the remaining ½ cup sugar until stiff peaks form. Fold the egg whites into the cooled yolk mixture.

10. Line the cooled pie crust with the sliced bananas. Pour the filling over the bananas. Refrigerate 1 hour or until firm. Whip the cream and sweeten slightly, if desired. Spread over the top of the pie and decorate with a few more banana slices, if desired.

Grasshopper Pie

Makes one 9-inch pie

Crust:

1½	cups chocolate-wafer cookie crumbs
¼	cup melted butter

Filling:

32	large marshmallows
½	cup milk
3	tablespoons green crème de menthe
3	tablespoons white crème de cacao
1¼	cups chilled whipping cream
	Few drops green food coloring, optional

1. To prepare crust: Combine the cookie crumbs and butter until mixture is crumbly. Reserve 2 to 3 tablespoons for topping.

2. Press the remaining crumb mixture into a 9-inch pie plate, pressing firmly against bottom and sides.

3. Chill in the refrigerator for 1 hour.

4. To prepare filling: Heat the marshmallows and milk in a saucepan over medium heat, stirring constantly, until marshmallows melt. Chill until thickened.

5. Blend the crème de menthe and crème de cacao into the chilled marshmallow mixture. In a chilled bowl, beat the cream until stiff, then fold into the marshmallow mixture. Fold in food coloring, if desired.

6. Pour into the crust, swirling the top of the filling. Sprinkle reserved crumbs into the swirls. Chill several hours until set.

Pumpkin Chiffon Tarts

Makes 12

Tart Shells:

2	cups flour
1	teaspoon salt
½	cup oil
¼	cup milk

Filling:

1	envelope unflavored gelatin
¾	cup firmly packed brown sugar
½	teaspoon salt
1	teaspoon ground cinnamon
½	teaspoon ground nutmeg
¼	teaspoon ground ginger
1¼	cups mashed cooked pumpkin
3	eggs, separated
½	cup milk
⅓	cup sugar
	Whipped cream

1. Preheat oven to 475°.

2. To prepare tart shells: Mix the flour and salt in a large bowl. Pour the oil and milk into a measuring cup; do not stir.

3. Pour the oil-milk mixture all at once into the flour. Stir with a fork until mixed. Dough will look moist but will not be sticky. Press into a smooth ball. Cut in thirds and flatten slightly.

4. Place one-third of the dough between 2 sheets of wax paper. Roll gently to ⅛-inch thickness. Fit dough into four 3½-inch tart tins. With a rolling pin, cut the dough even with the shell edges. Repeat with remaining dough. Pierce dough with tines of a fork.

5. Bake 8 minutes. Cool and remove from tart tins.

6. To prepare filling: Blend thoroughly the gelatin, brown sugar, salt, cinnamon, nutmeg, ginger, pumpkin, egg yolks and milk in a saucepan. Cook over medium heat, stirring constantly, until it boils. Remove from heat.

7. Place the pan in cold water. Cool until the mixture mounds slightly when dropped from a spoon.

8. Beat the egg whites until soft peaks form. Slowly add the sugar, beating until egg whites are stiff but not dry.

9. Fold the pumpkin mixture gently into the egg whites. Pour into the prepared tart shells. Chill until set, about 2 hours. Garnish with whipped cream.

Pecan Chiffon Pie

Makes one 9-inch pie

½	cup coarsely chopped pecans
½	cup firmly packed brown sugar
2	tablespoons cornstarch
⅞	cup water
2	egg whites
2	tablespoons sugar
1	teaspoon vanilla
1	(9-inch) pie shell, baked (see index)
½	cup whipping cream, whipped
	Additional finely chopped pecans

1. Preheat oven to 250°.

2. Spread the pecans on a baking sheet and bake for 10 to 15 minutes or until nuts barely begin to brown. Watch carefully that they don't burn.

3. Combine the brown sugar, cornstarch and water in a saucepan. Cook, stirring constantly until mixture becomes clear and is the consistency of a thick pudding. Remove from heat.

4. Whip the egg whites at high speed until soft peaks form. Slowly add sugar and beat until stiff peaks form.

5. Reduce mixer speed to low and gently add the hot brown sugar mixture, nuts and vanilla. As soon as everything is blended, shut off the mixer. Do not overmix.

6. Spoon the filling lightly into the baked pie shell.

7. Spread the whipped cream over the pie. Sprinkle a few additional finely chopped nuts over top for garnish.

Frozen Margarita Pie

Makes one 10-inch pie

Crust:

½	cup butter
1½	cups finely crushed pretzels
⅓	cup sugar

Filling:

1	(14 ounce) can sweetened condensed milk
½	cup fresh lime juice
2	tablespoons tequila
2	tablespoons Triple Sec or Grand Marnier
2	teaspoons grated lime peel
1	cup whipping cream, whipped
2-3	drops green food coloring
	Additional whipped cream
	Mint leaves

1. To prepare crust: Heat the butter in a small saucepan over low heat until melted. Stir in the pretzel crumbs and sugar. Mix well. Press the crumb mixture into a buttered 10-inch pie plate. Chill.

2. To prepare filling: Mix the condensed milk, lime juice, tequila, Triple Sec and lime peel in a medium bowl until well mixed. Fold in the whipped cream and food coloring. Pour into the crumb crust. Freeze until firm, about 4 hours.

3. Let stand 5 minutes before cutting. Garnish with whipped cream and mint leaves.

Kahlua White Russian Pie

Makes one 9-inch pie

Kahlua Brown Butter Crust:

2	tablespoons sugar
2½	cups crushed shortbread crumbs
¼	cup butter
1	tablespoon Kahlua

Filling:

1	envelope unflavored gelatin
¼	cup cold water
3	large eggs, separated
7	tablespoons sugar
¼	cup Kahlua
3	tablespoons vodka
½	cup whipping cream

Kahlua Cream Topping:

1	cup whipping cream
3	tablespoons Kahlua

Grated white chocolate

1. To prepare crust: Mix the sugar and shortbread crumbs.

2. Heat the butter over moderate heat until lightly browned. Remove from heat; stir in the Kahlua, then mix well with the crumbs.

3. Reserve ½ cup crumbs for the pie center. Press the remainder over the bottom and sides of a buttered 9-inch pie pan. Chill.

4. To prepare filling: Sprinkle the gelatin over cold water and let stand 5 minutes to soften. Dissolve over hot water.

5. Beat the egg yolks with 4 tablespoons sugar at high speed with electric mixer until thick. Beat dissolved gelatin slowly into the egg mixture. Stir in the Kahlua and vodka. Cool, stirring occasionally, until the mixture begins to thicken slightly.

6. Beat the egg whites to soft peaks, then beat in 3 tablespoons sugar, one at a time, to make meringue. Fold into the gelatin mixture.

7. Beat the cream until stiff. Fold in the gelatin mixture. Chill the mixture a few minutes until it mounds on a spoon. Turn half into the chilled shell. Sprinkle evenly with the ½ cup reserved crumb mixture. Top with remaining filling. Chill several hours or overnight.

8. To prepare topping: Beat the whipping cream to soft peaks. Beat in the Kahlua, 1 tablespoon at a time, until topping is stiff. Swirl over the pie. Garnish with grated white chocolate.

Purple Plum Cheese Tart

Makes one 9-inch tart

Tart Shell:

1½	cups flour
1	tablespoon sugar
⅛	teaspoon salt
½	cup butter, softened
1	egg yolk
¼	teaspoon vanilla
2-3	tablespoons water

Filling:

1	(8 ounce) package cream cheese, softened
2	eggs
1	cup sugar
¼	teaspoon ground cinnamon
¼	teaspoon almond extract
1	cup water
12	purple prune plums, halved and pitted

1. To prepare tart shell: Combine the flour, sugar and salt. Beat the softened butter and egg yolk together. Work them into the flour. Add the vanilla and water to form a ball. Dust with flour, wrap in wax paper or plastic wrap and refrigerate about 30 minutes.

2. Preheat oven to 400°.

3. Roll the dough on a lightly floured surface and fit into a 9-inch tart pan with removable bottom. Trim excess dough and pierce the shell with a fork. Bake 15 minutes or until slightly brown. Cool. Reset oven to 375°.

4. To prepare filling: Combine the cream cheese, eggs, ½ cup sugar, cinnamon and almond extract and mix until smooth. Pour into the prepared tart shell. Bake 15 minutes or until set. Cool.

5. Bring the water and ½ cup sugar to a boil; add the plums and simmer about 30 seconds or just until tender. Remove with a slotted spoon, drain and cool.

6. Continue boiling the syrup until thickened or volume is reduced to one-third. Cool. Arrange the plums on the baked cheese filling. Spoon the glaze over the plums.

Rum Cream Pie

Makes one 9-inch pie

5	egg yolks
1	cup minus 1 tablespoon sugar
1	envelope unflavored gelatin
½	cup cold water
½	cup rum
2	cups whipping cream, whipped
1	(9-inch) pastry shell, baked and cooled (see index)
	Bittersweet chocolate shavings

1. Beat the egg yolks until light. Add the sugar gradually, mixing well.

2. Soak the gelatin in the cold water in a saucepan for a few minutes. Bring the gelatin-water mixture to a boil, stirring until gelatin is dissolved.

3. Pour gelatin mixture slowly over the egg yolks and sugar, stirring constantly. Add the rum and let cool to room temperature.

4. Stir the mixture, then fold in the whipped cream gently but thoroughly. Gently pour the filling into the pie shell. Chill 4 to 5 hours or until the pie has set.

5. Sprinkle the top with chocolate shavings. Return to the refrigerator until serving time.

This pie recipe is one of Dawn Clark's favorites.

Strawberry-Almond Pie

Makes one 9-inch pie

Almond Pie Shell:

1 cup flour

½ teaspoon salt

2 tablespoons ground almonds

⅓ cup plus 1 tablespoon shortening

2-3 tablespoons ice water

⅓ cup sliced almonds, toasted

Almond Filling:

½ cup sugar

½ teaspoon salt

⅓ cup cornstarch

1½ cups milk

½ cup half-and-half

1 egg, beaten

½ cup whipping cream

1½ teaspoons almond extract

2½ cups halved fresh strawberries

Glaze:

1 cup sliced strawberries

½ cup water

¼ cup sugar

2 teaspoons cornstarch

1. To prepare shell: Sift the flour and salt together, then stir in the ground almonds. Cut in the shortening until pieces are the size of small peas.

2. Sprinkle 1 tablespoon water over part of the mixture. Gently toss with a fork and push to one side of the bowl. Repeat until all is moistened.

3. Form into a ball. Flatten on a lightly floured surface and roll into a 12-inch circle.

4. Fit the pastry into a 9-inch pie plate. Trim ½ to 1 inch beyond edge. Fold under and flute the edge. Pierce the bottom and sides well with a fork. Chill for 30 minutes.

5. Preheat oven to 475°.

6. Bake for 6 to 8 minutes or until golden brown. When cool, sprinkle with toasted almonds. Set aside.

7. To prepare filling: Combine the sugar, salt and cornstarch in a saucepan. Add the milk and half-and-half slowly, beating with a wire whisk. Cook over medium heat, stirring until thick and boiling.

8. Remove from the heat. Add some hot mixture to the egg, beating well. Return egg mixture to saucepan. Return to heat and bring almost to a boil. Cool and refrigerate until cold.

9. Whip the cream, then fold, with the almond extract, into the filling. Spread evenly over the crust.

10. Beginning at the center, arrange halved berries, cut side down, in a spoke fashion over the filling.

11. To prepare glaze: Combine the sliced berries and water in a saucepan. Bring to a boil and cook 2 minutes. Purée in a blender.

12. Combine the sugar and cornstarch in a saucepan. Add the strawberry purée and cook until thick and clear. Cool 5 minutes. Spoon the glaze over the berries. Refrigerate 4 to 6 hours or overnight.

Creamy Peach Pie

Makes one 9-inch pie

¾	cup sugar
¼	cup flour
¼	teaspoon salt
¼	teaspoon freshly grated nutmeg
4	cups peeled and sliced fresh peaches
1	(9-inch) pie shell, unbaked (see index)
1	cup whipping cream

1. Preheat oven to 400°.

2. Combine the sugar, flour, salt and nutmeg. Add to the peaches and toss lightly. Turn into the pie shell. Pour the whipping cream evenly over the top. Bake for 35 to 45 minutes or until firm and golden brown on top.

3. Chill for several hours before serving.

Pear Almond Tart

Makes one 9-inch tart

Pâte Sucrée:

1	cup flour
2	tablespoons sugar
½	teaspoon salt
6	tablespoons unsalted butter, softened
1	egg yolk
½	teaspoon vanilla
1	tablespoon lemon juice or water

Almond Filling:

½	cup unsalted butter
½	cup sugar
1	egg
1	cup finely ground blanched almonds
3	tablespoons rum
1	tablespoon flour
1	teaspoon almond extract

Poached Pears:

½	cup sugar
1	cup water
3-4	pears

Apricot Glaze:

½	cup apricot preserves
2	tablespoons rum

1. To prepare pâte sucrée: Combine the flour, sugar and salt in a bowl. Cut in the butter using a pastry blender. Make a well in the center and add the egg yolk, vanilla and lemon juice. Stir with your fingers until the mixture forms one blended ball and no longer adheres to your hands. Cover the dough and refrigerate for at least 30 minutes.

2. Roll the dough on a floured board into an 11-inch circle, about ⅛-inch thick. Line a 9-inch tart pan with the dough. If the dough cracks, press it together with your hands. Trim edges and chill.

3. To prepare almond filling: Cream the butter and sugar with an electric mixer. Add the egg, almonds, rum, flour and almond extract. Beat

until well combined. Spread evenly in the chilled tart shell. Refrigerate until the pears are ready.

4. Preheat oven to 425°.

5. To poach pears: Bring the sugar and water to a boil and simmer 5 minutes. Peel the pears. Cook the pears in the syrup just until tender. Cool.

6. Cut the pears in half, core and slice crosswise. Arrange on top of the filling. Bake the tart 45 minutes. If the top browns too quickly, cover with foil. Remove from oven and cool on a wire rack.

7. To prepare glaze: Melt the preserves with the rum in a small saucepan, stirring constantly. Strain through a mesh strainer. Brush the glaze on top of the tart. Cool completely, then refrigerate several hours or until set.

Blackberry Pie

Makes one 9-inch pie

Pastry for 1 (9-inch) two-crust pie (see index)

Filling:

4	cups clean, fresh blackberries
1	cup sugar
⅓	cup flour
½	teaspoon cinnamon
1½	tablespoons butter

1. Prepare the pastry and divide in half. Roll one half out and fit into a 9-inch pie plate.

2. To prepare filling: Mix the blackberries lightly with the sugar, flour and cinnamon. Pour the blackberries into the pastry-lined pie plate. Dot with butter.

3. Preheat oven to 400°.

4. Cover the pie with a top crust or weave strips into a lattice design. Cut vents in the top crust to allow steam to escape. Bake the pie 35 to 40 minutes or until the crust is nicely browned and juice begins to bubble through the slits or holes in the top crust. Remove to wire rack to cool.

Peach Chantilly Pie

Makes one 9-inch pie

3-4	large peaches
1½	tablespoons lemon juice
1	envelope plus 1 teaspoon unflavored gelatin
½	cup sugar
2	tablespoons orange-flavored liqueur
⅛	teaspoon salt
1	cup whipping cream
1	(9-inch) pie shell, baked and cooled (see index)
	Extra whipped cream
	Peach slices

1. Peel, halve and dice the peaches to measure 2¾ cups. Turn into a food processor or blender and process to measure 2 cups purée.

2. Combine ½ cup purée with the lemon juice in a medium saucepan and sprinkle with the gelatin. Let stand 5 minutes to soften, then set in a larger pan of hot water and heat, stirring constantly until gelatin dissolves.

3. Stir in the remaining puréed peach, sugar, liqueur and salt. Cool in the refrigerator until the mixture begins to thicken, about 2 hours.

4. Beat the cream stiff and fold into the gelatin mixture. Chill until the mixture mounds on a spoon, about 45 minutes. Turn into the pie shell and chill until firm, 3 to 4 hours or overnight.

5. At serving time, decorate top of pie with small puffs of whipped cream and slices of fresh peaches.

Fresh Fruit Tart

Makes one 9-inch tart

Tart Shell:

1	cup flour
2	tablespoons sugar
½	teaspoon salt
6	tablespoons softened butter
1	egg yolk
½	teaspoon vanilla

1	tablespoon lemon juice or water
1-1½	cups dried beans or pie weights

Filling:

1	(8 ounce) package cream cheese at room temperature
1	tablespoon sugar
1	tablespoon Grand Marnier

Topping:

Fresh fruit such as strawberries, nectarines, grapes, raspberries

Glaze:

½	cup apricot preserves
1	tablespoon orange juice or Grand Marnier

1. To prepare tart shell: Sift together the flour, sugar and salt in a bowl. Using a pastry blender, cut in the butter.

2. Make a well in the center and add the egg yolk, vanilla and lemon juice or water. Stir with your fingers until the mixture forms one blended ball and no longer adheres to your hands. Cover and refrigerate for at least 30 minutes.

3. Preheat oven to 400°.

4. Roll the dough to ⅛-inch thickness and line a 9-inch tart pan with it. Place foil over pastry and fill with dried beans or pie weights. Bake 7 to 10 minutes, or until lightly browned. Remove beans and foil.

5. To prepare filling: Beat the cream cheese until it is smooth and soft. Add the sugar and liqueur and mix thoroughly. Spread the filling in a smooth layer over the bottom of the crust and refrigerate.

6. To prepare topping: Wash the fruit and drain well on paper towels. Slice the nectarines into thin wedges. Arrange the fruit in concentric circles on top of the filling.

7. To prepare glaze: Melt the preserves over low heat. Strain through a mesh strainer. Thin with the orange juice or Grand Marnier. Brush over the fruit. Refrigerate.

French Peach Custard Tart

Makes one 9- or 10-inch tart

Crust:

6	tablespoons butter, chilled
1½	ounces cream cheese, chilled
¾	cup flour

Filling:

1½	cups milk
½	cup sugar
¼	cup cornstarch
¼	teaspoon salt
1½	teaspoons vanilla
½	teaspoon grated orange peel
2	eggs
1	cup plain yogurt
2	large fresh peaches, peeled and thinly sliced, dipped in lemon juice
	Mint sprigs

1. To prepare crust: Combine the butter, cream cheese and flour in a bowl. Cut with a pastry blender until the mixture is formed into lumps and is just beginning to get sticky. Shape with your hands into a ball and let stand for 10 minutes, uncovered.

2. Preheat oven to 400°.

3. Turn the dough onto a floured board and knead gently for 1 minute, about 40 turns. Work in extra flour as needed to prevent sticking. Roll out the dough to a 14-inch round. Fold carefully in half (pastry is tender) and lay in a 9-inch glass quiche dish with 1-inch upright sides or a 10-inch glass pie plate. Fold the edges of pastry under and pinch lightly to smooth the edge. Pierce the crust with a fork. Bake 12 minutes or until light golden. Cool.

4. To prepare filling: Whisk together the milk, sugar, cornstarch, salt, vanilla and orange peel in a saucepan. Cook, stirring over medium heat until the mixture comes to a boil. Boil gently, stirring vigorously with a wire whisk for 1 minute.

5. Beat the eggs in a small bowl. Beat some of the hot mixture into the eggs, then pour back into remaining hot mixture in saucepan. Cook, stirring, 4 minutes longer or until thick. Remove from heat and place a piece of plastic wrap directly on the pudding to keep a skin from forming. Cool slightly.

6. Beat in the yogurt with a wire whisk or rotary beater until smooth. Spoon into the cooled pastry crust. Chill until set.

7. Top with the sliced peaches. Garnish with mint, if desired.

Lemon Curd Tartlets

Makes 24

Pastry for 1 two-crust pie, unbaked (see index)
1 cup sugar
6 egg yolks, slightly beaten
½ cup lemon juice
½ cup butter
3 tablespoons grated lemon peel

1. Preheat oven to 475°.

2. Line 24 small tartlet pans with pastry and bake 8 to 10 minutes. Cool.

3. Combine the sugar and egg yolks in a medium saucepan. Gradually stir in the lemon juice. Cook over low heat, stirring constantly, until the mixture coats the back of a spoon. Do not let the mixture boil.

4. Remove from heat and stir in the butter and 1 tablespoon grated lemon peel. Cool completely.

5. Fill the tartlet shells and garnish with remaining lemon peel.

Strawberry Tart

Makes one 12-inch tart

Short Pastry:

2	cups flour
¼	cup sugar
¾	cup butter, cut into chunks
2	egg yolks

Pastry Cream:

1	(3 ounce) package cream cheese at room temperature
1	cup whipping cream
½	teaspoon vanilla
½	teaspoon grated lemon peel
1	teaspoon lemon juice
3-4	tablespoons powdered sugar

Strawberries and Glaze:

6	cups strawberries
1½	cups red currant jelly
2	tablespoons kirsch

1. Preheat oven to 300°.

2. To prepare pastry: Stir together the flour and sugar. Mix in the butter with your fingers until smooth.

3. With a fork, stir in the egg yolks until dough holds together. Work the dough with your hands to make a smooth ball, then press dough into a 12-inch tart pan or flan pan with removable bottom.

4. Bake 30 to 40 minutes or until golden. Let the shell cool in the pan.

5. To prepare pastry cream: Beat the cream cheese in a bowl with an electric mixer. Gradually blend in the whipping cream. Add the vanilla, lemon peel and lemon juice and beat until mixture is like stiffly whipped cream. Add the sugar and beat until well blended. Chill covered up to 24 hours.

6. To assemble tart: Wash berries and dry well.

7. Boil the jelly and liqueur in a small saucepan until jelly "sheets" from a spoon into drops. Then paint the inside of the shell with a thin coating of the glaze. Allow to set for 5 minutes. Reserve remainder of the glaze.

8. Spread the pastry cream over the bottom of the pastry shell. Place the berries on the cream with the largest ones in the center. Be sure to cover the entire surface of the cream.

9. With a spoon or pastry brush, apply reserved glaze over the berries, warming up the glaze if necessary for easy spreading. Refrigerate until ready to serve, but no longer than 2 or 3 hours. Remove from pan to serve and cut into wedges.

Rhubarb-Strawberry Pie

Makes one 9-inch pie

1½	cups sugar
4	tablespoons flour
2	teaspoons tapioca
	Dash salt
2	cups fresh strawberries, sliced
2½	cups cut-up fresh rhubarb
	Grated peel of 1 orange
	Pastry for 1 (9-inch) two-crust pie (see index)
1	tablespoon butter
	Milk
	Sugar

1. Combine the sugar, flour, tapioca and salt and mix well.

2. Place the strawberries and rhubarb in a bowl and add the sugar-flour mixture. Stir well to combine, then stir in the orange peel.

3. Preheat oven to 425°.

4. Roll out half the pastry and fit it into a 9-inch pie pan. Pour in the filling and top with dabs of butter.

5. Roll out the top crust. Adjust over the filling and seal by crimping the edges in your favorite manner. Cut vents in the top crust to allow steam to escape.

6. Brush the top crust with a little milk and then sprinkle lightly with sugar. Bake for 15 minutes, then lower heat to 400° and bake about 30 minutes longer.

Brandy Pumpkin Mousse Pie

Makes one 9-inch pie

Mousse Pie:

1	envelope unflavored gelatin
⅓-½	cup brandy
2	cups pumpkin purée
4	eggs, separated
½	cup firmly packed brown sugar
½	cup sugar
¼	cup butter, melted
1	teaspoon ground cinnamon
½	teaspoon salt
¼	teaspoon ground cloves
⅛	teaspoon cream of tartar
	Pinch salt
¾	cup whipping cream, whipped
1	(9-inch) pie shell, baked (see index)

Pecan Nut Topping:

½	cup sugar
½	cup coarsely chopped pecans
	Additional whipped cream

1. To prepare pie: Soften the gelatin in the brandy and set aside. Heat the pumpkin, egg yolks, brown sugar, sugar, butter, cinnamon, ½ teaspoon salt and cloves in a saucepan over medium heat, stirring constantly, until slightly boiling and thickened. Remove from heat. Beat in the gelatin mixture until gelatin is dissolved, about 1 minute. Cool.

2. Beat the egg whites, cream of tartar and pinch of salt until stiff peaks form. Fold the beaten egg whites and whipped cream into the pumpkin mixture. Pour into the pie shell, mounding slightly in the center. Chill 6 hours or overnight.

3. To prepare topping: Heat the sugar in a saucepan until a light caramel color. Stir in the pecans. Spread on a buttered baking sheet and cool. Crush into small pieces.

4. When ready to serve pie, garnish the top with whipped cream and crushed pecan nut topping.

Note: When using fresh pumpkin, cook down the mashed pulp over low heat until it is a very thick purée.

Golden Apple Meringue Tart

Makes one 9-inch tart

Pastry:

1	cup flour
2	tablespoons sugar
⅓	cup softened butter
1	egg yolk, beaten
¼	teaspoon vanilla
1	teaspoon milk

Filling:

3-4	golden Delicious apples, pared, cored and sliced
¼	cup water
1	tablespoon sugar
2	teaspoons cornstarch
¾	teaspoon ground cinnamon
	Dash salt

Topping:

3	egg whites
¼	teaspoon cream of tartar
¼	cup sugar

1. Preheat oven to 400°.

2. To make pastry: Combine the flour and sugar. Cut in the softened butter. Stir in the beaten egg yolk and vanilla and mix well. If the mixture is too dry, add milk. Press in the bottom and 1 inch up the sides of a 9-inch springform pan. Bake 8 to 10 minutes. (Pastry may also be pressed onto the bottom and sides of a 9-inch flan pan with removable bottom.) Leave oven at 400°.

3. To prepare filling: Combine the apples and water in a saucepan. Simmer, covered, 5 minutes or until apples are tender. Combine the sugar, cornstarch, cinnamon and salt and stir into the apples. Cook and stir until thickened. Turn mixture into the baked pastry crust.

4. To prepare topping: Beat the egg whites with the cream of tartar until foamy. Gradually add the sugar and beat until stiff peaks form and sugar is dissolved. Spoon the meringue over the apples, sealing to the edges of the pastry.

5. Bake 5 to 7 minutes or until lightly browned. Serve warm or cool.

Pear Fruit Flan

Makes one 9-inch flan

Topping:

4-5	large fresh pears
1½	cups sugar
3	cups water

Crust:

1	cup sifted flour
2	tablespoons powdered sugar
½	cup unsalted butter, softened

Filling:

1	(3 ounce) package cream cheese, softened
3	tablespoons sour cream

Glaze:

½	cup apricot or raspberry preserves, strained
1	tablespoon brandy

1. To prepare topping: Peel and halve the pears. In a skillet, blend the sugar and water; heat, stirring until the sugar is melted. Add the pear halves in only one layer and poach for 20 minutes or until tender. Remove from the syrup and drain. When cool enough to handle, cut each half in half again. Cool completely.

2. Preheat oven to 450°.

3. To prepare crust: In a medium-size bowl, combine the flour and sugar. Blend in the butter with your fingertips. Press evenly on the bottom and sides of a 9-inch flan pan or a 9-inch pie plate. Pierce the bottom of the crust with a fork. Bake 10 minutes. Cool on a wire rack.

4. To prepare filling: Blend the cream cheese and sour cream together and spread into the cool crust. Arrange well-drained pears on cream cheese layer.

5. To prepare glaze: Heat the preserves in a small saucepan. Remove from heat and stir in the brandy. Brush over the fruit and edges of the crust. Chill until ready to serve.

Strawberry Angel Pie

Makes one 9-inch pie

Meringue Shell:

3	egg whites
¼	teaspoon cream of tartar
¾	cup sugar

Lemony Cream Filling:

3	egg yolks
¼	cup butter, melted
¼	cup warm water
¾	cup sugar
	Dash salt
3	teaspoons grated lemon peel
3	tablespoons lemon juice
2	pints strawberries, stemmed
1	cup whipping cream, whipped

1. Preheat oven to 275°.

2. To prepare meringue shell: Draw a 9-inch circle on a greased and floured baking sheet. Beat the egg whites and cream of tartar until foamy. Add the sugar, 2 tablespoons at a time, beating until very stiff and glossy. Spread on the 9-inch circle, building up the sides (or pipe through a pastry tube). Bake for 1 hour. Turn off the oven but leave the shell in 1 hour more. Remove and cool. Place on a serving platter.

3. To prepare lemony cream filling: Put the egg yolks, butter, water, sugar, salt, lemon peel and lemon juice in a blender. Whirl until smooth. Pour into the top of a double boiler placed over simmering water. Cook, stirring constantly, until thickened, about 8 minutes. Cool and chill.

4. Halve the berries, reserving a dozen whole berries for garnish.

5. Swirl together the lemony cream filling, halved berries and whipped cream. Spoon into the meringue shell. Chill 6 hours or overnight.

6. Top with the reserved berries and serve.

Cookies

The eating revolution that has dotted our shopping malls and downtown streets with cookie stores was founded mostly on a growing awareness that, if we are going to snack our way through life, what we eat should be wholesome, if not low-calorie.

While store-bought cookies fill the bill as snacks, homemade cookies in the hands of an inquisitive cook are loving adventures in adding fillings, toppings and ingredients to dough.

In the process, they can become as complex as a dessert while keeping them portable enough to be carried into the mountains in a backpack or be packed lovingly in a tin and sent off to someone away from home.

Cookies have always meant something special, whether it was a family holiday tradition, the treasured sweet in a brown-bag school lunch, or a childhood lesson in learning how to cook. The growing anticipation as the delicious smells escaped from the oven was enough to etch it permanently on the memory.

The recipes in this chapter take a skillful home baker a long way beyond the standard offerings and well along the road to becoming a neighborhood legend.

Swedish Almond Butter Cookies

Makes 3 dozen

1	cup butter at room temperature
½	cup sugar
¼	teaspoon salt
2	cups flour
1	scant teaspoon almond extract
	Additional sugar

1. Beat the butter and sugar until creamy. Blend in the salt and flour and flavor with almond extract. Chill dough in the refrigerator for about 30 minutes.
2. Preheat oven to 350°.
3. Pinch off pieces of dough and roll into 1-inch balls. Roll the balls lightly in additional sugar. Place on cookie sheets and stamp with a cookie stamp in your favorite design. Bake 12 to 15 minutes, or until a light gold. Watch carefully so they do not get brown. Cool on wire racks.

Kringles

Makes 6 dozen

¾	cup butter
½	cup sugar
1	egg yolk
	Dash salt
1	teaspoon vanilla
1¾	cups flour
6	dozen blanched almonds

1. Preheat oven to 325°.
2. Mix together the butter, sugar, egg yolk, salt, vanilla and flour until well combined.
3. Pinch off small amounts of the dough and form into small balls. Place on cookie sheets and flatten by pressing an almond into the top of each.
4. Bake 20 minutes. These cookies should not brown. Cool on wire racks.

Lemon Bars

Makes 32

½	cup butter
1	cup plus 2 tablespoons flour
1	cup powdered sugar
2	eggs
1	cup sugar
4	tablespoons lemon juice
1	teaspoon grated lemon peel
½	teaspoon baking powder

1. Preheat oven to 350°.
2. Mix together the butter, 1 cup flour and ¼ cup powdered sugar. Press into an 8-inch-square pan. Bake 15 minutes.
3. Mix together the eggs, sugar, 3 tablespoons lemon juice, lemon peel, baking powder and 2 tablespoons flour. Pour on top of the baked crust. Bake 25 minutes longer.
4. Mix 1 tablespoon lemon juice with ¾ cup powdered sugar until smooth. Use to frost lemon bars while still warm. Cool completely and cut into 1-by-2-inch bars to serve.

Thumb-Print Cookies

Makes 2 dozen

½	cup butter
¼	cup sugar
1	egg yolk
1½	cups sifted flour
1	tablespoon rum
	Raspberry or apricot jam for filling

1. Cream the butter and sugar, then add the egg yolk, flour and rum. Refrigerate dough for 5 minutes before making cookies.
2. Preheat oven to 350°.
3. Form the dough into small balls and place on an ungreased cookie sheet. Make a thumb print in each cookie and add a dab of jam.
4. Bake 10 minutes or until a light gold. Cool on wire racks.

Chocolate Mint Squares

Makes 4 dozen

Cookie Layer:

2 ounces unsweetened chocolate

½ cup butter

2 eggs

1 cup sugar

½ cup chopped almonds

½ cup flour

Filling:

1½ cups powdered sugar

3 tablespoons butter, softened

2 tablespoons whipping cream

¾ teaspoon peppermint flavoring

Drop of green food coloring, optional

2 tablespoons crushed peppermint candy, optional

Chocolate Glaze:

4 ounces semisweet chocolate

4 tablespoons butter

1 teaspoon vanilla

1. Preheat oven to 350°.

2. To prepare cookie layer: Melt the chocolate and butter together over hot water.

3. In a bowl, beat together the eggs and sugar until thick. Add the nuts, flour and chocolate-butter mixture and stir until smooth.

4. Pour the batter into a buttered 9-inch-square pan and bake 30 minutes or until done. Let cool.

5. To prepare filling: Beat together the sugar, butter, cream and flavoring until smooth. Add a drop of green food coloring and/or 2 tablespoons crushed peppermint candy, if desired.

6. Spread over the cookie layer; cover and chill until firm, about 1 hour.

7. To prepare glaze: Melt together the chocolate, butter and vanilla over hot water and mix well. Drizzle it over the mint topping. Cover and chill again until firm.

8. Cut into bite-size squares to serve.

Walnut Dessert Cookies

Makes 2 dozen

Cookies:

2 cups walnuts

1 cup butter

⅔ cup sugar

2 teaspoons vanilla

2 cups sifted flour

Walnut Filling:

1 cup walnuts

½ cup raspberry or apricot jam

Chocolate Glaze:

2 ounces semisweet chocolate

2 tablespoons butter

1 teaspoon vanilla

Garnish:

Large walnut pieces

1. To prepare cookies: Finely grind the walnuts in a food processor or blender and set aside.

2. Cream the butter, sugar and vanilla. Gradually blend in the flour, then add the walnuts. Chill the dough for easier rolling.

3. Preheat oven to 350°.

4. Roll the dough on a floured board to about ¼-inch thickness and cut with floured 2½-inch cutters. Place on ungreased cookie sheets. Bake above the center of the oven 15 minutes, or until the edges brown very lightly. Using a wide spatula, remove to wire racks to cool.

5. To prepare walnut filling: Process the walnuts in a food processor or blender, then mix with the jam.

6. To prepare glaze: Melt the chocolate and butter over low heat. Add the vanilla, stir and cool slightly.

7. When the cookies are cold, put 2 together, sandwich fashion, using about 2 teaspoons walnut filling for each. Spread half of the top cookie of each sandwich with the cooled chocolate glaze. Top the glaze with a piece of walnut.

Kahlua Fudge Mounds

Makes 2½ dozen

½	cup chopped red candied cherries
¼	cup Kahlua
2	ounces unsweetened chocolate
1¾	cups sifted flour
¾	teaspoon baking soda
¾	teaspoon salt
1	cup firmly packed brown sugar
⅓	cup shortening
1	large egg
1	teaspoon vanilla
⅓	cup milk
⅓	cup chopped pecans

Kahlua Buttercream Frosting:

2	cups sifted powdered sugar
2	tablespoons soft butter
1	tablespoon Kahlua
1	tablespoon half-and-half

Garnish:

15	red candied cherries, halved
7-8	green candied cherries, quartered

1. To prepare cookies: Combine the chopped red candied cherries and Kahlua. Let stand while preparing the batter. Melt the chocolate over warm water and cool slightly.

2. Resift the flour with the baking soda and salt. Beat the sugar, shortening, egg and vanilla together until fluffy. Stir in the flour mixture alternately with the milk, then stir in the melted chocolate and mix well.

3. Add the cherries and Kahlua, then the pecans. Mix well and let stand 5 minutes.

4. Preheat oven to 375°.

5. Drop the batter by rounded tablespoonfuls onto lightly greased cookie sheets, making about 30 small mounds.

6. Bake above the center of the oven about 10 minutes, until the tops spring back when touched lightly in the center.

7. Let stand 1 minute, then remove to wire racks to cool.

8. To prepare frosting: Beat the sugar, butter, Kahlua and half-and-half until smooth.

9. When the cookies are cool, top each with frosting pressed through a pastry tube fitted with a rosette. Center each frosting rosette with a red candied cherry half and a quarter of green candied cherry to look like a leaf.

Pumpkin Spice Cookies

Makes 6 dozen

2¼	cups flour
2	cups quick or old-fashioned oats, uncooked
2	teaspoons baking powder
1½	teaspoon pumpkin-pie spice
½	teaspoon salt
1	cup firmly packed brown sugar
¾	cup butter, softened
2	eggs
1¼	cups pumpkin purée
¾	cup raisins
¾	cup chopped nuts

1. Preheat oven to 375°.

2. In a small bowl, combine the flour, oats, baking powder, pumpkin-pie spice and salt.

3. In a large bowl, beat together the sugar and butter until light and fluffy. Blend in the eggs and pumpkin. Add the flour mixture and mix well. Stir in the raisins and nuts.

4. Drop by rounded teaspoonfuls onto greased cookie sheets. Bake 12 to 14 minutes or until light golden brown. Cool 1 minute on the cookie sheets. Remove to wire cooling racks. Store in a loosely covered container.

Note: When using fresh pumpkin, cook down the mashed pulp over low heat until it is a very thick purée.

Marbled Brownies

Makes 3 dozen

Chocolate Mixture:

4	ounces semisweet baking chocolate
3	tablespoons butter
1	teaspoon vanilla extract
¼	teaspoon almond extract
2	eggs
¾	cup sugar
½	cup flour
½	teaspoon baking powder
¼	teaspoon salt
½	cup chopped walnuts

Cream-cheese Mixture:

1	(3 ounce) package cream cheese at room temperature
2	tablespoons butter at room temperature
¼	cup sugar
1	egg
1	tablespoon flour
½	teaspoon vanilla

1. To prepare chocolate mixture: Combine the chocolate and butter in a small heavy saucepan. Melt over low heat, stirring until thoroughly mixed. Cool.
2. Stir in the vanilla and almond extracts.
3. In a large bowl, beat the eggs until light. Add the sugar gradually and beat until thick.
4. Combine the flour, baking powder and salt. Add to the egg mixture, stirring until smooth.
5. Stir in the chocolate mixture until well mixed. Fold in the nuts.
6. To prepare cream-cheese mixture: Cream the cheese and butter together until smooth. Add the sugar and cream until fluffy. Add the egg and beat well. Add the flour and vanilla, beating until smooth.
7. Preheat oven to 350°.
8. To assemble brownies: Spread half of the chocolate mixture in a greased 9-inch-square baking pan. Smooth the cream-cheese filling over the top.
9. Place spoonfuls of the remaining chocolate mixture evenly over

the top of the cream-cheese mixture. Swirl a knife through the batters to create a marbled effect.

10. Bake 25 to 30 minutes or until brownies test done.

11. Cool completely on a wire rack. Cut into 1½-inch squares to serve. Store, covered, in the refrigerator.

Soft Center Chocolate-Chip Cookies

Makes 5 dozen

½	teaspoon salt
2½	cups flour
1	teaspoon baking soda
1	cup butter, melted
¾	cup firmly packed brown sugar
¾	cup sugar
2	eggs
1	teaspoon vanilla
2	cups chocolate chips
1	cup nuts

1. Stir together the salt, flour and baking soda.

2. Beat the melted butter until it is homogenized. Add the brown sugar, sugar, eggs and vanilla and blend well. Add the flour mixture, mixing until well blended. Stir in the chocolate chips and nuts.

3. Preheat oven to 350°.

4. Drop the dough by teaspoonfuls on cookie sheets lined with slightly greased parchment. Bake 15 minutes or less, or until cookies still feel soft to the touch when pressed with a finger. Remove from parchment and cool on wire racks.

This recipe is one of Judy Borreson Groom's favorites.

Walnut-Cherry Holiday Squares

Makes 5 dozen

Crust:

½ cup butter

2 tablespoons firmly packed brown sugar

1 cup sifted flour

Filling:

½ cup finely chopped coconut

1 cup firmly packed brown sugar

1 cup chopped walnuts

15 candied red cherries, chopped

12 dates, chopped

2 tablespoons flour

¼ teaspoon baking powder

1 teaspoon vanilla

2 eggs

Frosting:

1 cup powdered sugar

2 tablespoons butter

1 tablespoon orange juice

1 tablespoon lemon juice

1. Preheat oven to 400°.

2. To prepare crust: Cream together the butter and brown sugar. Add the flour and mix thoroughly. Pat the dough into the bottom of an 8-inch-square pan.

3. Bake 10 minutes. Remove from oven and cool. Reduce oven to 350°.

4. To prepare filling: Combine the coconut, sugar, walnuts, cherries, dates, flour, baking powder, vanilla and eggs. Spread over the cooled crust.

5. Bake 30 minutes. Remove from the oven and cool.

6. To prepare frosting: Cream together the powdered sugar and butter. Thin frosting to spreading consistency with equal parts of orange juice and lemon juice as needed.

7. Frost the cookies, then cut into small squares.

Spicy Pear Drop Cookies

Makes 3½-4 dozen

½	cup butter
¾	cup sugar
¾	cup firmly packed brown sugar
2	eggs
1	teaspoon vanilla
2	cups finely chopped pears
3	cups flour
2	teapoons baking powder
1	teaspoon baking soda
1	teaspoon ground cinnamon
¼	teaspoon ground nutmeg
¼	teaspoon ground ginger
⅓	cup chopped nuts

1. Preheat oven to 350°.
2. Thoroughly beat together the butter and sugars. Add the eggs and vanilla and mix well. Stir in the pears.
3. Sift together the flour, baking powder, baking soda, cinnamon, nutmeg and ginger. Add to the creamed mixture. Stir in the nuts.
4. Drop the batter by heaping spoonfuls onto greased baking sheets.
5. Bake 10 to 12 minutes or until golden brown. Cool on wire racks.

Candies

In professional kitchens, candy making is a skill all to itself. The basic ingredient is sugar, but the artful practitioner can make it hard or brittle, soft or chewy, spun out into fluff or almost liquid. It can be a solid piece, a filling or a coating.

It takes a practiced sense of time and temperature to know when the recipe is going as it should. But once the techniques are mastered, few other types of cooking combine as much delicacy and elegance in their products.

While candy always has been a messenger of Valentine's Day and Mother's Day love, it has been sending mixed messages in some of its other societal roles recently. Dieters shun it for its calories, but others praise it as a means of quick energy.

Most of us regard candy with varying degrees of pleasure and guilt, but we seem to agree that, if we are going to eat candy, we might as well have the best. Witness the vigorous sales of $10-a-pound-and-up chocolates from around the world.

The recipes in this chapter will challenge your candy-cooking skills. They are a mix of textures and flavors that span the whole range of the candy maker's skills. And they are guaranteed to keep candy lovers happy the year around and make those who "really shouldn't . . . have well, maybe just one."

◇

Mint Truffles

Makes 8 dozen

6-8	ounces semisweet chocolate
1	(12 ounce) package chocolate chips
½	cup butter, softened
½	cup powdered sugar
2	eggs
2	teaspoons vanilla
½-1	teaspoon peppermint extract

1. Melt the semisweet chocolate in the top of a double boiler over hot, not boiling, water. Spread evenly in a foil-lined 8-inch-square pan. Refrigerate until set.

2. Meanwhile, melt the chocolate chips in the top of the double boiler over hot, not boiling, water. Cool. Blend the butter and sugar in a blender or a food processor. Add the eggs and blend well. Add the melted chocolate chips, vanilla and peppermint extract and blend well.

3. Spread the chocolate chip mixture over the hardened chocolate layer and refrigerate again until firm, about 1 hour. Lift the truffle out of the pan; remove the foil and cut the truffle into small pieces. Serve immediately or return to refrigerator. Truffles will keep for a couple of weeks in the refrigerator, covered with plastic wrap.

This recipe is from Ruby Wyman.

Mocha Truffles

Makes 2½ dozen

1	(6 ounce) package chocolate chips
⅔	cup butter, softened
1	egg yolk
1¼	cups powdered sugar
1	tablespoon rum
1	teaspoon instant coffee
	Chocolate shots

1. Melt the chocolate chips in the top of a double boiler over hot, not boiling, water. Remove from heat and set aside to cool briefly.

2. Cream the butter, egg yolk and powdered sugar. Add the rum, instant coffee and melted chocolate chips. Chill 1 to 2 hours in the refrigerator or until the mixture can be formed into balls.

3. Roll into 1-inch balls, then in the chocolate shots. Place in confectioners' paper cups on a plate. Refrigerate 1 to 2 hours before serving. They will keep a couple of weeks in the refrigerator, covered with plastic wrap.

Brandied Truffles

Makes 4 to 5 dozen

6	ounces semisweet chocolate
4	ounces milk chocolate
½	cup whipping cream
3	tablespoons butter, softened
¼	cup brandy
	Chopped nuts, chocolate shots or powdered cocoa

1. Combine the semisweet chocolate and milk chocolate in the top part of a double boiler and melt over warm, not hot, water. When chocolate is melted, heat the cream to scalding.

2. Slowly beat the cream into the melted chocolate, blending until smooth. Beat in the butter, 1 tablespoon at a time, then stir in the brandy.

3. Turn the mixture into a small loaf pan and chill thoroughly. Scoop out small balls, working quickly and place them in the freezer to firm up.

4. Remove the chocolate balls from the freezer and smooth each one by rolling it quickly between your palms. Return to the freezer to chill.

5. When ready to coat the chocolate balls, roll them in finely chopped nuts, chocolate shots or powdered cocoa. If using cocoa, roll just before serving. If they stand, the cocoa will be absorbed and the candies won't look as attractive.

Divinity

Makes 2½ dozen pieces

2½	cups sugar
½	cup water
½	cup light corn syrup
¼	teaspoon salt
2	egg whites
1	teaspoon vanilla
1	cup chopped nuts
¼	cup chopped green candied cherries or pineapple
¼	cup chopped red candied cherries

1. Place the sugar, water, corn syrup and salt in a saucepan. Cook to 260° F. on a candy thermometer, or until a small amount of the syrup forms a hard ball when dropped into cold water.

2. Beat the egg whites until stiff peaks form. Slowly add the syrup, beating 1 minute with a mixer on high speed. Add the vanilla and continue beating until the mixture begins to hold its shape and to lose its gloss. Quickly stir in the nuts and candied fruit.

3. Drop by the teaspoonful onto wax-paper-lined cookie sheets. Let set until cool.

Note: It is best not to make divinity on a rainy day, but if you must, pick a day that is barely raining and cook the syrup about 2° higher.

Chocolate Mint Squares

Makes 12 dozen

1	(12 ounce) package semisweet chocolate chips
4	tablespoons vegetable shortening
5	tablespoons butter
½	cup light corn syrup
4½	cups sifted powdered sugar
1	teaspoon peppermint extract

1. To prepare bottom layer: Combine half the chocolate chips and 2 tablespoons shortening in the top part of a double boiler. Place over hot, not boiling, water and heat until the chips melt and the mixture is smooth.

2. With the back of a spoon, spread the mixture evenly in a foil-lined 10-by-15-inch pan. Chill in the refrigerator about 20 minutes or until firm. Carefully invert the chocolate onto a wax-paper-lined cookie sheet. Gently peel off the foil and return the chocolate mixture to the refrigerator.

3. To prepare the center layer fondant: Combine the butter, corn syrup and 2½ cups powdered sugar in a large saucepan. Bring to a full boil over medium-low heat, stirring constantly. Add the remaining sugar and peppermint extract. Stir vigorously until well blended, 2 to 3 minutes.

4. Remove from the heat. Pour the fondant onto a greased cookie sheet. Cool just enough to handle, or it could get too stiff to knead. Knead until soft, about 2 to 3 minutes.

5. Roll out the fondant ⅛-inch thick between two pieces of plastic wrap to form a 10-by-15-inch rectangle. Remove the top sheet of plastic wrap. Carefully place the fondant on top of the chocolate layer. Remove the second sheet of plastic wrap. Chill 15 minutes.

6. To prepare top chocolate layer: Melt the remaining chocolate chips and shortening in the top of the double boiler over hot, not boiling, water until the chocolate melts and the mixture is smooth. Spread the melted chocolate evenly over the fondant filling. Chill 15 to 20 minutes. Cut into squares or fancy shapes, if desired.

Hazelnut Fondant Roll

Makes 1 roll

1½	cups shelled hazelnuts (also called filberts)
1	pound powdered sugar
	Dash salt
¼	cup melted butter
1	teaspoon vanilla
2-3	tablespoons half-and-half

1. Preheat oven to 250°.

2. Toast the hazelnuts in a pan for 15 minutes or until crisp. Chop coarsely.

3. Add the sugar and salt to the melted butter. Gradually mix in the vanilla and half-and-half. Stir in 1 cup hazelnuts and shape into a log. Roll the log in the remaining ½ cup hazelnuts.

Cream Sherry Candied Walnuts

Makes 3½ to 4 cups

1½	cups sugar
1	teaspoon light corn syrup
¼	teaspoon salt
½	cup cream sherry
1½	teaspoons grated lemon peel
1	(12 ounce) package walnut halves or quarters

1. In a saucepan that will hold 2 quarts comfortably, mix the sugar, corn syrup, salt, sherry and lemon peel. Stir well to mix and bring to a boil. Cook the mixture to soft-ball stage, 234° to 240° F. on a candy thermometer.

2. Stir in the walnuts; remove from the heat and stir until creamy and the nuts are well coated. Quickly turn out on wax paper and, using two forks, separate the nuts. It sets up fast, so work quickly.

3. When cool, store in airtight containers until ready to serve.

Peanut Brittle

Makes 3½ pounds candy

2	cups sugar
1	cup light corn syrup
½	cup water
½	teaspoon salt
4	cups raw peanuts, skins on
2	tablespoons butter
2	teaspoons baking soda

1. In a heavy saucepan, heat the sugar, corn syrup, water and salt to a rolling boil. Add the peanuts. Reduce heat to medium and stir constantly. Cook until the syrup spins a thread, 293° F. on a candy thermometer. This will take about 45 minutes.

2. Add the butter, then the baking soda. Beat rapidly and pour the mixture onto a buttered surface, spreading it to ¼-inch thickness. When cool, break into pieces. Store in an air-tight container.

Brandied Pecan Butter Creams

Makes 9 dozen

½	cup finely chopped pecans
3	tablespoons brandy
4½	cups sugar
½	cup corn syrup
1	cup water
½	cup butter
1	pound semisweet or milk chocolate, grated

1. Marinate the nuts in the brandy for 2 hours or overnight.

2. Combine the sugar, corn syrup and water in a large, heavy saucepan and bring to a boil. Cook to 220° F. on a candy thermometer.

3. Add the butter and stir. Cover for 2 minutes. Uncover; continue cooking until the mixture reaches the soft-ball stage, 234° to 240° F. on a candy thermometer.

4. Pour the mixture onto a marble slab or large platter; cool to 98° F. Fold the sides to the middle with a wide spatula. Continue this process until the candy changes color. This will take about 30 minutes.

5. Mix in the brandied nuts using your fingers to distribute them thoroughly. Divide the candy into 6 parts; roll each into a 1-inch log. Wrap in plastic wrap and let ripen at least overnight at room temperature.

6. When ready to coat with chocolate, cut the candy into ¾-inch chunks and form into balls.

7. Melt the grated chocolate in the top of a double boiler over hot, not boiling, water. Dipping chocolate should maintain temperature of about 86° F. Dip each candy in the melted chocolate. Set on foil and let the chocolate coating harden.

Maple Almond Candy

Makes 1½ pounds

½	cup whole blanched almonds
1	cup firmly packed brown sugar
1	cup sugar
⅔	cup half-and-half
¼	cup butter
2	tablespoons light corn syrup
¾	teaspoon maple flavoring
⅓	cup almond paste, crumbled

1. Preheat oven to 300°.

2. Spread the almonds in a shallow pan and toast lightly about 15 minutes or until light gold. Chop finely while still warm and set aside.

3. In a 2-quart saucepan, combine the sugars, half-and-half, butter and corn syrup. Heat to boiling, stirring until the sugar dissolves. Cover and cook over low heat 5 minutes.

4. Uncover, place a candy thermometer in the pan and cook over moderate heat until the mixture reaches the soft-ball stage, 234° to 240° F. on the candy thermometer.

5. Remove from the heat and allow to stand undisturbed until lukewarm. Add the maple flavoring and start beating with a heavy spoon. Beat until the mixture thickens and becomes creamy. Quickly stir in the chopped almonds, then the almond paste.

6. Turn out into a buttered 8-inch-square pan. Let stand until firm before cutting.

Peanut Clusters

Makes 35

1	(6 ounce) package semisweet chocolate
⅔	cup sweetened condensed milk
1	teaspoon vanilla
1½	cups Spanish peanuts

1. In the top of a double boiler, melt the chocolate over hot, not boiling, water.

2. Remove from the heat and add the milk, vanilla and Spanish peanuts. Mix together well. Drop by spoonfuls onto wax paper. When cool, store in a container with a tight fitting lid and keep in a cool place.

Baked Caramel Corn

Makes 5 quarts

1	cup butter
2	cups firmly packed brown sugar
¼	cup light corn syrup
¼	cup dark corn syrup
1	teaspoon salt
½	teaspoon baking soda
1	teaspoon vanilla
6	quarts popped corn
2	cups peanuts

1. In a large, heavy saucepan, melt the butter; stir in the brown sugar, corn syrups and salt. Bring to a boil, stirring constantly; boil without stirring, 5 minutes.

2. Remove from heat; stir in the baking soda and vanilla. Gradually pour the sugar mixture over the popped corn and nuts, mixing well.

3. Preheat oven to 250°.

4. Turn the popped corn mixture into two large shallow baking pans. Bake 1 hour, stirring every 15 minutes. Remove from the oven and cool completely.

5. Break apart and pack in an airtight container.

Breads & Rolls

One of the Northwest's distinctions is that marketing studies show we do more baking than most regions of the country. Home baking is a regular part of life for thousands of families, and the number of small bakeries, each with its own following, increases steadily.

At almost any party in the area, you can find a roomful of people trading notes on the specialties of their favorite bakeries and perhaps sparking a friendly debate as to which one is best.

Reader response to baking recipes in the Food section tells us that Times readers are always on the lookout for something new to try, particularly recipes that mix the region's bounty of fruits and nuts into the breads and rolls and muffins that parade out of our ovens.

Whether it is a festive way to grace a holiday table or a way of ensuring that whole grains find their way into the diet of a generation of eat-on-the-run active family members, bread is an enduring part of our eating patterns.

The breads in this chapter also provide accompaniment for meals in several ethnic cuisines which have flourished in this region. Most of them, from Mother O'Donnell's Irish Soda Bread to the Scandinavian Lila's Aebelskivar, were contributed by immigrants or children of immigrants with the baking of their homelands still vivid in their memories.

◇

Rye Bread

Makes two 9-by-5-inch loaves

2	packages dry yeast
1	cup warm water
2	tablespoons sugar
1	tablespoon salt
4½	cups unbleached flour
1½	cups lukewarm water
¼	cup dry milk
¼	cup molasses
2	tablespoons vegetable oil
2	cups rye flour
	Melted butter to brush tops of loaves

1. In a mixing bowl, dissolve the dry yeast in warm water (105° to 115°F.). Add the sugar, salt and ½ cup unbleached flour. Beat until smooth. Cover and set in a warm place until it looks bubbly and foamy, about 1 hour.

2. Add the lukewarm water, dry milk, molasses, 2 cups unbleached flour and oil. Beat well.

3. Add the rye flour and remaining 2 cups unbleached flour, turning out on a floured board and kneading while adding the last of the unbleached flour. Knead until the dough is smooth and elastic, about 10 minutes.

4. Place the dough in a buttered bowl, turning once to grease all sides. Cover and let rise until double in size, about 1 hour.

5. Punch the dough down and let it rise again until double, another hour.

6. Divide the dough in half and flatten each piece into a rectangle. Roll up like jelly rolls and place each roll into a greased, 9-by-5-inch bread pan. Cover and let rise again until double, about 1 hour.

7. Preheat oven to 350°.

8. When doubled, bake 50 minutes. If bread pans are glass, lower heat to 325°. Remove the bread from the pans and let cool on a rack. While still hot, brush the tops of the loaves with melted butter.

Stout Rye Bread

Makes 2 large loaves

3	cups	Guinness beer
⅓	cup	shortening
½	cup	firmly packed light-brown sugar
½	cup	light molasses
1½	tablespoons	salt
2	tablespoons	grated orange peel
2	tablespoons	caraway seeds
2	packages	dry yeast
½	cup	warm water
5	cups	rye flour
5-6	cups	white flour

1. Heat the beer until it just bubbles, then add the shortening, brown sugar, molasses, salt, orange peel and caraway seeds. Set aside and let cool to lukewarm.

2. Dissolve the yeast in warm water (105° to 115°F.). Add to the beer mixture. Beat in the rye flour and enough white flour to make a soft dough.

3. Turn out on a heavily floured board and knead until smooth and elastic, about 10 minutes.

4. Place the dough in a greased bowl, turning so as to grease the top. Cover loosely with a towel and let rise in a warm place until double in bulk.

5. Punch down the dough and knead again. Divide in half. Shape each portion into a round or long oval on a greased cookie sheet. Slash the tops of loaves with a sharp knife. Let rise until double in bulk.

6. Preheat oven to 350°.

7. Bake 40 to 45 minutes or until done. Remove from the cookie sheet and cool on wire racks.

Steamed Brown Bread

Makes 2 loaves

1	cup dark stone ground rye flour
1	cup whole-wheat flour
1	cup cornmeal
½	teaspoon salt
2	teaspoons baking soda
¾	cup molasses
2	cups sour milk (made with 1⅞ cups milk and 2 tablespoons vinegar or lemon juice)

1. Combine the rye flour, whole-wheat flour, cornmeal, salt and baking soda. Mix well.

2. Stir the molasses into the milk and pour into dry ingredients. Stir thoroughly.

3. Pour the batter into two greased 1-pound coffee cans, filling the cans no more than two-thirds full. The cans can be covered with aluminum foil or left uncovered.

4. Place the cans in a kettle; add boiling water to a depth of 3 or 4 inches. Cover the kettle and steam for 2½ to 3 hours, replenishing the water as necessary to keep it partway up the cans. Remove the bread from the cans, handling them with potholders. Cool and slice.

Walnut Bread

Makes 4 round loaves

5	cups unbleached flour
1	tablespoon salt
2	tablespoons sugar
2	packages dry yeast
2	cups warm milk
½	cup walnut oil
1	cup walnuts, roughly chopped

1. Measure the flour into a sifter; add the salt and sugar. Sift together into a large warm bowl. Dissolve the yeast in ½ cup of the warm milk (105° to 115°F.) stirring until dissolved.

2. Make a well in the center of the flour and pour in the milk-yeast mixture, walnut oil and the remaining milk. Stir until combined enough to make a moist dough. Scrape the dough out onto a well-floured board. The dough will be moist. Flour your hands well and begin to knead the dough.

3. Knead for about 10 minutes or until a smooth springy dough forms, using more flour as needed. (It will take about ⅓ to ½ cup more flour during the kneading process.) The dough will be soft, but won't stick to your hands.

4. Lightly grease a large bowl with walnut oil and place the dough in the bowl, turning once to oil both sides. Cover and let rise until double in size, about 1 to 1½ hours, or until the indentation of two fingers remains when inserted ½ inch in the dough.

5. Punch down the dough and work in the walnuts, as well as possible, by kneading them in. Don't try to distribute them too evenly or the dough could get overworked. Some walnuts will stick out on the surface.

6. Divide the dough into 4 even pieces and shape each piece into a round loaf. Place the 4 dough rounds on a lightly greased baking sheet. Cover and let rise again, in a warm place, until double, about 45 minutes.

7. Preheat oven to 400°.

8. Bake 35 minutes or until the loaves sound hollow when tapped. Check after 15 minutes of baking and if the bread is getting too brown, place a piece of foil loosely over the top. This bread will look quite dark and have a crispy crust, but it will have a wonderful texture.

Note: If a whole-wheat bread is desired, use 2 cups whole-wheat flour and 3 cups white flour. Sift the white flour with the salt and sugar and then stir in the whole-wheat flour to mix well. Then proceed with the recipe as above.

Two-Grain Bread

Makes two 9-by-5-inch loaves

2	cups rolled oats
2	cups milk
½	cup oil
1	tablespoon dry yeast
1	cup warm water
½	cup plus 1 tablespoon honey
1	cup white flour
1½	teaspoons salt
5-6½	cups stone ground whole-wheat flour

1. In a medium saucepan, combine the rolled oats and milk. Cook over medium heat until the oats are softened, about 5 minutes. Remove from heat. Stir in oil, then cool to lukewarm.

2. In a large bowl, dissolve the yeast in warm water (105° to 115°F.) and 1 tablespoon honey. Stir into the oatmeal mixture.

3. Add 1 cup of white flour, salt and ½ cup of honey to the oatmeal mixture. Blend on low speed of an electric mixer until moistened; beat 3 minutes at medium speed.

4. By hand, stir in enough whole-wheat flour to form a stiff dough. On a floured surface, knead in as much remaining flour as necessary until the dough is smooth and elastic, about 10 minutes.

5. Place the dough in a greased bowl, turning to grease all sides. Cover loosely with plastic wrap and a cloth towel. Let rise in a warm place until light and double in size, about 1¼ to 1½ hours.

6. Punch down the dough. Cover, let rise a second time until light and double in size, about 45 to 60 minutes.

7. Grease two 9-by-5-inch loaf pans. Punch down the dough. Divide in two and shape into two loaves. Place in prepared pans. Cover and let rise in a warm place until light and double in size, 40 to 45 minutes.

8. Preheat oven to 375°.

9. Bake loaves 30 to 40 minutes or until they sound hollow when lightly tapped. Remove from pans immediately and cool on racks.

Jarlsberg Cheese Bread

Makes 2 large loaves

3½-4½	cups flour
¼	cup sugar
1	teaspoon salt
1	package dry yeast
1	cup water
⅓	cup milk
¼	cup butter
1	egg at room temperature
2	cups shredded Jarlsberg cheese

1. In a mixer bowl, blend together 1 cup flour, sugar, salt and yeast. Heat the water, milk and butter until lukewarm (105° to 115°F.). Add to the dry ingredients and beat 2 minutes at medium speed.

2. Add the egg, ½ cup cheese and ½ cup flour and beat 2 minutes at high speed.

3. Stir in additional flour to make a soft dough. Knead on a floured surface until smooth and elastic, about 10 minutes. Cover and let rise in a warm place until double in size, about 1 hour.

4. Punch down the dough and divide in half. Roll out one half on a lightly floured board to a 12-by-15-inch rectangle. Spread the rectangle with ¾ cup of cheese. Roll up from the short side. Cut in half lengthwise and braid. Tuck the ends under. With spatulas, gently move the braid to a greased baking sheet.

5. Repeat the process with the remaining dough.

6. Let the braided bread rise in a warm place, until it doubles in size, about 1 hour.

7. Preheat oven to 375°.

8. Bake 20 minutes or until done and the top is golden brown.

Note: For a bread with a Mexican flavor, substitute cheddar cheese for the Jarlsberg and sprinkle 1 diced green chili over the rectangle of dough before it is rolled up.

Casserole Dill Bread

Makes 1 round loaf

1¾-2¼	cups flour
2	tablespoons sugar
1	teaspoon salt
1	tablespoon fresh minced green onion
3	tablespoons fresh minced dill
¼	teaspoon baking soda
1	package dry yeast
1	tablespoon softened butter
¼	cup hot water
1	cup small-curd cottage cheese at room temperature
1	egg at room temperature

1. In a large bowl, thoroughly mix ¼ cup flour, sugar, salt, onion, fresh dill, baking soda and undissolved yeast. Add the softened butter.

2. Gradually add the hot water (125° to 135°F.) and beat 2 minutes at medium speed of an electric mixer, scraping the bowl occasionally.

3. Add the cottage cheese, egg and ½ cup flour or enough flour to make a thick batter. Beat at high speed 2 minutes, scraping the bowl occasionally.

4. Stir in enough additional flour to make a stiff dough. You will have to stir the last of the flour in by hand. The dough will be fairly stiff but still sticky (not as thick as a kneaded dough). Cover the dough and let rise in a warm place, free from draft, until double in bulk, about 1 hour and 15 minutes to 1 hour and 45 minutes.

5. Stir the batter down. Turn into a greased 1½-quart casserole. Cover; let rise in a warm place, free from draft, until double in bulk, about 50 minutes.

6. Preheat oven to 350°.

7. Bake about 35 minutes, or until done. Remove from the casserole and cool on a wire rack. If the bread gets too brown on top toward the end of the baking time, place a piece of foil over the top.

Note: The best way to let the dough rise is to place the casserole of covered dough on the middle rack in the oven and place a pan of hot water on the rack below. Close the oven door and let it rise.

◇

Focaccia

Serves 6 to 8

1	clove garlic, peeled and crushed
1/3	cup olive oil
1	teaspoon dried rosemary, crushed
1	teaspoon dried oregano, crushed
1	teaspoon dried basil, crushed
1	package dry yeast
1	cup warm water
2	teaspoons sugar
1/2	teaspoon salt
2-3	cups flour
	Cracked pepper

1. Add the garlic to the olive oil and set aside.

2. Grind the rosemary, oregano and basil in a mortar and set aside.

3. In a large bowl, sprinkle the yeast over warm water (105° to 115°F.) and let stand until softened. Stir in the sugar, salt, 4 tablespoons of seasoned oil and 1 teaspoon of mixed herbs. Add 1 cup of flour and mix well. Add enough more flour to make a soft dough.

4. Turn the dough onto a floured board and knead until the dough is smooth and elastic, about 10 minutes, adding flour as needed. Place in a greased bowl and let rise until double in size, about 1 hour.

5. Punch down the dough, turn onto a floured board and roll into a 12-inch circle. Fit into a well-greased 12-inch pizza pan. With a fork, perforate the dough at 2-inch intervals. Brush with seasoned olive oil and sprinkle with the remaining herbs and freshly ground black pepper. Let rise 20 minutes.

6. Preheat oven to 450°.

7. Bake 15 minutes. Cut into wedges and serve at room temperature.

Apple Ring
Serves 8

Dough:

¾	cup lukewarm milk
¼	cup sugar
1	teaspoon salt
1	envelope dry yeast
¼	cup lukewarm water
1	egg, slightly beaten
¼	cup soft shortening
3½	cups sifted flour
2	tablespoons melted butter

Filling:

¾	cup cooked dried prunes, cut up
1½	cups cored, peeled and diced golden Delicious apples
1	tablespoon lemon juice
½	cup brown sugar
1	teaspoon cinnamon
¾	cup chopped walnuts

Powdered Sugar Glaze:

½	cup powdered sugar
1	tablespoon milk
¼	teaspoon vanilla

1. To prepare dough: Combine the milk, sugar and salt in a bowl. Dissolve the yeast in lukewarm water (105° to 115°F.). Add the dissolved yeast to the milk mixture and stir. Add the egg and shortening. Stir in just enough flour to make the dough easy to handle.

2. Turn out the dough on a lightly floured board and knead until smooth and elastic, about 5 to 10 minutes.

3. Place in a greased bowl, turning once to bring greased side up. Cover and let rise in a warm spot until double in bulk, 1½ to 2 hours. Punch down; let rise again until double, 30 to 45 minutes.

4. Roll the dough into a 9-by-18-inch oblong. Spread with melted butter.

5. To prepare filling: Combine the prunes, apples, lemon juice, brown sugar, cinnamon and walnuts. Spread over the dough. Roll up from the long side, seal edge and form into a circle, sealed edge down, on a lightly greased baking sheet. Seal the ends together.

6. Using scissors, cut through the top layer of the dough two-thirds of the way into the ring from the outer edge at 1-inch intervals. Turn each section slightly to the side. Cover and let rise until double.

7. Preheat oven to 375°.

8. Bake 25 minutes or until done.

9. To prepare glaze: Sift the powdered sugar in a small bowl. Add the milk and vanilla. Drizzle over the warm ring.

Corn Bread

Serves 12

2	cups	flour
2	cups	cornmeal
⅓	cup	sugar
2	tablespoons	baking powder
1½	teaspoons	salt
4	eggs	
2	cups	milk
½	cup	shortening

1. Preheat oven to 425°.

2. Mix the flour, cornmeal, sugar, baking powder and salt together in a large bowl. Add the eggs, milk and shortening. Beat with an electric beater until just smooth. Do not overbeat.

3. Pour into a greased 9-by-13-inch pan. Bake for 25 minutes or until done. Cool.

Potato Rolls

Makes 3 dozen

1	package dry yeast
½	cup plus 1 tablespoon sugar
⅓	cup warm water
¼	cup shortening
½	cup butter, softened
2	teaspoons salt
½	cup scalded milk
½	cup hot potato water
1	cup cooked, mashed potatoes
3	eggs, beaten
5	cups flour

1. Combine the yeast and 1 tablespoon sugar in warm water (105° to 115°F.). Stir until the sugar and yeast are dissolved. Combine the shortening, butter, ½ cup sugar, salt, scalded milk, hot potato water and mashed potatoes in a large mixing bowl and mix well.

2. When cool, add the yeast mixture and beaten eggs and mix well.

3. Add the flour a little at a time, mixing well. When flour is mixed and it's hard to add more, turn out on a well-floured board and knead until a soft, pliable dough that doesn't stick to hands is achieved. More flour might have to be kneaded in, depending on the size of the eggs.

4. Place in a well-greased bowl and brush the top with melted butter. Cover and place in the refrigerator overnight.

5. Working with small amounts of dough, shape into small balls about the size of large walnuts. Using muffin tins with 2½-inch cups, place 3 balls of dough in each cup to form a cloverleaf. Put remainder of dough back into refrigerator until ready to use. Let stand at room temperature for about 1 hour or until the dough is double in bulk. The time will depend on how cold the dough is.

6. Preheat oven to 400°.

7. Bake 12 to 15 minutes. Brush with melted butter after baking, if desired.

Mother O'Donnell's Irish Soda Bread

Makes 1 loaf

4	cups sifted flour
¼	cup sugar
1	teaspoon salt
1	teaspoon baking powder
2	tablespoons caraway seeds
¼	cup butter
2	cups seedless raisins
1⅓	cups buttermilk
1	egg
1	teaspoon baking soda
1	egg yolk, beaten
	Cream

1. Preheat oven to 375°.

2. Sift the flour, sugar, salt and baking powder into a large bowl. Stir in the caraway seeds. Cut in the butter with a pastry blender until it resembles coarse cornmeal. Stir in the raisins.

3. Combine the buttermilk, egg and baking soda. Stir into the flour mixture until just moistened.

4. Turn the dough onto a floured board and knead a few minutes. Shape into a ball and place in a greased 1½-quart casserole. With a sharp knife, make a cross ¼-inch deep in the center.

5. Combine the egg yolk and cream and brush the bread with it before baking.

6. Bake 1 hour and 10 minutes or until a cake tester inserted in the center comes out clean.

This recipe was passed on to us by Margaret Harkin O'Donnell who was born and raised in County Donegal, Ireland. This is her adapted recipe for the Irish version of a scone.

Raisin-Cinnamon-Swirl Bread

Makes 2 loaves

3-3¾	cups flour
1	envelope fast-rising yeast
6	tablespoons sugar
1	teaspoon salt
¾	cup plus 1 tablespoon water
⅔	cup evaporated milk
½	cup raisins
½	teaspoon cinnamon

1. Combine 3 cups flour, the yeast, 2 tablespoons sugar and salt in a bowl.

2. In a saucepan, heat the water and evaporated milk to 120° to 130°F. Pour the warm liquids into the flour mixture and stir. Add the raisins and stir.

3. Knead the dough on a floured board until smooth and elastic, about 10 minutes, working in additional flour as needed. Place the dough in an oiled bowl and turn to coat the top. Cover; allow to rise in a warm place until double in bulk, about 45 minutes.

4. Punch down the dough and divide in half. Roll the first half of the dough into an 8-by-12-inch rectangle.

5. Combine the remaining sugar and cinnamon and sprinkle half of it over the surface of the dough. Roll up tightly, starting at the short end; seal the edges. Place seam side down in a buttered 8½-by-4½-by-2½-inch loaf pan. Repeat with the second part of the dough. Cover and let rise in a warm place until double in bulk, 45 minutes to 1 hour.

6. Preheat oven to 350°.

7. Bake 20 to 25 minutes.

Note: If using regular yeast, allow approximately 1½ hours for each rising.

Spoonbread

Serves 6 to 8

2	cups half-and-half
⅓	cup whipping cream
4	tablespoons butter
1½	tablespoons sugar
1	tablespoon honey
¾	teaspoon salt
1	cup white cornmeal
4	eggs, separated
1	teaspoon baking powder
⅛	teaspoon white pepper
	Syrup or butter
	Salt and pepper

1. Preheat oven to 375°.

2. In a large, heavy saucepan, combine the half-and-half, cream, butter, sugar, honey and salt. Cook over low heat until the butter melts, but do not bring mixture to a boil.

3. Add the cornmeal, very slowly, stirring constantly, over low heat until the mixture gets thick, about 5 minutes. Do not boil.

4. Quickly pour the mush mixture into the large bowl of an electric mixer. Add 1 egg yolk, beating until smooth. Continue adding remaining egg yolks, one at a time, beating well each time. Stir in the baking powder and pepper.

5. Beat the egg whites until stiff peaks form. Fold them gradually into the mush mixture. Pour the batter into a buttered 2-quart soufflé dish.

6. Bake 35 minutes or until a cake tester inserted near the center comes out clean.

7. Remove from oven and serve immediately while hot. Cut in wedges and top with syrup or butter and salt and pepper.

Christmas Stollen

Makes 2 loaves

Stollen:

1	package dry yeast
¼	cup warm water
6	tablespoons milk, scalded
¼	cup butter
¼	cup sugar
½	teaspoon salt
2¼-2½	cups flour
½	cup cornmeal
1	egg
¼	cup diced mixed candied fruit
¼	cup golden raisins
¼	cup candied cherry halves
¼	cup blanched almond slices
1½	teaspoons grated lemon peel
	Butter, softened

Powdered Sugar Glaze:

½	cup powdered sugar
2	teaspoons hot milk
¼	teaspoon vanilla

Candied cherries and almonds

1. To prepare stollen: Dissolve the yeast in warm water (105° to 115°F.). In a large bowl, pour the milk over the butter, sugar and salt; cool to lukewarm. Stir in the dissolved yeast, ½ cup flour, cornmeal and egg.

2. Add the fruits, nuts and lemon peel. Stir in enough additional flour to make a soft dough.

3. Turn out the dough on a lightly floured surface; knead about 8 to 10 minutes or until smooth and elastic.

4. Divide the dough in half. Roll out each half to a 7-by-9-inch oval. Spread each with about ½ teaspoon softened butter; fold in half lengthwise. Spread the top of each bread with ½ teaspoon butter.

5. Place both loaves on a large greased cookie sheet. Cover with plastic wrap. Let rise in a warm place about 1½ hours or until double in size.

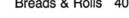

6. Preheat oven to 350°.

7. Bake 20 to 25 minutes or until golden brown. Cool.

8. To prepare powdered sugar glaze: Sift the powdered sugar. Add the hot milk and vanilla. Stir until smooth. Drizzle the glaze over the stollen and garnish with candied cherries and almonds, if desired.

Pineapple Zucchini Bread

Makes 2 loaves

3	eggs
1	cup salad oil
2	cups sugar
2	teaspoons vanilla
2	cups shredded zucchini
1	(8¼ ounce) can crushed pineapple, well drained
3	cups flour
2	teaspoons baking soda
1	teaspoon salt
½	teaspoon baking powder
2	teaspoons cinnamon
1	cup finely chopped nuts
1	cup raisins

1. Preheat oven to 350°.

2. Beat the eggs. Add the oil, sugar and vanilla., Beat until light and foamy. Stir in the zucchini and pineapple.

3. Sift together the flour, baking soda, salt, baking powder and cinnamon; gently stir into the zucchini mixture. Add nuts and raisins.

4. Line the bottom of two 9-by-5-inch loaf pans with wax paper. Grease the sides of the pans and the wax paper. Pour the batter into the pans. Bake for 1 hour or until bread tests done when a toothpick inserted in center comes out clean. Cool the bread in the pans 10 minutes, then remove from the pans and continue cooling on racks.

Christmas Apricot Ring

Makes 1 large ring

Filling:

¾	cup dried apricots, packed
¼	cup butter
¼	cup chopped, blanched almonds
¼	cup sugar
¼	cup orange marmalade

Bread:

1	package dry yeast
2	tablespoons warm water
⅓	cup milk
2	tablespoons butter
2	tablespoons sugar
1	teaspoon salt
1	egg, beaten
1⅔	cups sifted flour
⅓	cup whole-wheat flour

Powdered Sugar Glaze:

½	cup powdered sugar
1	tablespoon milk or cream
¼	teaspoon vanilla

Red maraschino cherries and green candied pineapple or
red and green candied cherries

1. To prepare filling: Chop the apricots and set aside. Combine the butter, almonds, sugar and marmalade in a saucepan. Bring to a boil and, stirring constantly, cook until thick, about 3 minutes. Add the apricots and set aside to cool.

2. To prepare bread: Combine the yeast with the warm water (105° to 115°F.) and set aside. Scald the milk. Remove from the heat and stir in the butter, sugar and salt. When lukewarm, add the egg and yeast.

3. Combine the flours and stir about 1¼ cups into the yeast mixture slowly, until a stiff dough forms.

4. Sprinkle a little of the remaining flour mixture on a board and turn

the dough out on the board. Knead the dough, adding the remaining flour while kneading, until dough is smooth and elastic, about 10 minutes. Cover the dough and let rest 15 minutes.

5. Roll the dough into a 6-by-18-inch rectangle. Spread with cooled filling. Roll up like a jelly roll, starting from the long side. Moisten the long edge of the dough with milk to seal.

6. Shape on a greased cookie sheet into a ring, securing the ends firmly by brushing with milk and pressing together.

7. With floured scissors, clip the ring all the way around at 1-inch intervals, cutting about three-quarters through the dough. Separate the clips by pulling every other one toward the center.

8. Cover and let rise in a warm place until almost double in bulk.

9. Preheat oven to 400°.

10. Bake 3 minutes. Reduce heat to 375° and bake about 15 minutes longer. Cool.

11. To prepare powdered sugar glaze: Sift the powdered sugar into a bowl. Add the milk or cream and vanilla, stirring until smooth. Drizzle the wreath with the powdered sugar glaze and garnish as desired with slivers of maraschino cherries and green candied pineapple or slivers of red and green candied cherries.

Braided Holiday Wreath

Makes 1 large wreath

4⅓	cups flour
⅓	cup plus 2 tablespoons sugar
1	teaspoon salt
1	teaspoon ground cardamom
2	packages dry yeast
½	cup butter
1	cup milk
3	eggs
2	tablespoons chopped almonds or other nuts

1. In a large bowl, combine 1 cup flour, ⅓ cup sugar, salt, cardamom and yeast.

2. In a small saucepan, melt the butter; add the milk and heat to 120°F. Add the milk to the flour mixture and beat with a mixer on medium speed for 2 minutes. Add 2 eggs, slightly beaten, and 1 cup flour. Beat on high speed for 2 minutes. Stir in enough remaining flour to make a soft dough.

3. Turn out the dough on a floured surface and knead 8 to 10 minutes or until smooth and elastic. Place in a greased bowl, turning to grease the top. Cover and let rise in a warm, draft-free place 1 hour or until double.

4. Punch down the dough. Turn out on lightly floured surface and, using more flour if necessary, knead until smooth and elastic.

5. Cut the dough in 3 equal pieces. Shape each into a 30-inch long rope. Braid the ropes loosely. Transfer the braid to a lightly greased baking sheet and shape into a wreath, pinching the ends firmly together. Place a 6-ounce custard cup, greased on the outside, upside down in the hole in the center of the ring. Cover and let rise in a warm, draft-free place about 45 minutes or until double.

6. Preheat oven to 375°.

7. Brush the wreath with 1 egg, slightly beaten. Sprinkle with a mixture of the remaining 2 tablespoons sugar and almonds. Bake 25 to 30 minutes or until golden and done. Remove to a rack to cool.

Hot Cross Buns

Makes 2 dozen

2	packages dry yeast
¼	cup warm water
½	cup boiling milk
½	cup butter
⅓	cup sugar
1	teaspoon salt
½	teaspoon cinnamon
4	cups bread flour
3	eggs, beaten
1	cup raisins
1	cup chopped candied fruits
	Melted butter
⅓	cup powdered sugar
1	egg white

1. Dissolve the yeast in warm water (105° to 115°F.) in a warm bowl. Stir together the milk, butter, sugar, salt and cinnamon. Add half of the flour and beat until smooth.

2. Add the yeast, beaten eggs, remaining flour, raisins and candied fruits. Mix to a moderately stiff dough.

3. Knead on a lightly floured board about 5 minutes, until satiny. Place in a greased bowl; turn over to grease the top. Cover and let rise in a warm place 1½ hours.

4. Roll on a floured board to ½-inch thick. Cut in 2½-inch rounds and shape each round into a ball. Place on a greased baking sheet; brush with melted butter. Snip a deep cross in each bun with greased scissors. Let rise 1 hour or until double in size.

5. Preheat oven to 375°.

6. Bake 15 minutes.

7. Combine the powdered sugar and egg white until thick enough to pipe through a decorating tube. Outline the crosses on top of the buns with icing. Serve warm.

Mile-High Orange Rolls
Makes 28

Dough:

2	packages dry yeast
½	cup warm water
½	cup sugar
1¼	cups milk
½	cup shortening
2	eggs, beaten
5	cups flour
1	teaspoon salt

Filling:

½	cup butter, softened
¾	cup sugar
	Grated peel of one orange

1. To prepare dough: Dissolve the yeast in warm water (105° to 115°F.) in a small bowl. Add the sugar.

2. Scald the milk, add the shortening and stir to melt. Pour into a large mixing bowl and cool to lukewarm. Stir in the eggs and yeast mixture.

3. Combine the flour and salt and slowly add to egg-milk-yeast mixture, stirring as you go, until it becomes too stiff to stir.

4. Turn out the dough on a board and knead in any remaining flour until dough is smooth, about 10 minutes.

5. Put the dough back in the bowl, cover and let rise at room temperature about 1 hour or until double and light.

6. Punch down the dough and place in the refrigerator. It usually rises again in the refrigerator in about another hour.

7. Punch down, if needed, and place dough on a lightly floured surface. Roll out with a floured rolling pin to a large rectangle, much longer than wide, and about as thin as it will roll out comfortably.

8. To prepare filling: Combine the butter, sugar and orange peel in a small bowl and cream together until light. Spread this mixture evenly over the dough.

9. Roll up from the long edge, like a jelly roll. Cut the roll crosswise in about ¾-inch to 1-inch slices.

10. Place each roll in a standard 2½-inch muffin cup. Cover and let rise until double, about 45 minutes to an hour.
11. Preheat oven to 425°.
12. Bake 8 to 10 minutes.

Lila's Aebelskivar

Makes 3 dozen pancakes

3	eggs, separated
2	teaspoons sugar
½	teaspoon salt
2	cups buttermilk
2	cups flour
1	teaspoon baking powder
1	teaspoon baking soda

1. Beat the egg yolks; add the sugar, salt, buttermilk, flour, baking powder and baking soda.
2. Beat the egg whites until stiff; gently fold them into the batter.
3. Brush an aebelskivar iron with oil. Heat the iron over medium heat until hot. (A few drops of water sprinkled on the iron will sizzle when it is hot.) Fill the indentations two-thirds full with batter. Cook over medium heat until bubbles start to form. Loosen around the edges, then turn with a cake tester or skewer to brown all sides. It will form a round ball.

This recipe is from Florence Ekstrand, author of Scandinavian Home Cooking.

Lemon Scones

Makes 2½ dozen

½	cup diced candied lemon peel
2½-2¾	cups flour
½	teaspoon salt
½	cup sugar
2	teaspoons baking powder
1	teaspoon baking soda
6	tablespoons cold butter
1	egg, lightly beaten
1	(8 ounce) container lemon yogurt
	Grated peel of ½ orange

1. Preheat oven to 425°.

2. Toss the candied fruit peel in 2 tablespoons of the flour and set aside. Sift the remaining flour with the salt, sugar, baking powder and baking soda into a large bowl.

3. Cut in the butter with a pastry blender until crumbly. Add the candied fruit, egg, yogurt and orange peel to the flour mixture and blend well.

4. Divide the dough into 30 balls. Flatten to ½-inch thick. Arrange on a lightly greased cookie sheet. Bake 12 minutes or until lightly browned. Cool on wire racks or serve warm with butter and jam.

Banana Tea Muffins

Makes 16

1½	cups flour
2	teaspoons baking powder
¼	teaspoon baking soda
¾	teaspoon salt
⅓	cup sugar
1	egg, well beaten
⅓	cup melted shortening or vegetable oil
1	cup mashed, fully ripe bananas

1. Preheat oven to 400°.

2. Sift together the flour, baking powder, baking soda, salt and sugar into a mixing bowl. Combine the egg, shortening and bananas.

3. Add dry ingredients to the egg-shortening mixture, mixing only enough to dampen all the flour. Turn into well-greased small muffin pans.

4. Bake 20 minutes, or until a cake tester inserted in the center comes out clean. Serve hot or cold.

Seven-Week Bran Muffins

Makes 8 dozen

2	cups 40 percent bran flakes
4	cups bran buds
2	cups boiling water
4	eggs
1	cup shortening
2½	cups sugar
1	quart buttermilk
5	cups flour
5	teaspoons baking soda
1	teaspoon salt
1½	cups raisins

1. Preheat oven to 375°.

2. In a very large bowl, combine the bran flakes, bran buds and boiling water. Mix well and let stand.

3. In another bowl, combine the eggs, shortening, sugar and buttermilk; mix well and add to the bran mixture.

4. Sift together the flour, baking soda and salt. Stir the flour mixture into the bran mixture. Add the raisins.

5. This can be refrigerated in well-covered jars up to seven weeks. When ready to bake, fill greased muffin pans two-thirds full and bake about 25 minutes, or until a cake tester inserted in the center comes out clean.

Country Pear Muffins

Makes 1 dozen

Sesame-Seed Topping:

1	tablespoon sesame seeds
1	tablespoon sugar
¼	teaspoon ground cinnamon
¼	teaspoon ground nutmeg

Muffins:

1	cup all-purpose flour
¾	cup whole-wheat flour
½	cup sugar
2	teaspoons baking powder
1	teaspoon salt
½	teaspoon baking soda
½	teaspoon ground cinnamon
½	teaspoon ground nutmeg
1	egg
¾	cup buttermilk
¼	cup butter, melted
1½	teaspoons grated orange peel
1	cup finely chopped, pared pears

1. Preheat oven to 450°.

2. To prepare topping: Combine the sesame seeds, sugar, cinnamon and nutmeg. Set aside.

3. To prepare muffins: Sift the flours, sugar, baking powder, salt, baking soda, cinnamon and nutmeg into a large mixing bowl.

4. In another bowl, beat the egg slightly with the buttermilk and melted butter. Add the orange peel and pears to the egg mixture. Gently stir the egg mixture into the dry ingredients until all ingredients are moistened.

5. Spoon the batter into 12 well-greased muffin cups. Sprinkle each muffin with ½ teaspoon reserved sesame-seed topping.

6. Bake 20 to 25 minutes or until a cake tester inserted in the center comes out clean.

Three-Grain Pear Muffins

Makes 12

1½	cups finely chopped, peeled and cored Bartlett pears
½	cup milk
⅓	cup vegetable oil
1	egg
¾	cup all-purpose flour
¾	cup yellow cornmeal
½	cup whole-wheat flour
½	cup old-fashioned rolled oats
⅓	cup sugar
¼	cup golden raisins
2	teaspoons baking powder
½	teaspoon salt

1. Preheat oven to 375°.

2. Stir the pears, milk, vegetable oil and egg in a bowl. In a separate large bowl, combine the all-purpose flour, cornmeal, whole-wheat flour, oats, sugar, raisins, baking powder and salt.

3. Add the liquid ingredients to the dry ingredients and stir just until blended.

4. Divide the batter between 12 greased 2¾-inch muffin cups. Bake 35 minutes or until browned and a cake tester inserted in the center comes out clean.

Blueberry Muffins

Makes 1 dozen

1¾	cups sifted flour
½	teaspoon salt
2½	teaspoons baking powder
½	cup sugar
1	egg, beaten
⅔	cup milk
¼	cup shortening
1	teaspoon vanilla extract
1	cup fresh blueberries

1. Preheat oven to 375°.

2. Sift together the flour, salt, baking powder and sugar into a mixing bowl.

3. In another bowl, beat the egg, milk, shortening and vanilla extract until smooth. Add to the dry ingredients and mix only until moistened.

4. Gently stir in the whole blueberries. Spoon into well-greased muffin tins and bake 20 to 25 minutes.

Cranberry Brunch Bread

Makes two 9-by-5-inch loaves

Bread:

⅔	cup boiling water
¾	cup butter, cut up
3	packages dry yeast
½	cup warm water
6¼-6¾	cups flour
2-2½	cups chopped (medium-fine) fresh cranberries
1	cup oats, regular or quick-cooking
1	cup sugar
2	large eggs
3	teaspoons salt
	Grated peel of 2 medium oranges

Glaze:

1   cup powdered sugar

1   tablespoon orange juice or more

1. To prepare bread: In a 4-quart bowl, pour the boiling water over the butter. Stir to melt and cool to lukewarm.

2. Sprinkle the yeast over the warm water (105° to 115°F.) and stir until dissolved.

3. Stir the yeast, 1 cup flour, cranberries, oats, sugar, eggs, salt and orange peel into the butter mixture until well blended. Stir in enough flour to make a stiff dough.

4. Knead the dough on a lightly floured surface until smooth and elastic, about 10 minutes. Shape into a ball. Place the dough in a well-greased bowl and turn to coat all sides.

5. Cover the bowl tightly with plastic wrap. Let rise in a warm place for 1½ hours.

6. Punch down the dough. Divide in half and place in two well-greased 9-by-5-inch baking pans. Cover with wax paper and allow to rise in a warm place, about 1½ hours.

7. Preheat oven to 375°.

8. Bake 50 to 55 minutes, or until a cake tester inserted in the center comes out clean. Turn out of pans and cool on a rack.

9. To prepare glaze: Combine the powdered sugar and orange juice. Add enough more orange juice, ¼ teaspoon at a time, to make the glaze medium-thin. Drizzle glaze over loaves.

Beverages

One of the most delightful ways to enjoy the fresh fruits of the Northwest is to incorporate whatever is at its seasonal best in a cooling drink. It doesn't have to be alcoholic, nor does it even have to be high-calorie, but it is guaranteed to deliver the essence of the flavor along with an excuse to sit down, take a break, and enjoy it.

Menu planning sometimes stops short of including the drinks in a well-coordinated sequence of flavor experiences, yet a fruit drink can add lightness to a heavy dinner or refresh the palate when you need to make a transition.

The selection of special coffees in this chapter also is invaluable for putting a hospitable touch at the end of a meal. It can be either an exclamation point after dinner or as an alternative to dessert for those who are watching their weight or have dined too well already.

In a region where informal entertaining is a frequent challenge to the gracious host or hostess, an assortment of hot and cold drinks easily made from what's at hand can make spur-of-the-moment parties memorable at little expense.

There's even a selection of liqueurs you can make yourself to cut even further on the cost of entertaining. If your reputation for out-of-the-ordinary drinks spreads, you'll need extra supplies of makings.

Holiday Fruit Punch

Makes 3 quarts

3	tea bags
1½	cups boiling water
1½	cups sugar
1	cup hot water
6-8	ice cubes
2	cups orange juice, chilled
1½	cups lemon juice, chilled
1	quart ginger ale, chilled
	Ice mold

1. Add the tea bags to the boiling water and let steep for 5 minutes. Discard the tea bags.
2. Dissolve the sugar in 1 cup hot water in a punch bowl. Add 6 to 8 ice cubes to cool. Mix in the tea and citrus juices. Stir well. Chill.
3. Just before serving, add the ginger ale and the ice mold.

Orange Eggnog Punch

Serves 24

6	eggs, separated
½	cup sugar
2	cups milk
2	cups whipping cream
1	cup frozen orange-juice concentrate, undiluted
	Nutmeg
	Grated orange peel

1. In a large mixing bowl, combine the egg yolks, sugar, milk, whipping cream and orange-juice concentrate. Beat with rotary beaters until slightly thick and foamy. Chill until serving time.
2. In a small mixing bowl, beat the egg whites until stiff but not dry. Gently fold the egg whites into the orange mixture. Serve in chilled punch cups. Garnish with nutmeg or orange peel.

Champagne Wine Punch

Makes 1 gallon

¼	cup brandy
1	quart lemon-flavored carbonated beverage
1	(750 ml) bottle dry white wine
2	(750 ml) bottles extra dry champagne
	Ice block

Pour all liquids over the ice block in a large punch bowl.

Hot Spiced Cider

Makes 1 gallon

1	gallon apple cider
1	orange, sliced
1	lemon, sliced
3	apples, each studded with 6 to 8 cloves
4	cinnamon sticks
1	teaspoon whole cloves
1	whole nutmeg, crushed
1	teaspoon whole allspice
2	whole cardamoms, crushed
1	tablespoon crystallized ginger

1. Bring the cider to a boil in a large pot. Add the orange and lemon slices, apples and cinnamon sticks.

2. Make a spice bag by tying the cloves, nutmeg, allspice, cardamom and ginger in a cheesecloth. Add to the cider mixture.

3. Simmer 2 hours and serve hot.

Nonalcoholic Eggnog
Makes 2 quarts

6 eggs, separated
½ cup superfine sugar
½ teaspoon nutmeg plus extra for garnish
¼ teaspoon salt
2 teaspoons vanilla
1 teaspoon rum extract
2 cups milk
1 cup whipping cream

1. Beat the egg yolks, ¼ cup sugar, nutmeg, salt, vanilla and rum extract together with a rotary beater or an electric mixer until very thick and light yellow. Slowly beat in the milk. Cover and chill overnight.

2. Shortly before serving, beat the egg whites to soft peaks. Gradually beat in the remaining ¼ cup sugar. With the same beater, beat the cream to soft peaks. Fold the meringue into the beaten cream.

3. Slowly pour on the chilled egg-yolk mixture, folding in gently. Sprinkle with nutmeg.

Note: Keep no longer than 2 to 3 days in the refrigerator.

Holiday Eggnog
Serves 12

6 eggs
1 cup sugar
½ teaspoon salt
1 cup golden rum
1 quart half-and-half
Ground nutmeg

1. In a large bowl, beat the eggs until light and foamy. Add the sugar and salt, beating until thick and lemon-colored.

2. Stir in the rum and half-and-half. Chill at least 3 hours. Stir and sprinkle with nutmeg before serving.

Tom Stockley's Sangria
Serves 6

1	(750 ml) bottle Northwest merlot
4	tablespoons sugar
	Juice of 1 lemon
1	orange, thinly sliced
1	stick cinnamon
½	cup brandy
1	(6 ounce) bottle club soda
	Ice cubes

1. Pour the wine into a pitcher and add the sugar, lemon juice, slices of orange and cinnamon. Stir well.

2. Just before serving, add the brandy, soda and ice cubes.

This recipe for Sangria was developed by Tom Stockley, Times wine columnist.

Pineapple-Cranberry Punch
Makes 5 to 6 quarts

½-1	cup sugar
1	(46 ounce) can pineapple juice
1	cup lemon juice
2	cups cranberry juice
1	(750 ml) bottle vodka
2	quarts ginger ale

1. Dissolve the sugar in the pineapple, lemon and cranberry juices. Chill.

2. Just before serving, stir in the vodka and ginger ale.

Irish Liqueur

Makes 1 quart

3	eggs
2	tablespoons chocolate syrup
2	tablespoons vanilla extract
1	tablespoon instant coffee powder (not granules)
⅓	cup water
1	(13½ ounce) can sweetened condensed milk
1	cup whipping cream
1⅓	cups Irish whiskey

1. Put the eggs, chocolate syrup, vanilla, coffee powder and water in a blender or the bowl of a food processor. Blend until mixed.

2. Transfer the mixture to a bowl and add the condensed milk, whipping cream and whiskey. Stir until well-blended. Pour into a container with a tight-fitting lid and keep refrigerated.

Note: This will keep up to 1 month in the refrigerator.

Coffee-Flavored Liqueur

Makes 2 quarts

4	cups sugar
4	cups water
1	cup instant coffee granules
1	vanilla bean or 1 tablespoon vanilla
1	(750 ml) bottle vodka

1. Bring the sugar and water to a boil in a medium-size saucepan. Add the coffee and bring to a boil again.

2. Split the vanilla bean lengthwise and add to the water-sugar syrup, or add vanilla. Cool completely. Add the vodka.

3. Pour into clean glass bottles or jars. Put on lids and store in a cool place for 2 to 3 weeks. Remove the vanilla bean.

Note: The liqueur will last indefinitely if stored in a cool place.

Orange-Flavored Liqueur

Makes 1 quart

1	cup sugar
½	cup water
3	cups brandy
2	teaspoons orange extract

1. Dissolve the sugar in almost-boiling water. Place over low heat for 3 minutes, stirring constantly. Allow to cool.

2. Add the brandy and orange extract. Pour into a container with a tight-fitting lid. Stir or shake the bottle each day to dissolve the sugar completely. The liqueur will be ready to use in five to 10 days. The longer it ages, the more mellow the flavor becomes.

Liqueur for Wallbangers

Makes 7 to 8 cups

2½-3	cups sugar
1½	cups water
2	tablespoons pineapple extract
1	tablespoon vanilla extract
½	teaspoon anise extract
1½	teaspoons banana extract
1	(750 ml) bottle 100-proof vodka

1. Boil the sugar and water 5 minutes. Add the extracts to the syrup and cool to room temperature.

2. Add the vodka. Place the mixture in a jar with a tight-fitting lid. It will be ready to serve within a couple of days but is better if aged at least one week. The liqueur will keep several months in a cool, dark place.

Blackberry Base

Makes 3 cups

8	cups blackberries
1	cup sugar

1. Whirl the blackberries in a food processor until partly puréed.
2. Heat the berry purée to a boil in a saucepan, then simmer for 5 to 8 minutes or until juice is released.
3. Set a sieve over a bowl and pour in the berry mixture. Gently press out the juice and pulp with a wooden spoon until mainly seeds are left in the sieve.
4. Return the thick juice to the saucepan and add sugar to taste. Bring to a boil and cook until the sugar is dissolved.
5. Chill and pour into a covered jar. Store in the refrigerator up to a month for use in blackberry drinks.

Blackberry Cooler

Serves 4

	Ice
2	cups blackberry base (see above)
2	cups carbonated water

1. Fill each glass with ice cubes.
2. Pour each glass half full of blackberry base.
3. Fill the remainder of the glass with carbonated water.
4. Stir and serve immediately.

Blackberries on the Rocks

Serves 1

Crushed ice
Blackberry base (see above)
Lemon twists

1. Fill a glass with crushed ice.
2. Pour blackberry base over the ice. Stir until chilled.
3. Add a lemon twist to each drink and serve immediately.

Cranberry-Grape Sparkle

Makes 2 quarts

6	cups cranberry-juice cocktail
1	cup white grape juice, chilled
1	(6 ounce) can frozen concentrated pink lemonade, thawed and strained
1	quart club soda, chilled
	Lemon slices

1. Pour half of the cranberry juice into an ice-cube tray. Freeze until hard.
2. Combine the remaining cranberry juice, grape juice, lemonade concentrate and club soda in a punch bowl. Add cranberry ice cubes. Garnish with lemon slices.

Orange-Strawberry Slush

Serves 8

1	(6 ounce) can frozen orange-juice concentrate, thawed
1½	cups ginger ale
¼	cup grenadine
1	cup crushed ice
1	(10 ounce) package frozen strawberries, partly thawed
	Additional crushed or shaved ice

1. Combine the thawed orange-juice concentrate, ginger ale, grenadine and crushed ice in a blender container. Process 10 seconds.
2. Add the partly thawed strawberries; process 5 seconds. Serve immediately, over additional crushed or shaved ice, if desired.

Spiced Mocha

Serves 6 to 8

2	ounces unsweetened chocolate
2	tablespoons water
½	cup sugar
1	tablespoon cornstarch
2	cups freshly brewed strong black coffee
1½	teaspoons ground cinnamon plus extra for garnish
½	teaspoon vanilla extract
⅛	teaspoon salt
3	cups hot milk
	Whipped cream

1. Grate the chocolate into the top part of a double boiler over hot, not boiling, water.
2. When the chocolate is melted, add the water and mix into a smooth paste.
3. Combine the sugar and cornstarch and stir into the paste.
4. Gradually stir in the coffee. Beat until smooth. Cook for about 5 minutes, stirring occasionally.
5. Stir in the cinnamon, vanilla, salt and milk and blend thoroughly. Cook the mixture for about 20 minutes, stirring occasionally.
6. Pour into cups; top with whipped cream and a sprinkling of cinnamon.

Irish Coffee

Serves 6

½	cup sugar
¾	cup Irish whiskey
4½	cups hot, strong coffee
½	cup whipping cream, whipped

1. Into each of six coffee cups, put 4 teaspoons sugar, 2 tablespoons whiskey and ¾ cup hot coffee. Stir until the sugar dissolves.
2. Top each serving with about 2 tablespoons whipped cream. Do not stir. Serve immediately.

Coffee Amandine

Serves 2

¼	cup whipping cream
1	teaspoon sugar
⅛	teaspoon almond extract
1½	cups strong coffee
2	tablespoons amaretto
2	teaspoons ground almonds

1. In a small bowl, combine the whipping cream, sugar and almond extract and beat until stiff. Set aside in the refrigerator.
2. Prepare the coffee; add amaretto and stir.
3. Pour the coffee mixture into 2 heat-proof mugs and top each with a dollop of almond whipped cream. Garnish the whipped cream with the ground almonds.

Café Brulot

Makes 6 to 8 demitasses

1	piece stick cinnamon
6	whole cloves
	Small piece lemon peel
	Small piece orange peel
6	cubes sugar
½	cup brandy
¼	cup rum
3	cups double-strength coffee

1. Combine the cinnamon, cloves, lemon and orange peels, sugar, brandy and rum in an attractive silver bowl or chafing dish. Light with a match.
2. Slowly stir to dissolve the sugar and blend the ingredients. Pour piping-hot coffee slowly into the mixture. Serve immediately.